Earthbound Perspectives

The Human Quest for Global Equilibrium and Growth

By Hugh M. Lewis

Copyright 2000

Hugh M. Lewis

ISBN

9798413571422

2000

Earthbound Primer #1

Lewis Micropublishing & Poor Hugh's E-Press

For the Human "Race,"
That it may not be so much a "race"
In a biological sense of different colors
And physical characteristics
Nor a "race" in the game sense
Of the first player to cross the finish line
But rather a single intelligent species
We have come to call
Homo sapiens

Contents

EARTH WORKS (1991) 1

Preface to Earth Works (2023) 2

PART I: ANTHROPOLOGICAL PROSPECTUS 4

PART II: NATURE'S CLOCKWORKS 32

PART III: EARTH STATE 67

PART IV: POPULATION BOMBS 96

PART V: GLOBAL SYSTEMS, INC. 125

PART VI. HIDDEN FACTORS 148

PART VII: FINAL SOLUTIONS 169

The Third Millennium (1999) 177

Preface to the Third Millennium (2023) 178

Introduction 182

Part I: Basic Problems and Prospects 187

Chapter 1: Basic Dilemmas of the Global Imperative 188

Chapter 2: Cultural Selection and
the Human Succession 196

Chapter 3: A Brief Natural History of Humanity 200

Chapter 4: The Population Bomb
and Global Circumscription 204

Chapter 5: Global Environmental Circumscription.... 210

Chapter 6: Militarism 214

Chapter 7: Authoritarianism 219

Chapter 8: Socio-Structural Inequalities 223

Chapter 9: Ethno-cultures 228

Chapter 10: World Systems—Open and Closed 233

Part II—Basic Principles and Progress.....................237

Chapter 11: Alternative Development.......................238

Chapter 12: Non-Violence & Pacifist Revolution 243

Chapter 13: Human Rights and States' Rights..........249

Chapter 14: Human Rights and
Anthropological Relativity 253

Chapter 15: Earthboundness...................................255

Chapter 16: Global Eco-culture 260

Chapter 17: Human Development.............................265

Chapter 18: Techno-Ecology and Eco-Technology...270

Chapter 19: The Information Revolution
and the Dawn of the Information Age 275

Chapter 20: Global Culture, Global Society
& Global Civilization...280

Chapter 21: Beyond the 21st Century 284

Afterward (2023)..287

Appendix A: Universal Natural Rights
& Human Responsibilities.......................................288

Appendix B: Statement on Techno-Ecology
and Eco-Technology...296

Appendix C: A Preliminary Definition of
the Global Commons...300

Appendix D: Notes and Queries
on a Minimalist Framework......................................304

For Life on Earth and Civilization in the Stars

EARTH WORKS (1991)

Essays on Human Development in Recent Earth History

Hugh M. Lewis

Preface to Earth Works (2023)

I wrote Earth Works about 31 years ago, in the Summer of 1992. Even after more than thirty years, the writing in this text represents more a set of living documents than something epigraphically bound to my past biography.

In a sense, all my work continues to consist of living documents, even in my senior years. I would not mind either, that they may continue to live through others' attention and efforts, than just becoming epigraphic at the end of my days.

But it is not the texts themselves that I would wish to live beyond myself in some corporate guise. Rather, it is the extension and elaboration of useful ideas and knowledge to the larger problem of human survival upon and beyond earth (and the even greater challenge of the earth's survival of humankind.)

We had just returned from China and in rereading the work now I am somewhat surprised that China then was not the reference point to some of the text that it has since become. In editing the work now for this publication of the work, I am also surprised somewhat that many of the ideas carried forward in an applicable way to unfolding realities in our contemporary world.

We just recently crested the estimate of 7.5 billion human souls on earth sometime around 2013-2015. Now in 2023, we have certainly surpassed the Club of Rome estimated "Limits to Growth" global carrying capacity set back in the early 1970s.

We are looking by United Nations 2017 population update for the global human population to reach between 8.4 and 8.7 Billion by 2030, and between 9.4 and 10.2 billion by 2050 (the lower estimated trajectories being the best possible scenario.)

Carrying capacity of the earth, for richer or poorer, will have to be able to accommodate between 9.6 and 13.2 billion human beings on earth, after which population is expected to "slow down in its growth and even off.

Of course global carrying capacity is inversely proportional to relative degree of global social-circumscription, and depends upon our cultural technological capacities and policies to effectively intervene and interfere with the natural world for the sake of human population growth.

A key set of factors governing these outcomes appears to be what might be referred to as human developmental momentum in certain socio-structural trajectories relating to urbanization, fertility, increasing quality and quantity of life, functional linkage between core and periphery (or urban and rural) contexts, and the capacity of urban core areas to effectively absorb population with employment opportunities for adults and educational, welfare and heath services for children.

This links to lowering infant mortality rates and lower fertility of young women overall, as well as with increasing average rates of longevity.

PART I: ANTHROPOLOGICAL PROSPECTUS

Whole Worlds in a Nutshell

Anthropology has long stood aloof from the common existential concerns of its principle object of study, humankind, as the academic arbiter of human understanding, as well as being the scientific referee of issues of human development and predicaments.

Though many individual anthropologists may express strong concern for the welfare and affairs of the other, Anthropology as a corporate enterprise dedicated to the scientific understanding of humankind has for the most part remained consistently along the sidelines of the unfolding events of human history in the making, and has, by itself, done next to nothing to alter the direction of recent developments on earth or to attempt to prevent the passing of many unfortunate episodes.

We can look to anthropology for documentation, assessments, analysis, information, interpretation, reporting and alternative points of view, but we can no longer naively believe that anthropology would ever provide the kind of assistance or intellectual support that will in the long run make a critical difference or a lasting contribution to the future of the world order. Of course the professional community of anthropologists in majority voice would disclaim any such mission in the first place. It is perhaps only people like myself who see anthropology as offering viable solutions to global dilemmas.

For the most part, anthropologists as field researchers and as empirical scientists have preoccupied themselves with the local and the microscopic lens of human minutia, and from this they have sought to derive definite general rules and principles of human culture and society, as well as the universal laws of human nature.

But they have for the most part eschewed the global or even the regional or interregional as themselves legitimate subjects of central focus, and currently appropriate frames of analysis by themselves, except perhaps in terms of a brief passing phase of 'hologeist' studies of cross-cultural comparison in that the ultimate units of analysis remain the problems of the other at a local level.

But hypothetically speaking, anthropology remains the appropriate 'possible' framework of understanding in a systematic and elucidating way many recent events that are of an earth shaking scale and for the socio cultural dynamics and problems of human development as both problem causing and potentially problem solving, and for the relatively recent events of human developments as critically bound up with the recent evolutionary and ecological history of the earth.

It is the traditional and methodological holism, relativism, synthetic holism and comparison that renders anthropology such a possible an integrative paradigm for the framing of larger-scale problems, as it provides anthropology with a powerful way of seeing and interpreting human realities in that the interrelatedness of things humanly and anthropologically significant can be understood within horizons beyond implicit ethnocentric biases and normal, conventional boundaries of knowing the world.

The inherent way of comparing elements and aspects cross culturally and trans-subjectively, and the ethnographic and ethnological instrumentality of integrating and configuring from a broad range of difference and diversity in the world general images and paradigms for understanding humankind, allows anthropology the potential power for stepping outside of its own academic boundaries and for coming to terms with the collective existential human problems in the whole world in such a way as to both provide substantial solutions for such problems as well as to provide increased understanding of such problems.

The world of anthropology, or what I've called Anthropologia, has been undergoing a major crisis within the last decade. For some it is a crisis of professional identity, for others it represents a major paradigmatic revolution, while for others it is the pre-paradigmatic birth throes of a fully developed, Mature Science of Humankind that will no longer be hooked upon the horns of self-definitional dilemmas.

<u>Earthbound Perspectives</u>

The problem with this paradigmatic perspective is that all departments and all communities of anthropologists cannot yet decide upon and settle down to a single common set of paradigmatic definitions and puzzle solving praxis. Nor would such uniformity be desirable in any more open anthropology.

Some think the way to such scientific unity and consensus is through cultural materialism, others believe it is in terms of a toned down political economy, still others believe it to be in terms of socio-biology and bio-cultural analysis. Still others believe that the future of scientific anthropology lies in more reliable cross-cultural comparisons.

Even others more theoretically and philosophically inclined believe that perhaps anthropology is non-paradigmatic or at best poly-paradigmatic anyway, or is actually a strange in-between mixture of too much science and not enough of the humanities. So the long sought after sense of unity, and the general unifying theory upon that such paradigmatic normalcy can be based, still eludes the fieldworker and researcher of any and all persuasions.

But the crisis of identity occurring within anthropology is not just a problem of its paradigmatic possibilities and its department dynamics or its professional politics. It is a more fundamental crises that is occurring throughout Academia, and that has roots much deeper in the history of ideology, understanding and in the earth itself, than many people yet realize.

Existential human realities upon an encapsulated earth have caught up with academia in general and with Anthropologia in particular. Anthropologia has run up against its own basic existential horizons if earthbound in a world that is changing more rapidly than its tradition bound methods allow it to comprehend or grasp.

Understanding of human reality, and the human realities of understanding, was never meant to be parsed up, and separated into different, exclusive disciplines and academic fields of study. Such realities are becoming increasingly complex and interrelated, cross disciplinary, such that boundaries and horizons of human understanding once neatly bound within academic tradition are rapidly becoming disrupted and fused together upon the peripheries of collective human consciousness, and upon the margins of the Academic mainstream.

The basic symptoms are the pervasive feelings of discontentment and dissatisfaction that the usual, time tested ways of doing things are no longer adequate or efficient enough to keep pace with the rate and number of changes happening in the human world. As a consequence, information and understanding between the said of the academic version of the world. The tried and the true of the time tested ways of the past, is the done of the wider world of humankind that no longer prizes the past in the quest for the new, the novel and the better, is growing wider and wider, and more and more unbridgeable.

In terms of Anthropologia, this crisis is experienced as an ex-colonial empire that has come home at least since the early 1970s. In the rectification of its identity, names have changed but the basic rules of the game remains the same. Economic imperialism has replaced earlier versions of political imperialism, in an ever shifting political-economic balance, but the underlying factors of military aggression and imperialistic predominance remain structurally the same, except for increasing lethality and destructiveness of modern weapons of war.

Political economic strategies and capitalistic systems of world order have relinquished their old charter of westernization for a new global charter of modernization. Bureaucratic encapsulation within a world system has co-opted and usurped the old ways of administrative colonialism.

Now there are more game players, and more pieces of the pie, and more people in the world who must be accounted for. What was once the Americana of manifest destiny and the new world, has become the Pax Americanization, Internationalization and capitalistic acculturation of the new frontiers of the whole world and the entire encapsulated earth. Developmental policies have become political economic domination by other means, and the need for 'defensive' military aggression is but a temporary lapse of normal political economic function.

As Empire returns home, Anthropologia has becomes increasingly reflexive in search of its lost sense of otherness that it had so long taken for granted in the world. Or, put another way, what is increasingly happening to anthropologists is that they are awakening to a world without a global commons or a shared sense of common good, in which only the sense of self remains.

The original other has become merged into our own sense of identity as other senses of the self. Anthropologists are no longer bent on making the strange seem familiar, but must now deal with a strangeness and estrangement of the familiar. And the anthropological sense of self that remains in the world, is neither monolithic nor monothetic.

Beneath a very thin veil of a very narrow ego identity might gain through association within the world system, the sense of self has become fragmented, shattered and disintegrated. The genuine identity of the multicultural anthropological self in the world has become culture shocked into a state of psychosocial schizophrenia. Losing an objective sense of otherness in the shared world, we have also lost and permanently challenged a subjective sense of self in our own worlds. All that remains is a thin veneer of professional ego identity in search of both self and other in the world.

Only if and when anthropology finally learns to step outside of the terminological and definitional battles of its own dialectics and beyond the sphere of influence of its own paradigmatic politics will it be able to recover an undivided sense of ego identity in the world.

Only then will it be able to relearn how to deal with both otherness and sense of self in the world without the dilemmas of a dichotomized reality. Anthropology as a corporate enterprise cannot accomplish this difficult task, but anthropologists as independently acting individuals and as members of a shared humanity can and must attempt this feat. The world may never have needed Anthropologia, but Anthropologia has always needed the world.

Anthropology, as an alternative way of understanding human possibility in the world, provides both a general framework for the theoretical understanding of the human world, and a realistic accounting of the general phenomenal patterning encountered in that world. Anthropology can offer a different way of seeing the world and a different way of relating to that world. As such, it can offer the promise of a different possible version of that world.

A general global model of recent developments of earth history is available for understanding the interrelationships of many otherwise quite disparate but nonetheless interdependent elements and events.

Simply put, continuing technological development in the directions of the past one hundred or more years, coupled with a rapidly increasing world population of 8 or 9 or more billion earthbound souls that is estimated to soon surpass the carrying capacity of lifeboat earth, is leading rapidly to basically un-rehabilitated degradation and destruction of many ecosystems of the earth's environment.

General global environmental circumscription in terms if decreasing available resources, imbalanced ecosystems and human induced erosion and pollution, will become coupled with increasing social circumscription of global over population to further squeeze the world political economic system and to create stresses and tensions that on one hand will induce greater degrees of authoritarianism, and on the other, increasingly destabilize the functional adaptability and coherence of the system.

The net consequence is that the world system has reached a supercritical zenith of its developmental growth beyond which periodic, expectable but wholly random and unpredicted damaging events will recur that functions to maintain the overall stability of the whole system.

Food prices will continue to climb, along with basic energy costs, and the whole cost of living will soar to become essentially unaffordable to more and more people who are driven outward and downward by a system of capitalistic development that has run out off control.

Increasing inequality coupled with decreasing availability will generate many minor revolutions of rising expectation, that either grow beyond control to induce drastic structural changes or else lead to extreme authoritarian reactions and much social violence.

<u>Earthbound Perspectives</u>

One expectable and likely consequence of this general development will be increasing global militarization in terms of horizontal escalation as opposed to continued vertical escalation of nuclear armaments.

Horizontal escalation could in the long run prove to be more inherently destabilizing that the vertical escalation of the past has been, but one very plausible scenario of an outcome of such escalation, of multilateral armaments, is the occurrence of another world war, the basic destructiveness of which surpasses the nuclear threshold.

Global nuclear holocaust would have sudden and drastic consequences for the future of human development and earth history. Humankind will be thrust literally into another dark ages from which there may be no any significant reemergence.

But even if a global holocaust never happens, there would be definite destructive long-term consequences of historically recent human events on earth. The quality of life for virtually everyone will continue to rapidly deteriorate, even for the fortunate few who struggle to remain in positions of control.

Their long-term success will hardly have been worth the net costs, and no amount of ideological delusion or deceit would be able to dispel the globally pervasive disillusionment for everyone that must inevitably be a consequence of the global environmental degradation of the earth.

For many more, life will only prove to be a matter of more poverty, violence, and opportunity-less than ever before. There will be fewer compensations or consolations for failure to make a modern living in the world. There will become fewer escapes or fewer ways out of the existential predicaments and entanglements that we shall find ourselves thrust deeper and deeper into.

The loss of quality of life will be reflected in the increasing spuriousness, alienation, anomie and aloneness in an increasingly impersonal, over crowded and complex social world. Fewer and fewer people will be able to afford to find themselves, to avoid increasing exploitation or else systematic exclusion and under employment. Life and living will become more bureaucratically encapsulated and more political economically controlled indirectly by people whom we will never have occasion to meet, challenge or even answer for.

Education, for example, will become increasingly consumption oriented and decreasingly productive per educational dollar spent. Education will entail economic and social institutional entrapment for many whose experience and personal development prevent them from entering the world system at a level commensurate to their level of education. Schools will become seen more and more as social reservoirs that serve to keep in suspended animation a larger, exploitable pool of human resources who might otherwise, if left un-isolated in the world, have a destabilizing effect.

No one really knows exactly how many resources are yet available, or actually how resilient the global ecology of the earth might be, or what its carrying capacity of the total population of humankind might really be.

Much less do we know what the long-term human responses to increasing levels of stress and circumscription, or social-functional-adaptive reverberations within the world system that might result, or what kinds of militaristic crises might eventually be precipitated from increasing conflict, tension and competition for fewer and fewer resources, coupled with the over shadowing doom of future diminishment, depletion and deprivation. But anthropological theory and evidence supports the general model of increasing dysfunctional equilibrium of a global system and ecology and a likely scenario of major systemic events that produces damaging reverberations worldwide.

Whether we might survive such a doomsday or not, whether intact or by bits and pieces, what role scientific and technological progress and economic development may play in both spurring forward these dire developments, and in further increasing our ability to adapt, remains to be finally discovered. As it is today, it is extremely difficult to look beyond the storm clouds upon our current earth horizon, to forecast brighter, better days ahead.

The kinds of question that will be of more and more concern for more and more people are existential problems of how the general global predicaments impact upon and affect elements of everyday life and living and what will be the daily signs and common manifestations of the changes that are rapidly taking place worldwide.

These are questions that affect except perhaps from a profit making perspective, neither the privileged elite at the apex of the progressive pyramid of world development, nor the many more who have fallen into the abyss of absolute poverty below the base of the pyramid. Life in-between the two extremes will become more or less attenuated and more and more fragile in its long-term stability, as well as increasingly over burdened by many different stresses and strains that pull in multiple, often opposite, directions.

It can be expected that everyday life will become more characterized by competition against more and more people for fewer and fewer resources, and that will mean that social pressures of downward social mobility will become stronger than the pulling forces of upward mobility. Fewer and fewer people will make it in ways that people used to in the past. And if does not prove to be true for many of us in our own generation, it will definitely prove more common in our children's generation.

Social institutions and services already strained to capacity will become more overloaded to the point that they become practically dysfunctional in meeting the needs in that they were designed to serve. Bureaucracy will grow in both size and inefficiency to deal effectively increasing numbers of human problems. Bureaucracy will come more and more institutionalized to serve a system reinforcing function rather than a social service role.

Its administrative priorities will tend to negatively outline social problem areas and thereby serve to maintain and perpetuate these problem areas in ways that render them relatively neutralized in relation to the larger social system.

On the down side this will entail erecting ever more complicated screens of obfuscation that shunt excessive people into circular networks that lead nowhere but back to the beginning. Ideologies of denial and closed-door policies will tend to permit the development of more intricate and entangled hidden secondary networks within the system that serves the real arbiter function of prioritizing private group vested interests.

The environment of the earth that surround us will begin evolving in ever more rapid transition, and the social environment will begin to crowd in upon our lives and become ever more threatening to individual sense of autonomy, control, power and security in the world.

Issues of relative powerlessness and the need for power, of lack of security and the search for security, of lack of control and autonomy and the need for exercising control and autonomy, will become greater concerns for the individual and the group, and non-being of human ego identity will come to replace in ever greater proportion the psychological sense of being of natural human self identity.

Electronic media and mechanisms of information manipulation will increasingly come to intermediate our environments and will assume an ever greater measure of influence, both directly and indirectly, in our lives.

We will become increasingly dependent upon such electronic intermediation and thus will become to rely less upon our own sensibilities and sensitivities and ego balance in making our own independent decisions. There will be a gradual usurpation upon an unconscious level of our normative independence in a general context.

Electronic media will become increasingly our artificial senses, our artificial intelligence, our artificial imaginations, our artificial voices and even our artificial actions. Direct perceptual access to significant environments will become increasingly distanced by such electronic intermediation.

We can witness the process happening even now as a whole world remains helplessly glued to television screens to watch the unfolding of military events that seem beyond anyone's control. The indirect and vicarious experience of the electronically intermediated events has come to serve as substitutes for our sense of control in the world.

What is even more problematic, that the long and complex networks of such electronic intermediation renders our basic perceptual horizon of the world subject to manipulation and interference and thus to control by agents, representatives, editors, reporters, cameramen, who cannot be accounted for and whose influence in our intermediation remains mostly hidden.

This entails that ultimate, impersonal and grand interests of social organization are in manipulative and subliminal control of our electronic perception and this control will always tend to be indirect, out of awareness and subversive to the very common sense ground of reality upon which our individual rights, freedoms and interests are rooted.

Common sense itself, as the basic ground of our existential pre-understandings, of our sensibilities, of our conceptualization and rationality of our collective values and collective imagination, and even of our conditioned consciousness and perception, is being socially rendered more and more subject to this kind of manipulative control and management, such that the very ground of our implicit and intuitive knowledge of the world is being directed and influenced by interests that are contrary to our own and over which we have slight powers or capacities to counteract or correct for.

While our collective existential electronically intermediated, environmental horizons of the world will expand and become enlarged, our own narrow personal normative horizons will proportionately shrink and diminish in relevance in relation to the world.

As our natural environments and being become replaced by artificially constructed social environment and sense of nonbeing in the world, we must face more and more the inevitable consequences of a basic individual atomization, alienation and aloneness, if not loneliness, in an overcrowded, and impersonal world. We have to learn to live with increasing existential indeterminacy and indecision, such that even the choices that we feel we must make are not clearly definable or discernible in our lives. We must act, but we will no longer know in what direction or exactly how to act.

We are on the verge of a mass oriented world society of a mass-oriented humankind defined in terms of increasingly technological mass oriented values and behaviors. Such mass orientation will be material but not spiritual; it will be collective but highly impersonal. It will be automatic and mechanical and participatory, but not voluntary; it will have great quantity but be significantly lacking in any quality.

We must learn to live collectively with the ideological delusion and mythological illusions of a cyborg humankind—a cybernetically, electronically intermediated, orgasmic body of humankind that combines in strange ways natural and artificial elements, and yet in which the natural is always subject of and subordinated to the functions of the artificial, the cosmetic, the material and hedonistic.

Our lives are becoming increasingly composed of a moiré patterning of both vegetable and organic elements and plastic and synthetic components. We yield more and more a true baseline sense of genuine mechanical organism for the overpriced, cheap promise of its pretension.

The future development of human civilization will not be all bad. It will mostly be just different, and much more difficult in some ways than it has recently been. Human flexibility, adaptability and creativity will respond in many unpredictable ways when genuine human needs become left unsatisfied by a grand and impersonal system. People will form loose and informal networks and associations that to some extent fill in the deficit and left over.

Humans can learn to cope with and endure situations of extreme stress and deprivation, and can rapidly readjust to changes if their survival depends upon such readjustment.

The rise of ad hoc, extemporaneous, and extra legal social organization will be something to look forward to when artificial and unnatural social environmental circumstances tend to cultivate increasing alienation, isolation and an underlying sense of anomie of individual personal existence. It will provide a missing sense of interpersonal identity and meaningfulness that will counteract the negative, anti-individual tendencies of the System.

Such organizations will provide screens of resistance and alternative opportunity that will break the 'totalizing' tendencies of the System, and if successful, will in the long run erode the base of social support of the private closed System.

<u>Earthbound Perspectives</u>

It will be from this direction that unpredictable change and potentially damaging, even catastrophic events will arise and provide a limiting influence to the growth and power of the world system. It can be expected that the world system will respond with violent force in order to control such uprisings and that this will become a primary source of conflict in the future.

It is possible that the world will undergo a global kind of civil war that will split world society into contraposed interest groups divided horizontally not so much along "ethno-national" lines as diagonally along lines of class-caste lines of global social structure—dividing the world internationally between first and third world nations, and domestically within countries between the upper and lower classes.

The long-term outcome of such a kind of conflict would be difficult to estimate, except to say that like most civil conflicts it is likely to be very bloody (and perhaps even more unnecessary.)

The point is that many people who are systematically excluded from normal participation within the world system, will not be left completely hopeless and helpless to struggle for themselves together against the dictates and over-determination by the elite of the system.

The main stratagem of the system will be to systematically divide and conquer social groups in order to turn the frustration of people against one another and to prevent aggression from becoming focused upon the system itself or its elite.. It does this through exaggeration and inflation of competition between individuals and groups in the struggle for limited basic resources.

Individuals will also tend to be selectively isolated or removed from normal participation within the system is a very surreptitious manner, and potential oppositional leadership will tend to be bought off or co-opted into the system to serve as administrative mediators on behalf of the interests of the system.

But people who find themselves still existentially apart from the system will eventually awaken to their common plight and must sooner or later coalesce together to form social movements in resistance to or outside of the normal boundaries of the system. Such groupings will find common ground for grievance and resistance against the system.

The only way that the system will be able to exert control and try to stem the rise of such unification of grass roots resistance to its dictates and determination will be to increasingly augment its mechanisms of programmatic behavior modification, brain washing, media manipulation and persuasion, and ideological conversion, by more and more authoritarian and totalitarian means.

The reaction of naked force and brutal violence to suppress popular resistance may work in the short term but in the long-term will tend to expose the raw inequities and naked power of the system, and will counteract to crystallize even more organized resistance against it.

The long-term consequences will be a vicious cycle of the escalation of violence and conflict as contraposed interest groups become more and more polarized between extremes and more and more people become caught in between in the crossfire.

It is hoped that the long-term outcome of this global civil war within the world system will be incremental democratization of the world system and a compromise and popular control of its power by increasing the level of popular participation within the system and by the elimination of socio structural exclusion.

It will either be this or the eventual disintegration of the world system as we know it now into a plethora of struggle and competing ethno-national states accompanied by increasing amounts of corruption the higher up the ladder of control and consumption.

The controlling elite will eventually be rendered incompetent to prevent the further fragmentation of the world system and the disaffection of its specialist functionaries.

There are one of two general directions that the world can go, on an earth the living spaces of which are becoming increasingly circumscribed by human activity and habitation.

One direction is towards increased polarization between the haves and the have-nots. This direction will entail attempts to maintain stability in core areas and to keep instability marginalized in the interstices and peripheries. As long as the illusion of peace can be fostered in the core, virtually any amount of trouble can be tolerated in the periphery.

Polarization will tend to create a two-tiered worldwide closed class society, the relations between which will be mediated by an in-between group that is part of neither tier. The upper tier will possess most of the wealth and control most of the capital and resources.

They will tend to own property and will be characterized by their long-term inhabitance of core areas. The mobility patterns of this tier will be quite different from the mobility patterns of the bottom tier. They will regularly travel in wide circles, but maintain fixed locations as places of long-term residence.

The lower tier will be characterized by its basic rootlessness and pervasive long-term homelessness. Their migration patterns will follow labor trails and routes of socio economic opportunity, but they will as a class-caste become characterized by their relative lack of property ownership, capital investment and wealth, and by their long-term transience and marginality at the edges of the core.

Any given area will become characterized by a local elite who are more or less interlinked with a virtually global cosmopolitan network of the elite, and by a movable mass that is characterized by its shifting distributions and its geographic mobility, and that is interconnected with its own international network of labor traffic.

Urban demographics and social distributions and patterns of consumption and lifestyle will be very different from surrounding rural areas, but urban areas globally will be more alike to one another around the world than they are to their proximate surrounding rural and functionally underdeveloped regions.

The in-between middle cosmopolitan and suburban class caste will be characterized by a lack of its own identity vis-à-vis the elite and the rootless masses, by its own internal stratification and divisions replicating the larger social structural pattern globally, and by its sacrifice of both mobility and ownership for a modicum of social security and extremely limited and restricted control.

In any area, it will compose the administrative bureaucracy; the functional, face-to-face intermediaries between the lower rungs of the upper class caste and the upper rungs of the lower class-caste.

From the perspective of the elite, they will be as specialized, but mostly part faceless masses, while from the standpoint of the underclasses and rootless masses of ground labor, they will be seen as if privileged elite.

It will be characterized by a shallow reactionary (or radical revolutionary) ideology of the system and by its pervasive superficial sense of false consciousness. From the standpoint of the upper class caste, it will be more like the lower class caste, but from the standpoint of the lower class caste it will reflect the values and symbolisms and authority of the upper class caste.

Its primary function will not be one of gate keeping so much as gate barring or locking, and the maintenance of mechanisms that create screens of obfuscation that effectively hide the activities of the upper elite and also glorify their status. It will also have the dirty job of enforcing the authority from above upon the lower classes.

Such a scenario would resemble somewhat South African social structure, except instead of enforced Apartheid, there would a worldwide cultural wasteland of shifting poor people, and many small defensive islands of the elite.

The elite and the have-nots will live and lead effectively separate lives, and the worldwide social structure will be characterized by class caste endogamy and occupational specialization, such that the lower classes castes will fill all menial and skilled labor positions at the bottom of the hierarchy, controlled by managers of managers of managers that forms its own marginal middle class hierarchy within a hierarchy, that is in turn controlled from above by the elite.

We are today not far from such a world order. It is one in that ethno-national identities are being crossed out and broken down by hierarchical diagonal loyalties within separate class caste positions, such that members of one class caste in one nation have more in common from a socio-structural standpoint with their counterparts in other nations, than with their own ethno-national elites.

From this standpoint, fostering ethno-national consciousness is a way of effectively sundering cross cutting ties between the lowest rank and file that might pose a problem to the elite, while the elite of different ethno-nations are becoming more and more interlinked with one another and are beginning more and more to form common interest groups.

It falls to the middle class caste managerial group again to interconnect the ethno national ideologies with the private interests of the controlling elite, such that they themselves tend to embody and act out the ethno-national ideologies and thereby themselves remain effectively fragmented and segregated along these lines. These groups will come to adopt a standard ethno-national cultural orientation that proclaims its own embodiment of tradition, mythology and values.

This kind of Pakistan scenario will stress the social distance and unbridgeable reality between the few haves and the many have-nots who are themselves organized in such a way as to keep one another from accomplishing anything in life.

Buying into the illusions of the ideologies and false consciousness reinforced by the mass oriented media, the lower rank and file will compete with one another to rise to the middle managerial positions, that, despite the promise of national leadership, will remain basically insecure and precarious in its inter-positioning vis-à-vis the global cosmopolitan elite and the ever shifting masses.

The other kind of direction that world order can go is in terms of bridging more effectively the gulf between the rich and the poor by the introduction and promotion of social programs, through socialization, of mechanisms that effectively redistribute wealth and level it in such a way as to demote its accumulation into the hands of a few.

Such a direction of development will lead to a formation of a strong, genuine middle class group, strong enough and wealthy enough to function separately and independently of any elite groups. Such a scenario would also depend critically on a global infrastructure of cheap and sustainable energy platforms.

In such a scenario, the middle managerial class will provide effective screens of opportunity and of support, that provide a means of escape from poverty at the bottom and that limits the accumulation of power and resources at the top.

Instead of being characterized by its bureaucratic gate barring function, as immigration authorities, and instead of the false consciousness and promotion of chauvinist ethno-national ideologies, this class will be rather well educated and will tend towards a multicultural orientation promoting attitudes of tolerance for diversity and difference and protection of human rights and freedoms.

An upper and lower class will always remain, but they will be more circumscribed than the middle classes that will be characterized by their diversity, and social forces will tend towards a convergence to the middle.

It is possible that some of both scenarios will be present in the future, and that world order will become characterized by a curious admixture of both directions of social development. It is impossible that in these contraposed tendencies the lines of stress and future conflict will appear—between local societies tending to merge in the middle and International Systems tending to polarize toward the extremes. There are also cases of varying degrees of mixed systems.

This kind of scenario depends upon the future diminishing importance of the cultural and geographical, and linguistic boundaries that have historically separated people into different groups, and the increasing power and significance of a worldwide socio political economic system that is symbolically reinforced through the use of electronic media.

Ethno-national identities, loyalties and interests will remain, but become encompassed by and encapsulated within a global framework of socio structural role status identity and personal interests within the world system.

Civilization as a global, inherently trans-cultural phenomena of socio structural integration, will tend to become more deeply embedded in the everyday life of each individual no matter what that person's relative position, to the point that these social forces tend to orient that individual more toward functional and symbolic solidarity within a world order than in terms of ethno-national or traditional loyalties to separate, distinct ethno-national and cultural orientations.

Ethno-national and cultural identity will remain, but it will become increasingly subservient to and functionally dependent upon the world system, as a principle mechanism of maintaining class caste hegemony and for promoting false consciousness and ideological disunity among the lowest classes.

Either direction of general social development depends upon the rise of a global civilization and of world consciousness that effectively transcends and overcomes the culture historical barriers between different peoples. These differences between groupings of people will be long maintained, but how the groups become interrelated within a global framework will become critical to determining the final long-term consequences of human development upon earth.

The Pakistani model will tend to promote chauvinism between such groups that serve a legitimating and reinforcing function of class caste polarization within a world system. The second general direction of development will lead, instead of chauvinism, to widespread pluralism and multiculturalism, and to general tendencies of social integration promoted by the brokerage and intermediating function of the middle class. Culture historical identity and heritage will remain important, but will become further relativized within an increasingly embedded context of a world wide multicultural continuum.

Also central to the understanding of these two general directions of human development is the validity of the notion of class-caste and the kind of diagonal solidarity that it is implicitly based upon.

Class caste is most generally reflected in the notion of first world, second world, third world, fourth world, fifth world and perhaps even a little recognized sixth world, that are most frequently used when describing world society.

Class caste also recognizes the consequences of long-term embedding of social stratification such that the definitional lines distinguishing clearly between a class and a caste are no longer sharp or even readily demarcated.

Global stratification within world society becomes effectively multi-tiered or in a sense triple canopied. Class-castes exist mutually side-by-side, and people lead functionally interrelated lives across boundaries, but at the same time they lead lives that are in every respect symbolically and structurally separated and different.

Important to this notion also is that international core periphery relations between upper and lower class castes will be reflective of and reflected by many similar domestic core periphery relations between the local level elite and the local poor. Even now we can find many such social correlates between a domestic analogy; say of homelessness, institutionalization, rural poverty, etc. and an international paradigm of refugees, immigrants, colonization, and displaced person of the "other" third-world.

More and more, the rise of global stratification and of world civilization will become characterized by an increasing structural isomorphism between international relations and domestic situations. International wars come to resemble more and more police actions to keep the peace, such that international differences between core and periphery will become reflected and embodied in domestic relations between core areas of key development and peripheral areas of underdevelopment.

These processes will come to superimpose a global hegemony of a world system cultural orientation in that separate ethno-national versions will come to resemble more and more minor variations upon a common theme of complex capitalist-authoritarian political-economic state development. Ethno-national cultures will become more and more oriented around the same focal standards of the world system.

The net affect of this is that in either direction, class caste differences within a global framework of a world system will come to increasingly override or undermine ethno-national cultural differences as the basis for political-economic and social determination.

If polarization occurs along lines of the diagonal stratification between ethno-class-caste, then it is likely that this difference will be symbolically and ideologically reinforced by a kind of fascism and social racism in that the elite ethno-class-caste becomes associated with conceptions of natural beauty, superiority, rationality, ability, while the lower class caste become associated with conceptions of natural ugliness, pollution, ineptitude, inferiority, irrationality, etc.

These may become socially racist to the extent that certain symbolisms of innateness become closely associated with certain body types, physique, facial appearance, manner of speech, etc. These racial preconceptions of superior natural fitness will cross cut old dividing lines of skin color or racial blood type, etc., such that selection will be on the basis of certain presumed natural physical characteristics etc.

That natural direction of development becomes predominant will be in part determined by that kind of cultural value orientation of a world ethno-class-caste becomes embedded—whether or not values emphasizing social difference, individual freedom, and distance, of hierarchy, authority and symbolisms.

I would add two more worlds—a fifth and a sixth world, and would add that the international paradigms for these worlds have domestic equivalents within the modern social structure of any region or nation-state territory.

Briefly the six worlds consist of the following:

1. The First World are the elite, or global alpha class, much less than one percent of the world's population, who occupy the very apex of the social pyramid and who control and consume most of the world's resources. Their primary function within the world system is that of consumption and symbolic reinforcement of the ethos of the system by sumptuary privilege. Typically, the economy of the first world is characterized as a professional, service related occupational structure within a consumer coordinator 'post industrial' economy. Service jobs are high paying with low supervision and facilitate the consumption of products of the capitalistic system.

2. The Second World consists of the middle class bureaucrat managers who are the next ten to twenty percent of the pyramid and whose jobs are had within a

redistributive centralized economy. Their function is to maintain symbolically the ideology of the system, to control and manipulate the dissemination of information, and to intermediate all relations between the first world and the rest. Their jobs tend to be low to medium paying but higher in security benefits. This world is characterized by its incorporation and embodiment of the values of the system, by its potential fascism, false consciousness, hypocrisy and hierarchy.

3. The Third World consists of the next sixty to seventy percent of the population pyramid whose primary function is labor production within the world system—production characterized by low pay for long and hard physical work, high supervision, lack of job security, transience. This is a plebeian-proletariat working class whose jobs range from unskilled to semi-skilled to skilled specialization. Though they make up the greatest bulk of the global population, they control proportionately the least amount of the world's resources. This group also comprises the rural peasantry of the world and consists of the greatest amount of intercultural diversity.

4. The Fourth World is the bottom ten to fifteen percent who are characterized by their joblessness or marginality within the world system. They may be groups either internally colonized or as in black American ghettos of the US or in apartheid in white South Africa, or else they may occupy the 'no man's land' of the very fringes of the World periphery in harsh environments in that only the very most basic forms of 'resource' production occur—forestry, mining, fishing, drilling, wild harvesting etc.

5. The Fifth World is the bottom, less than ten percent of the pyramid, representing the very base of this pyramid. They are the international refugees who lack a permanent residence or a homeland, and the domestic homeless who have been systematically excluded from participation within the world system. These are the sacrificial victims of the world system that represent mechanisms of population control. These people have been selected out

of the system as relatively unemployed and unemployable.

6. The Sixth World is a marginal residual category comprise only of two to five percent of the world's population. These are people who are permanently removed from participation within the system, or are forcibly isolated in prisons, asylums or as the inhabitants and street people of skid row.

The last three Worlds represent the black hole of absolute poverty—people whose lives are caught within a inescapable and vicious cycle of lack of resources, opportunities and early violent death.

The Third World contains the bulk of the population and are characterized by their relative deprivation and the exploitability of their existential situations. Their life is a grand lottery game in that their little money is exchanged for high hopes and grand disappointments within the world system.

It has been common to rank nations along this kind of scale depending upon the relative positions and proportions of population within these countries when compared nomothetically with others, of sumptuary wealth and privilege, or else values emphasizing social equality, pan-human commonality, individual identity etc.

The defining features of ethno-class-caste within the world system will be the coexistence of functionally integrated yet socially separate worlds that work and define themselves counter-referentially in relation to one another and yet that lead and live separate but parallel lives in separate socially constructed sub-worlds.

In essence the social structure of the world system will be a two tiered society in that the world of the upper and lower classes are functionally separated by one another by an intermediate class caste that defines its own functionality and marginality within the world system in maintaining this uneven class-caste structure, the system in which it is reinforced and institutionalized.

It is interesting that as this system develops, what in one set of circumstances might appear to be ethno-national exogamy or interracial marriage, may actually be instances of class-caste endogamy.

Social mobility and stratification can be described as diagonal within multiple overlapping hierarchies rather than as vertical within a single hierarchy or horizontal within multiple but separate hierarchies.

Whether polarization increases between the upper and lower classes, or a direction of convergence towards the middle is achieved, would be reflected by the amount of class caste intermarriage and integration of the middle class, and by the degree of social mobility that can be achieved by way of the middle class.

If the direction towards increased polarization occurs, then the middle class would become more and more functionally marginalized, and the amount of social interaction between the groups will be minimized. This group will then be characterized by its downward social mobility and its delegation of negative authority as a rigid bureaucratic hierarchy. It will then tend to become endogamous and hypergamous.

Within the social structure of the world system it has been typical to divide society up into four worlds defined by their separation and by their functional interrelation within the countries of the world. But it must be remembered that all six worlds can be found within any and all nations in differing proportions and degrees of difference and social distance.

It is also true that the position of any person or group or nation within such a framework is always relative to the local, regional or international context in that it is framed. It is the basic relativity of the positioning within the world system that renders such a typological scheme problematic, over-simplifying and blind to many expectations to its paradigmatic rule.

People move between worlds quite frequently; boundaries between worlds are frequently porous, undetermined and unclear. There exist structural in-betweens or inter-position in that people may share in more than one world at the same time. It is the case that the quality of life for many third world people may be relatively superior to that of many first world inhabitants, and that people of the third world living in core areas may have more materially and quantitatively than many first world people living in peripheral zones.

Positing two alternative directions for human social development within the World System focuses upon an alternative theory of social change and structuration that emphasizes the central determining role played by the social structural middle ground, occupied by the intermediate functioning of a middle "beta" class, rather than by either the material substructure or the ideological superstructure. In this version of this version of the historical dialectics of the development of human civilization, the central inter-position of the intermediate groups are critical to the direction of change within the society at large.

It represents the fulcrum, the center of gravity around which the social extremes teeter totter for control. In this regard the middle classes can function hierarchically and reactively, and itself becomes effectively sundered and nonexistent in the polarization between the extremes. Else it can on its own coalesce to create the major oppositional force to the predominant structure of any society. Change impacts upon and comes from the relative position and functioning of the middle classes in the articulation of the social system.

The center of gravity provides the source of leadership in alternative social movements, and can provide the loci of power and center of balance about that change within a society. In their intermediating function, in their articulation of social process and change, and in their controlling function within the system and symbolic role of ideological reinforcement and embodiment, this class becomes the focal point of the stresses and conflicts within any social structure and paradoxically also represent the group with the greatest power and strategic control to effect changes, if it can be organized and mobilized.

The history of human civilization, of the rise, fluorescence, decay and demise of societies on earth, can be seen as an accordion effect of contraction and expansion of social structure, such that one period of growth is characterized by convergence to the middle, followed in dialectical counterpoint by a phase of expansion and polarization towards the extremes that effectively splits the middle class and leads to social movement and structural change.

The development of human civilization has represented the spread of this historical dialectic of expansion/contraction, polarization/convergence, or mobilization/relaxation, such that more and more groupings of humankind become incorporated within this process as in the long run it tends toward convergence in centers of development that organizes ever-greater aggregations of people around its sphere of influence.

In this sense, civilizations are part of a culture historical process of selection. Civilizations compete with one another in access to resources, power, control, until eventually a single state will win out and monopolize the world order, except that in the process of culture historical competition the nature and structure of civilization will itself become transformed through processes of acculturative assimilation and integration of differences.

The primary function of the middle class within human civilization has been the intermediation of differences and the process of social mobilization and mobility. As such the middle class is always inter-positional and somewhat precarious on its relation between upper and lower classes, and its relative status will be a marker of the structural state of a given society.

One final consideration of anthropological importance in relation to the world system concerns the mechanisms that are readily employed for cultivating and maintaining conformity within the system and for controlling or eliminating nonconformity from the system. These mechanisms may be glossed as the following:

Propagandistic persuasion, deceit, manipulation, and control of information, official jargon, legalese, bureaucratese and double speak, designed to deceive, mislead, distort information, and to convince people of the legitimacy and authority of the System.

Behavior modification, punishment, negative and positive reinforcement, social ostracism, scapegoating, in group/out group consciousness etc., are all examples of social control, as is the inducement of conversion through stress.

Media manipulation of people's psyche, consciousness, motivation, levels of aggression, symbolic violence, unconsciousness and even their perception of the world. The use of subtle and subversive techniques of sublimation and symbolization is one example.

Ideological brainwashing to produce conversion experiences and to breakdown psychological resistance to ideological conformity provides yet another avenue of social manipulation and deliberate, premeditated control.

Widespread use and misuse of different drugs and narcotics lower people's rational resistance to the system and to induce passivity and controllability.

Control, legitimization and professionalization of intelligence and information possession is yet another mechanism. Access to kinds of information is graded and restricted, and a great deal of censorship and editorship goes on behind closed doors to control what people know and think about.

Symbolic promotion of values of material mass consumption that tends to hook people into dependency patterns within the world system in the long run to deprive them of actual or apparent independence from the system.

Promotion of attitudes and actions reflective of authority, hierarchy, dominance, fear, guilt, aggressiveness, competition that tend to reinforce predominant orientations and the status quo of power structure within the world system.

All of these mechanisms, as well as others, become interrelated and inter-functionally dependent in the reinforcement and structuration of the individual within the system. It is sometimes very difficult to tell where one kind of mechanism leaves off and another takes over.

It is important to emphasize the difference between manifest and latent purpose of the system, to foster ideological support and false consciousness on one hand, and on the other to hide or systematically obfuscate the realities of power and transaction that goes on within the system, and to legitimize the persecution, exclusion or destruction of out-groups or nonconformist individuals in the promotion and protection of the private, special interests that drive and control the system.

These mechanisms have all been technically developed and improved through trial and error and research and development, and have become much more effective in their power to subversively control the individual psyche and to render individual behavior more predictable.

PART II: NATURE'S CLOCKWORKS
Unwinding Time for Humankind

It is of paramount importance that we learn to see ourselves evolutionarily and ecologically in relation to larger spatiotemporal contexts of nature, and come to understand how the predicaments of our current global situation is part of a longer and larger natural history of life on earth that has had its own recurrent patterning and its own sense of timing and its own scales of duration and cycles and rhythms of events and process of which we are ourselves but a very small part to play.

It is not without relevance that we see how disproportionate our own brief span of culture historical consciousness is when compared to the much longer time scales involved in the bio-cultural evolution of human prehistory, in the evolution epochs of the dinosaurs and of the great mammals on earth, or of the still much longer span of the first primeval evolution of life on earth, or of the geophysical evolution of the earth itself from the stardust of that we are ultimately all composed.

The spans of time involved in the natural unfolding of life have been so immense in comparison to our own diminished historical experiences that we really have no sound way of comprehending or coming to terms with its vast scale of change or the enormity of its long duration. So much has happened in the earth's past that we lack any proportionate frame of reference by that to relate or compare our own relatively brief breath of existence on earth.

And yet our brief moment of human history and consciousness, but a few millennia of many millions of years, has had a special significance for the natural history of the earth. The rise of human civilization on earth has effectively stopped the natural clockwork of evolution and has interfered with and altered irremediably many of the natural rhythms and processes of the earth's fragile but flexible and enduring ecology.

Life on earth will continue evolving on long after we have left it on its own, in spite of and because of our interference and destructiveness. It will evolve but not as we have come to know it, and not in the same way as it had in the deep, long past.

We will become but another evolutionary episode of its evolving history, but the climax of another of its long epochs. There may in the future be some strange creature that may refer to the Age of the Dinosaurs, the Age of the Mammals, the Age of Man, and the Age of Global Extinction. This is not meant in an apocalyptic or millennial sense of religious eschatology, but in a scientific sense of global circumscription and strangulation.

And it is impossible to tell now whether we are at the dusk of our age or really at the dawn of a new one. The twilight of our collective consciousness—whether we are just awakening from a deep evolutionary sleep or we are but the sudden psycho biotic climax of the evolution of sentience, presents us with a dilemma of how we shall regard both our deep sense of the past and the way we shall seek to know our future becoming.

We are historically in a critical period of transition that is going on all around us and that is happening within us which radically relativizes our own awareness of ourselves in relation to the world and confers upon our self-conscious identity a fundamental sense of disorientation and of being basically out of place with the larger scheme of things.

We are individually, in our own brief span of four score and ten years, insignificant in relation to the whole history of the earth. We are but frozen instances of a long march of changing events who can scarcely know or measure the slow rates of change in the world around us that in any larger framework of history would seem quite rapid. In all our will power, in all our science and technological skill, in the height of our own most modern state of civilization, we must yet bow to the mercy of historical and natural forces of change that we can yet barely understand.

These changes are as likely to become realized through us as around us in our world, and to involve us in ways we cannot control and over which the direction of which our influence will be only slight. And in the natural structure of the long run, we can never know whether our actions are helping or hindering such change, or have a consequence or are inconsequential in the grander scheme of things. Our sense of history and consciousness are just brief fragments of memory and dreams of being awake and aware in the long night of the natural world, soon to become buried over and forgotten in the dust of cosmic time.

We do not know yet how evolution works, either at a microscopic level of ontogenetic cell differentiation or organismic development of the individual nor at the macroscopic level of exactly how speciation as a process of phylogenic differentiation actually happens, nor exactly how the different levels of evolution must be interrelated as a systemic process.

Even more, we are missing a conception of evolution as an evolving ecosystem of the environmental contexts of the Earth—of interspecies co-evolution that might create in the environment new eco-niches and new possibilities of evolutionary development for different species.

We are learning to see that the coeval evolution of all interdependent forms of life, of the evolutionary ecology of the entire web of life within the earth's biosphere, provides a handle on the long-term structure of evolutionary patterning.

In this framework, the evolution of individual species does not happen in isolation nor as a separate selection process from the evolution of many other species. At any given moment in time, the entire earth's ecosystem provides a cross section of an epigenetic landscape of many different, interacting life forms. Individual and species selection always happens within this larger evolutionary framework of self-organized systemic, and inter-specific, super-species selection.

From the standpoint of this environmental context of the earth as ecosystem, we can see the fabric of life is for the most part continuous and seamless. We can furthermore speak of differential rates of selection at different periods of development, of different kinds of selection, of different levels of selection, at the sub-species, species and super species level, and of different actors that combine to create selective pressures.

We can speak of exogenous and endogenous directions and pressures of selection, and we can also speak of different alternating phases of a selection, dialectic. Generalization and adaptive radiation imposes a stable selective regime, over populations and consequentially over specialization leads to a contraction phase in that more rapid, dynamic and basically different kinds of selection become inaugurated.

A species may subsequently be reduced back down to minimal threshold below which it must either develop a new generalized program of adaptation or face probable eventual extinction.

Furthermore, we can say that alongside of different gradients of selection, for some specially adapted species selective factors may become effective eliminated and in the entire species or phylogeny essentially stops evolving for a long period of time.

It has reached a very stable evolutionary plateau in that its development is frozen. Randomizing forces of genetic mutation become counterbalanced by the positive selective profiles of previously existing genotypic/phenotypic matrices. Previous successful adaptation slows or negates further selective drift until environmental changes within the ecosystem accumulate to the point of rendering the adaptation more and more genetically dysfunctional.

We may speak of certain kinds of wide margins or of relatively high tolerance limits that work in several ways at several levels of speciation that renders the entire evolutionary process relatively adaptive, flexible and capable of withstanding a large amount of change and selective pressures and still assure genetic reproduction of its life forms.

In a broad sense, the environmental ecosystem evolved these kinds of safety margins in order to promote and protect the evolutionary survival of its life forms. Only when particular individuals or groups or species overstep their safety margins, whether genetically, environmentally, or behaviorally, do selective mechanisms kick in like a thermostat to 'over determine' and select them out as adaptively dysfunctional for the interests of maintaining equilibrium within the entire ecosystem.

We can speak of the evolutionary development of the earth's ecosystem as a cybernetic system of information process and regeneration and also of creation. The basic information is genetic—the instructions of life itself. Selection may work as first order and as second order feedback mechanisms to either kick on or turn off various directions of evolutionary development.

The entire system can be said to be maintaining long-term dynamic equilibrium, and the logic of this systemic order is embedded in its long-term historical patterning.

In this sense we can speak of the evolution of life upon earth as not being only the blind subject of random chance, but as inherently directive and deliberative.

Evolution and some forms of selection serve definite purposes within the total scheme of things, whether this is the maintenance of long-term eco-systemic equilibrium or shorter-term selective development of particular species. Life has evolved towards greater responsiveness, interactivity and reading and controlling of its environment.

The purpose of life on earth has not only been the transmission and regeneration of the information and process maintaining its own long-term patterning, but also is an evolutionary feeling out, exploration and active experimentation with its environments, in order to expand the radius of its own possibilities of patterning.

Systemic selection has by and large served these functional purposes in creating environmental margins and possibilities that confer direction and the freedom of development to given species.

From this alternative standpoint, speaking of purely genetic evolution discounts the contribution of phenotypic adaptation and behavioral influences upon selection, whether individual or group ordered patterns.

It makes greater evolutionary sense to speak of certain ranges and horizons of phenotypic/genotypic profiles that form the basis of species selection. Selection for phenotypic traits can lead to selection of linked genotypic matrices underlying such profiles. Acquired behavioral traits, like instinct or even less ritualized patterns of adaptation, must have a sub-species' selective impact upon the reproductive gene pool of the species.

All organisms, from the simplest prokaryotes to humankind, form complex behavioral patterns throughout their life sequences. No species is purely, passively, molded by the environment in which it is situated. The interactive component of the processes of living of an organism must some way or another have an influence upon the adaptive fitness and selective forces of an individual and its species.

It is by this interactive process of living that a species, and life as a whole, participates in and explores the living environments of the earth, through which directions of selection and alternative adaptation open up or are created. Through such environmental interaction, it is not the acquired phenotypic traits that become genetically transmitted, but the successful genotypic profile underlying this successful adaptive acquisition that becomes selected for.

Furthermore, from social insects to most forms of animal life, individuals are never born wholly autonomously and ready made to survive in the environment. Different species have a group life or a natural culture that is the net product of a history of group adaptation, and that exists independently of, but functionally interrelated to, the genotypic transmission of individual traits.

Individual organisms are conditioned adaptively within such natural cultures in certain specific ways, and such cultures are transmitted as corporate, environmental contexts of group adaptation, alongside of and along with genetic reproduction and transmission.

Individuals live and reproduce, and die, but species as whole groups evolve. For most species, reproduction depends upon some form of group life and behavioral organization. And such group life or community cannot be discounted as a set of selective factors in the evolutionary process of life on earth.

For most species, this kind of natural culture cannot be totally fixed or instinctually determined (instinctively derived perhaps) or else the inflexibility of such group behavior would spell long-term adaptive disaster for the group as a whole.

All groups must have a flexible factor in their behavioral complexes that enables them to adjust, learn and incorporate into their way of life environmental changes that would otherwise interfere with their adaptation.

<u>Earthbound Perspectives</u>

In this sense we may hypothesize that even social insects must somehow learn and modify their own behavior through reconditioning to adapt to new environmental arrangements. Such adaptive flexibility of phenotypic acquisition must itself be programmed as part of the organism as a constituent of the species.

We may speculate that even at the microbiological level of the genetic matrix and process of development of an organism, there is a range of flexibility of possible patterning in phenotypic and ontogenetic expression that must feed back to phylogenic development.

Some kinds of genetic traits or trait complexes may have wider margins of phenotypic expression than others, or else be inherently more plastic. Other traits or trait complexes may be inherently more resistant and fixed that may confer an overall robustness and stability to the evolutionary process.

Slight alterations might lead to rather dramatic redesign or reconfiguration of either genotypic or phenotypic matrices of traits, such that a whole new horizon of phenotypic/genotypic profiles may be produced in relatively short and small increments of genetic variation. This may help explain the apparent saltational, punctuated equilibrium of long-term species evolution as a self-organizing patterning of genetic possibilities.

We may also speculate that fundamentally different selective and evolutionary processes are at work for the plant kingdom than for the animal kingdom, that a more stable and static, classical Mendelian process of evolution predominates within the plant kingdom, and this form of evolution provides the ecological substratum for the more active and dynamic form of behavioral evolution found in the animal kingdom, in which more complex selective systems and process are at work.

In this sense we may speak of fundamentally different environmental levels at that ecological co-evolution happens. Bacteria occupy a different environmental level than do plants or animals, in the same way that aquatic or terrestrial adaptation makes a difference in evolutionary development.

We may also say that speciation events are only apparent in hindsight than actually existing or happening in the present.

What is actually happening is a different kind of historical process. At any given time a species exhibits continuous variation, and all extant living species represent however remotely and indirectly, continuous lines of evolutionary development back to the very primeval beginning of the first experience of life.

We cannot know evolutionary process exclusively on the basis of extinct lines of development that proved dead ends in natural history and that no longer exist today except perhaps as rather fragmentary and incomplete fossil records. It is the variety, diversity and functioning of life as it exists in the present that we must seek to understand the unfolding process of evolutionary development and change.

At any given time a species represents not so much a genetically homogenous grouping but a horizon of a range of continuous variation that extends unendingly backward through time. Its present boundaries are always spatial and population shifting.

Within such boundaries, multiple variations are moving in different evolutionary directions. The selective center of the species comprises, at any given time, the locus of the successful phenotypic/genotypic profiles. Perhaps statistically determinable, and from that the margins of deviation can be determined.

What shifts through time is this selective locus or center—its shifts or drifts, converges or diverges in time. Differential loci within a single species may merge or converge, or a single loci may split or fission in time. The margins of these loci always represent relative genetic isolation or "social distance" from the reproductive core of the species. As the loci shifts, so also do the margins surrounding such loci continuously change.

A cross section of a species at any point in time, what we basically find in the fossil record, will also appear to us as monolithic and relatively homogenous, because of the relatively overall constant and continuous range of genetic variation comprised by the genetic totipotency of the species.

We cannot actually see speciation happening or catch a speciation event in the act except as a complicated complex of interactive patterns within a species range of variation, in that some individuals may be consistently selected for, while others may become ruthlessly deselected.

The boundaries of the locus may be usually fuzzy or actually comprise multiple sub-foci in interrelation. It is only in the long-term of hindsight that we can see the divergence of a single life form into two or more different life form, divergent and distinct, or the change of a single species from one form to a basically different but phylo-genetically descendant form, and we recognize or infer from this speciation as an historically evolutionary process.

We look for speciation on the ground and find only trophic systems of death and reproduction.

In these ways we have an alternative long-term view of evolution as an ecologically comprehensive process of earth history. Evolution can be seen as the exploration and subsequent patterning of the possibilities of life that are in part created by being within the evolving possibilities of the earth's environments.

We know speciation in forms of life on earth if we are lucky from our photo album's frozen photographs taken in form of life on earth animated with many sets of sequel shots seen through the rear view mirror—sets of sequel shots that we can turn into a cartoon flip book.

Evolution is as much responsive to its environments as it is spontaneous within the environment of the earth. Evolution always appears in the present as the epigenetic unfolding of all life forms on earth. Evolution not only explores environmental possibilities of being but it creates both the environments for being and the possibilities of being. It is the long-term patterning of the past history of evolutionary development as selectively directive and purposive as a self-organizing, system maintaining, patterning creating process of Life.

Speciation has always been a process of divergence. By definition, two separate species cannot converge to create a single species of life. Even if the species received a chance endowment in its genome of genetic material from a foreign virus, the chances of its adaptive success would be extremely slight.

It is this single fact of biological divergence of the speciation process that renders the whole of evolution historically irreversible as a processual patterning of possibility. It is this irreversibility of its history that means that what came before will never come again. And what comes after is only made possibly by what came before.

It is in this sense that the past patterning of evolutionary process can only be recognized as a history of divergences of separate species from a common ancestral form, after the fact of parsing the continuous structure of speciation.

It can be said that divergence did not have to necessarily entail geographic separation or isolation between groups before they could speciate into different forms. Rather, functional adaptive divergence between different reproductive loci within a single range of a species only need to have resulted in relative social distance between the loci such that the two loci become "functionally isolated" for a period long enough for speciation to be relatively complete.

Once begun, such a process probably tended to become self reinforcing as different systems of adaptation—social distance, already enough, leads into far greater and greater functional differences until reproductive separation became complete.

Divergence must be a long-term consequence of certain polarizing selection pressures that impact upon a species differentially, tending to separate and eventually sunder the single population of species into two, reproductively inbound groups. Such separation itself might effectively bottleneck one or both sub-groups that might result in an accelerated rate of genetic differentiation.

Any combination of a variety of factors may have contributed to such splitting processes of selection. Geographic distance alone, within a relatively extensive range of environmental radiation of a single species, such that members at one end of the range was effectively isolated from contact with members at the other end, even though there may have been continuous interaction and reproduction with intermediate members. Two ends of a long chain may in time become functionally isolated enough to result in speciation.

Geographic radiation would eventually result in local adaptive specializations of phenotypic/genotypic profiles, especially if the range of adaptive radiation of a single species crosses several different eco-tones.

Minor differences of functional adaptation itself in different eco-tones may be enough to eventual erect a functional reproductive barrier. It may be a direct consequence of a relative phenotypic plasticity and flexibility of the natural sub-cultures of the different groupings that leads to an eventually unsurpassable threshold to crossing over.

Divergence of different loci may even be a long-term consequence of differential local population densities within a region of radiation of a species. Dense regions of population spell at least short-term adaptive success and more rapid rates of reproduction.

Peripheral regions of relative population scarcity could entail greater natural selective pressures against adaptation, lower rates of survival of parents or offspring, and a lower frequency of reproduction and a high threshold of relative reproductive isolation. In such scenarios, crossing over may have occurred at a certain random rate, its homogenizing effect may be still inconsequential to reverse the overall process of heterogeneous divergence between the two groups.

Such instances of crossing over would likely be one way, and though statistically counterbalanced by the reverse crossing over of other individuals, the net consequence may have been not so much a homogenization as a dissimilar genetic re-composition between both groups.

It is also likely that successful members of one loci would be less likely to cross over than less successful members that for one reason or another fail to realize their reproductive capacity in a given vicinity, and so must move on. We must understand that selection may be as much neutral in outcome as it may be positive or negative, which can only be inferred in hindsight.

Such marginal types would either fail consistently to find an in-group and thus become selected out, such that their cross-over had no net effect, or else their adaptation in the new location may have been superior such that they successfully fit in and contribute positively to the selective adaptation of the other group.

It is also possible, and in the long-term likely, that species divergence occurred within a single broadly based species within a single given region without factors of distance or functional isolation or disproportionate or differential population densities to explain the divergence. It may just be a long-term consequence of species change, of unilineal drift and shift and the ever-present state of continuous variation.

Differential selective forces may impact differently upon individuals or sub-groups, or intra-specific competition between individuals or sub-groups for the same resources or for reproductive access may lead to local functional isolation or segregation that may be behaviorally and reproductively reinforced to the point that it sooner or later results in the populations divergence into two different, but closely related species.

Differential selective forces may impact upon individuals or sub-groupings of a single species population in such ways as to drive their functional separation and reproductive isolation. Extreme types may face different but favorable selection, while in-between intermediate types face negative selection, though the actual differences may only be slight or mostly phenotypic, it could have long-term reverberations that are quite biologically determinative.

It is to be wondered whether even a relatively homogenous population upon a relatively 'flat' epigenetic landscape will nevertheless, if given enough time, end up as two or more separate varieties—whether or not there is some mysterious mechanism of differentiation that drives the whole process of speciation inherent to the biological makeup of the species itself. It seems, though, that what will be observed is the drift of a single species in a given direction, and the unilineal direction of the species into a derivative form.

It seems that in order for divergence to occur, it must occur across space and there must occur some kind of relatively isolating boundary, border, barrier, whether this is a river, an ocean, a mountain chain, a forest, a wall, or an eco-tone, a differential epigenetic gradient, distance, inference by a predator species, competition, population differentials, etc. Such divergence seems to require first that a species adaptively radiate over a fairly wide and ecologically diverse region such that such relative, environmentally related boundaries occur to subdivide the population.

There is a sense that for the horizon of phenotypic/genotypic profiles of any given species, or even of a genus or phylum, there are certain kinds of constraints that function to ultimately limit the range and kinds of possible structural patterns that can be realized, and that in time, these patterns will eventually exhaust themselves if all other changes are controlled for.

The genetic totipotentiality for any given time of life form is always so constrained by a ceiling of its possible developments. Within such structural constraints, for a species to develop in any one direction, must entail that it sacrifice possible development in other directions. To add a little here may mean subtracting from somewhere else.

The genome or genetic matrix of any species is always fixed and finite—new material cannot be readily added, and the net amount cannot be increased or decreased, except perhaps over a very long frame of time.

The irreversibleness of its historical transformations means that once a species has chosen a given pathway of development, it is no longer free to choose alternative pathways leading in other directions.

This means that a species within a given horizon will eventually exhaust its possibilities for development and its evolutionary clock will wind out—a species may become trapped at an evolutionary cul-de-sac without a way of backing out.

We may refer this perhaps as overspecialization within a habitat of adaptation, but such biological winding out or evolutionary exhaustion of the possible patterns of a given species may be something more than too adaptively fine tuned to fit in any longer to environmental changes. An environment may not have to become radically altered before a species begins to no longer functionally it into its old habitat.

One way of seeing this is to consider that for any given horizon of a species, there is a corresponding range of environmental adaptation. The extensiveness of this range will be proportionate to the degrees of freedom offered by the horizon. When a species overextends its own range, it must run up against negative selection pressures that tend to bind its advance.

Over time, within such a range, increasingly successful adaptation will lead to population increase and to higher population densities. Such increase could lead to overreaching the carrying capacity of the range, and to a slow but irreversible process of environmental degradation.

Such an Easter Island scenario would mean that the whole species might eventually climb a step evolutionary gradient only to suddenly step over a sheer precipice into oblivion.

But even such a scenario might not be necessary to explain the mechanism of how a relatively homogenous species becomes eventually frozen and inflexible in its evolutionary development. Selective forces favoring convergence and homogenization of profiles, rather than divergence and heterogeneity, must be seen in the evolutionary long-run as headed in the wrong direction toward overspecialization, susceptibility to climatic environmental shift, and leading to an evolutionary cul-de-sac and eventual extinction.

Such tendencies towards convergence could result in an overriding cycle of development that reinforces itself to the exclusion of alternative avenues of development with tendencies favoring convergence could resist or counteract any tendencies towards diversification and divergence. A species may eventually find itself sitting on top of an epigenetic mesa or island from that it has not escaped as a natural group culture.

Even then, we must ask if there aren't fundamental differences between young species composed of basic, general traits and old species that are ossified by derivative, specialized traits that it cannot simply unburden itself from. In a similar vein, it is to be wondered whether there may also not be younger evolutionary worlds with fresh environments, and essentially old evolutionary worlds whose environments are inflexible and eroding.

One seemingly irreversible tendency in evolution that must be noted is that in the long run there has been a general increase in the amount of genetic information and organizational complexity of the genome.

Evolution has tended to augment and increase the amount of life, but it has never been observed to adaptive subtract or reduce the amount of genetic information. Another way of saying this is that basic, simple forms lead inevitably towards more derived and complex forms, but not the other way around. Perhaps individual extinction events in evolutionary history are merely instantiations reflecting this general trend.

There seems to be another, related tendency at work upon individual species or phylum. Once a horizon or range of profiles becomes relatively fixed and stable in its adaptive selection, it must naturally tend to be more highly resistant to internal reconfiguration in a way that enhance adaptation rather than eliminates adaptability.

Changes that become more likely to occur then are radical and catastrophic damaging that tends toward maladaptation and negative selection. The patterned possibilities settle into a plateau or into a "channel" of development, from which further alteration is more likely to become disruptive rather than constructive, and will tend to be further resisted.

It makes sense to posit the functioning of the clock- like mechanisms constraining evolutionary development and perhaps superimposing or predetermining time frames of duration for any given direction or line of development. In the development of new phylogenies, these time clocks become wound up and in the unilineal unfolding of a phylogeny's patterned possibilities, it eventually winds back down.

In a sense, such clocks are inherent latent in the undeveloped potentiality of primitive forms of life. These evolutionary undeveloped forms of life are the rough, uncarved blocks of nature that are yet waiting to become shaped and formed and eventually eroded away.

The irreversibleness of certain directions of development—of divergence, of overspecialized adaptation, of complex, derivative traits from simple, general primitive ones, of evolutionary convergence upon an island or plateau of development, all are evidence of the unwinding process of such clockwork.

It is possible to see in the process of continuous divergence and speciation the rewinding of such biological clocks. Offspring species of a single parent stock are like the procreation of children from the parents.

They are the regeneration and natural exchange of new fresh and young life for old. In this loose sense, phylogeny recapitulates ontogeny. We can find in the evolutionary development of new life forms a reflection of the individual reproduction of new life.

We can find the rewound clockwork in our own Neotonous development—in the vestiges of embryonic development in a watery world of a womb, in the brief appearance of gill slits, in our young chimpanzee like skulls that take us back to the earliest hominid of the *Taung* Child. From this basic traits, are derived the complex biological organisms we believe ourselves to be.

It is possible that we can find in nature latent and hidden clocks whose evolutionary process of development has not yet been inaugurated. Such clocks wait like perennial seeds within an enduring shell for just the right kinds of environmental conditions to be suddenly set in motion.

These clocks might be disguised to our sophisticated sensibilities as relatively primitive trait complexes of life forms, their potentiality for evolutionary development transparent and invisible within a world that as itself been growing much older.

It is also possible that many such seeds that have been dormant for so long may have been dead—the environmental conditions appropriate to the evolutionary inauguration of their development long since irreversibly lost in its own evolutionary unwinding.

If we are to find evidence for such clockwork we must find it in the irreversibleness of its directional development—in its function of unwinding possibility. Some such lines suggest themselves— the irreversible development of increased body mass, the trend to K-selective adaptation that may confer such short-term competitive or selective advantage but may entail a long-term impasse.

Another candidate is in the functional specialization of basically primitive appendages or body extremities—of turning limbs into fins, wings, legs and feet, arms and hands, or as apparatus for swinging from trees, or in the loss of limbs and a basic lack of limbs in adaptation to a life underground or on the surface of the ground.

Yet another possibility is in the development of derived sense organs, and corresponding sensitivities, from rather crude to more sophisticated and specialized forms. This can be eyesight, hearing or acoustical reception, voice, touch, or smell. Another kind of irreversible line might be in terms of the development of warm blooded, exothermic metabolisms, of lungs, of specialized alimentary systems, or of skin coverings that permit transpiration or perspiration or prevent dissipation.

Certain kinds of bone structures may also be basically derivative and irreversible in their evolutionary development—skulls, teeth, jaws, spines, hips, fingers, toes, etc. Finally, we must look to evidence for the development of the brain as somehow a irreversible direction toward more complex and derivative organization from simpler and more primitive forms.

It is also worth wondering whether all of life is set to a grand clock like mechanism that is slowly ticking away. Certain near universal characteristics shared by all life form the basic constraints to that biology must adhere.

Besides the genetic structure of DNA itself, we have evidence in the bilateral symmetry of almost all life forms, in the carbon and water composition of all life forms, in the primary dependence upon the light of the sun as the engine of the entire food chain. Yet what are the underlying principles and the basic clockwork of all life, remains yet an insoluble mystery even to our science.

Death and the longevity of an individual organism are other constraints that are universal to all life.

It must be wondered whether the clock of all life will eventually wind out in the exhaustion of its own possible patterning— whether life itself will grow old and inflexible with great age, and will, with decreasing capacity to adjust to environmental changes, eventually wilt away into the dust of the earth.

To look at the genetic structure of the DNA and of the genome as a biological clockwork mechanism that reproduces and transmits itself with each pass generation of life on earth, and in the process become itself irreversibly altered—a mechanism that governs the rhythms and timing of process and change of all life forms.

This genetic structure itself is moving in a direction of irreversible change, perhaps not in a straight direction, but it has become something in all life forms now extant different than what it was in size and in the amount of extra genetic material that it contains.

Having more information than any organism really may need is perhaps to the species long-term advantage, but it is also possible that the long-term accumulation of too much such material may adversely alter or affect the patterned structure of a species long-term development, or the ability to continue to diverge and differentiate successful into new forms of life.

Examples of this may exist in the over breeding of some forms of domestic animals or plants, in the genetic engineering and experimentation that produces new hybrid wonder strains of certain kinds of plant, but at a certain cost in the hybrids adaptive or procreative capacities.

We can say that there are now no underived or primitive forms of life that have remained essentially unevolved or unaltered from the beginning of all life. This must mean that all genetic structures today are more fine tuned and fixed in adaptive pattern than their great, great, great ancestors.

It is extremely unlikely that whole new life forms are being created spontaneously today, except perhaps in some scientific laboratory. So it must be assumed that life universally is evolving its patterned possibilities,, and has a last horizon on earth for its own evolutionary range of variation. A limited lump of clay can only be molded and remolded into so many different shapes—if each shape cannot be repeated again, then it will eventually become increasingly difficult to mold newer and newer shapes.

The clockwork of life may not only be situated in the structure of the genome, but may in fact exist super-organically in the self creating evolving environmental contexts of life itself. The evolution of the living environments and natural ecological contexts of life may in the grand scheme also be somewhat directional and irreversible, such that the kinds of selection forces and tolerance limits allowed are continuously developing.

Life that was possible in an earlier epoch of earth, may no longer be possible in the present epoch, not so much because of constraints imposed by the physical environment, but the lack of the biotic web of interdependency that originally fostered the evolution and supported its survival in the first place.

Once having evolved from one state to another, it becomes extremely unlikely that the previous state will ever be remodeled or recapitulated again. As such, the biospheric environment and ecology of life on earth is itself evolving and cycling in the patterning of its possibilities for development, and though this grand scheme of evolving life may be infinitely variable, it is not without its own structural limits that define the ultimate evolutionary horizon of its growth and development.

All life tends to grow until it over reaches the carrying capacity of its natural substrate upon that it depends for its energy and resource requirements. Such growth tends towards a super critical mass that becomes inherently destabilizing for the continued survival of the species.

Bacterium grown in the agar of a petri dish increase exponentially until they exhaust the limited amount of nutrient supply available to them, or else they poison their own substrate by their own waste. Many ecosystems and natural cycles of nature are basically conservational and therefore quite stable and enduring.

These are self-limiting systems that tend to replace and repair the damage to the physical substrate upon which they depend. Such cycles did not just happen full blown, but emerged very gradually over time as the most successful strategy of long-term survival and adaptation on earth.

It is necessary that forests or the plankton of the surface of the ocean consume carbon dioxide, produce oxygen and in the process recycle water on earth. It is important that certain fungi or lichen clear away the face of hard rocks, that insects continue to cross pollinate many plants, and that many animals continue to eat the insects.

In a sense many natural evolutionary experiments may in the long-term structure of things prove to upset such natural balances and economies of life and thus either become selected against, or also destroy the basis of its own existence.

The evolution of predator species high up the food chain, may not themselves be such mistakes but the development of the huge biomass prey species—of huge herds of animals that consume tremendous amounts of vegetable matter, and in the process of movement, mechanically destroy whatever may be growing in their path.

Nature must somehow act evolutionary to control the development of such life forms unless these upset the very cycles and balances upon which Nature itself depends for continued survival. Large predators, packs of small predators, scavengers, disease organisms, parasites, and even biotoxin-producing fungi all serve to keep the growth of such species in control.

There are certain broad margins within that the continuum of evolutionary development is defined. Evolution can work within these horizons, perhaps even to extend its range a little upon the horizons, but it cannot grossly overstep or violate such margins without adverse consequences to its own future ward development.

There are perhaps greater reasons than these to systematically seek to delimit global human population and human cultural interference with the natural landscape and its evolutionary and bio-geophysical processes.

These margins themselves may fluctuate from epoch to epoch with the changing conditions of the earth's physical environment—some eras may have much narrower ranges of adaptation than others. Periodically recurrent ice ages may be the primary candidates for explaining such fluctuations, as may be earlier periods of increased volcanism or of meteoritic activity, or of general atmospheric alterations.

Evolution of life is not guaranteed or certain to continue. Extinction of species represents of unrecoverable loss of evolutionary material and biological potential for future development. Life must continuously compete in evolutionary development of its own potential against randomizing processes of entropy that leads inexorably toward extinction.

If the margin of life goes through a period of contraction in which the rate of extinction tends to overtake the rate of evolutionary development, then there occurs a net loss of biological evolutionary potential, such that natural rhythms and balances are being degraded or upset.

It may be that during such contractive phases, life in general may work within relatively wide safety margins of its own, in that positive selection pressures tend to kick on to increase the rate, rapidity and diversity of evolutionary development. It may also be that in expansion phases selection pressures reverse themselves and become negative controls to further evolutionary development and that the rate of divergence and development slows down in proportion.

There is an important lesson for the modern development of humankind on earth. Our own genetic success has not been achieved without disproportionate costs to all of life on earth. For every extinction event of a different species that can be accounted for by our own continuing, exponential development, there is a net loss in the evolutionary and reproductive capacity for all of life.

We have artificially stepped beyond the natural selective pressures of nature and have induced a general 'contraction phase of life on earth, in the process upsetting irreversibly many of the natural eco-systemic checks and balances that in the long-term maintain the equilibrium of the whole system.

It may be that nature reacts in its own way to select against our own future development. It may act through us as well as around us. It may be as well that we precipitate a natural contraction phase at the same time artificially lowering beforehand life's ability to adjust and evolve to re-establish its natural harmonies. It may be that we can step in scientifically and make the difference or it may be that we ourselves have already made the critical difference.

It can be assured, though, that in the evolutionary structure of the long run, the loss of life of earth will become our own loss, that the continued survival and evolution of life on earth will become our continued survival and evolution. In all our civilization and developmental progress, we are still of life. In all our cultural artificiality, we are still fundamentally and necessarily composed of and by nature.

Our future will depend ultimately upon our ability to maintain and support the natural checks and balances, the natural harmonies that sustain life on earth and maintain its eco-systemic equilibrium on a finite planet earth. As we work to irreversibly destroy such harmonies and balances, we are working to destroy not only life on earth, but the possibilities for our own future survival and development.

We cannot trust or depend upon our somewhat myopic science to make up the difference or to correct the imbalances our development has caused. It cannot be relied upon to repair the damages that its own progress and technology has lead to. It cannot restore rhythms of life that took many millions of years to create. The lesson of our modern epoch to be learned is that it is always much easier to destroy than to create. We have mastered the arts of destruction, but are amateurish children in the natural arts of creation.

In a cosmological perspective, the evolution of life itself is but an extension of the evolution of the earth and the evolution of the whole universe. Our own evolution is but a complex elaboration of the physical processes underlying the changing patterns of the whole universe. The evolution of life may have been exceptional, but not physically impossible.

Life will come to an end, as will earth, the sun and the cosmos as we know it. In a sense, the reductionists of science who seek to define all of life in terms of bio-chemical or physical process are correct in their fundamental presuppositions that physical principles ultimately underlie and constrain biological principles of life.

But the realization of these constraints may prove to be in ways that they little anticipated, especially with loss of systems integration and the emergent properties in association with such living systems—our own human systems especially.

We must learn to see in the evolution of the earth, in its earthquakes, volcanism, in its erosive forces, its wind and rain, in its rivers and waves of the ocean, the limits of our own development.

We are special and extremely exceptional in the Universe, but not so special to forget our natural limits and needs.

A general story of the evolution of life on earth goes something like this. Life began, perhaps by fits and starts, as small eukaryotic forms that in their original adaptation became very successful and rapidly spread out in every direction, perhaps to encompass the globe. In the process of its adaptive radiation, these primitive life forms quickly differentiated into various interacting kinds—biotic environments began to form on the basis of this first interaction.

Slowly, but surely, multi-cellular life forms began to emerge in ever-greater degrees of complexity. These multi-cellular creatures had complex organismic metabolisms within which cells began to perform certain specific vital functions. Once these more complex organisms got started, they radiated out in every direction possible, as well.

At that point, life on earth became multi-tiered. The biotic environment began to develop a depth to its diversity and extremely complex chains of interdependency. As these multi celled organisms radiated out in every possible direction, they also began to differentiate and diverge, resulting in more complex and varied range of creatures.

These initial phases were perhaps long in happening compared to later evolutionary epochs. Life on earth was yet embryonic in its watery world, tiny, changing rapidly, gradually filling out the spaces of its womb.

At some point, life separated into animals and plants—quite early on two distinctly different, yet mutually interdependent, directions of evolutionary development became realized. By the time life forms began emerging from seas onto the land, life of the seas was already quite evolutionarily complex and in a sense complete.

Plant life took much more rapidly to land than animals, but once animals firmly established a capacity for surviving on land without needing to be in the water, its evolutionary development became quite rapid.

There was an overall tendency for life forms to grow in size to tremendous proportions. These large masses required a tremendous amount of energy consumption for their own maintenance and metabolism, movement and reproduction. It is without a doubt that these epochs witnessed a tremendous evolutionary expansion of life on earth.

It is possible that the general tendency to increase in morphological size eventuated in several extinction episodes when the biotic substrate upon which such evolution depended became exhausted or no longer provided the base of support for these leviathans of the land.

Could it have been that the plants evolved gradually under selection pressures created by this massive and continuous consumption, into life forms that became less susceptible to such mass harvesting?

It seems likely that once extinction began among the big plant feeders, it rapidly worked its way up the food chain to finish off all the giant predators that were dependent upon these big feeders for their own sustenance. It is possible that these big predators eventually found nothing more to eat than their selves, and in the last phase, ended up within a vicious cycle of intra-trophic cannibalism.

The mystery of these events is whether or not outside factors are necessary or enough to explain their apparent suddenness or rapidity. Though it is possible a huge comet might have struck the earth, it seems implausible that such an event alone could have eventuated in near complete biotic extinction. The dropping of the earth's temperature a few degrees might have made such huge levels of biomass unbearable, or imposed certain constraining conditions that mostly endothermic creatures could no longer tolerate. The earth went almost overnight from being a greenhouse to an icebox.

But it is also possible that life as it was might have withstood such changes or environmental catastrophes, had it not become too evolutionarily overdeveloped and thus that could not cope with minor alterations in certain fundamental environmental relations upon that its systemic patterning was based. Removing a single brick in the edifice might have inaugurated a whole chain reaction of extinction events that culminated in the near total destruction of life as it was then developed.

When dinosaurs ruled the earth, they were driven by blind libidinal forces and lacked the cunning to allow them to behaviorally adapt their instincts and habits and natural cultures to a changing set of environmental circumstances.

The later age of the great mammals in a sense repeated many of the mistakes of the past, in their huge biomass. Their lives too were governed by instinct, but perhaps it was instinct that was less blind than before.

For all their apparent slowness and clumsiness, the dinosaur had to have done something right to have lasted their 125 million years on earth. We have, in our own wise state, have only been around for less than a million years, and our whole hominid line is probably less than four million years old, and we have long been hunting whole species into extinction, irreversibly despoiling whole habitats, and now, in place of our own slight size, built new mechanical monsters that are rapidly transforming the whole landscape of the earth's surface.

The greatest mystery about evolution has been our own past and our own future. To explain why and how we have been led by events to our present anti-evolutionary state, and where exactly it will be that we are headed with our own artificial version of global civilization and of progressive development, that has become our species wide answer to the ages old problem of evolutionary survival against the forces of natural selection.

We have inaugurated forces of artificial selection that have effectively stemmed and cut off most, if not all, natural processes of evolution, and that have grown beyond our own severely limited ability to control.

And this sense of our brief history of human civilization has not even been the greatest mystery of our past. It has all been a rather simple and straightforward social process to understand.

The real mystery is how we acquired the capacities evolutionarily that we then sooner or later learned how to wisely use to our best advantage. After all has been said and done, this has been what our science has long been all about anyway. The real mystery is in the puzzle of anthropogenesis. The evolutionary origin mythology of our own biological beginning in nature endowed us with our birthright to rule the earth once and for all.

The kind of origin mythology that we choose for ourselves must inevitably say a lot about how we ourselves want to be remembered in the past, about the kinds of traits and "embodied values" that we find important enough to emphasize about our own evolution. Such stories abound in the literature, whether it is scientific, anthropological, theological, or "fringe."

The missing linkages of our past present us with a grand sense of critical absence within which we can configure what seems most "essential" and therefore important about ourselves that we can legitimate because it has always been there since the beginning.

In our stories reconstructing our own common past, we must learn to be cautious and critical about finding in the ground mere reflections of our own being in the present. If anything, we must learn to look within ourselves to find what might be vestigial impressions if a long lost sense of the primordial past. This will not be found in our own currently hyper-developed state of violence, aggressiveness or irrational impulse.

These are after all the analysis but the by-products and components of our own collective state. Nor will we find it in our own presupposed primitiveness—in our fossilized aboriginal others or our closest biological cousins among the primates.

All our artifacts and fossil fragments are in the last case but anachronisms and splintered survivals from a fuller sense of the past that has long been lost to our consciousness. But one way or another, in whatever symbolism we prefer, we must find our lost sense of the past if we are to continue to meet the future with a deep sense of purpose and reason for our being on earth. And humans never seem to live too well without some symbolic sense of purpose.

Perhaps respect for our own future lives on earth can be found rooted in reverence for all life that exists.

<u>Earthbound Perspectives</u>

We must see our own anthropogenesis in the development of a whole complex set of interrelated, and uniquely human characteristics—among these traits are bipedality, our vocal tracts, our hands, our hand-eye coordination, our large brains, our prolonged period of infant-child dependency, and our symbolic behavior.

It is likely that all of these trait complexes arose more or less together in time, as an increasingly human super-system, and each developed gradually along with the others to what they are today. The problem is not to ask that ones arose first, but to ask how these traits became interrelated as a complex in the first place, and what kind of conditions preceded this development and selected for its improvement over time.

There are also other associated sets of traits that surround this "core" but that are not necessarily exclusively our own possession in nature. This includes our upright body posture, our omnivorous, diurnal feeding patterns, the shape of our teeth with reduced canines, molars and incisors, our peculiar skeletal structure with reduced prognathism, the shape of our hips that widen at birth to accommodate a relatively wide skull, and our relatively gracile bone structure that is relatively light in weight yet strong in stamina and arduous in prolong activities.

It seems that we were designed by Nature to accommodate to a relatively wide and diverse range of natural habitats. Our general, unspecialized body structure allowed us to move rapidly over wide ranges and to seek out a wide variety of natural food resources.

Our designs, especially of our primary complex, seems to have preconditioned us for our peculiar sociability and for an early emergence of small group culture that depended upon vocalizations, hand signals, emotional expressions, and body postures and movements for communication.

Proto-human reproductive cycles were probably 10-20 years to begin with, growing thirty years with passing millions. Human beings spread more rapidly, tending toward population saturation

The way we seem to almost universally parse and categorize experience at a basic symbolic level that is non-specific and yet not too general—conceptual gestalts that predispose us to recognize similarity relationships in the environments and to carry information of past experience to the encounter of new environments. The movement to new environments required that we carried our natural culture and our group life with us wherever we wandered to, or else that could replicate it in new worlds full of strangers.

Such movement and continual adaptation also tended to include selection pressures that consistently favored just the kind of trait complex that we actually evolved. Young pregnant mothers who could walk relatively great distances; endure certain kinds of psychological-physiological stress responses; use hands with opposable thumbs and dexterous fingers; and hands free to carry things or to make things or to easily pick things up in the environment; voices that could penetrate the distances and travel about visual obstacles to make sure that one didn't wander too far from the group—voice patterns that carried instant recognition of individual identity at a distance, with omnidirectional hearing to match.

It included brains that store and rapidly process and learn a fairly large amount of experientially embodied information that could then be transferred to new settings and situations. It meant longer periods of infant dependency that favored bonding, learning and the acquisition of social skills, tending to confer upon small groups a center of gravity, and a focus of group life.

We were designed to be general jacks-of-all trades but masters of none. We are meat through our adaptive trait complexes both specialized and generalist. If we had been confined exclusively to a single mode of adaptation in a single kind of environmental configuration, we would never have survived to evolve into the kinds of things we became.

We have an innate capacity for aggressiveness and violence, but also for love and empathetic relation with our world. We must look to the kinds of traits and dispositions that we sacrificed in order to evolve into what we are now. We slowly gave up physical strength for a more gracile structure that was preeminently designed for streamlined endurance.

We developed a predisposition for the accumulation of excessive body fat that enabled us to store energy for long periods of stress. We gave up large protruding jowls and vicious arcades of fangs for the effectiveness of sonorous voices.

We gave up padded paws made to protect movement from sharp object for relatively fine and nimble fingers that could more carefully manipulate environments.

We gave up the speed, the power, the stability, and the protection of being on all fours for the agility, long distance running, climbing and reaching ability, and 'prairie dog' scouting of being upright and vulnerable. Finally, we gave up the assured predictability and natural efficiency of instinctual controls for the greater learning capacity and sentience of larger brains.

It seems that we evolved in an intermediate range of an environmental mosaic—upon the periphery of any single kind of environment. We did not evolve in any single spot, but upon the peripheries of whole regions or even continents—filling in the interstices of the natural environment with our population. We evolved in relative isolation, effectively separated from any selective competition by better-adapted species.

It was the relative sparseness that conferred upon us our natural mobility and advantage. We were neither wolf nor hyena; not tiger or a buffalo or bear. It assured us of frequently running into other groups of proto people with that we might establish some form of contact—exchanging information, genes, artifacts, stories, blows, etc. We may have evolved patterns of movement, of scattering and re-aggregation, in response to seasonal cycles that necessitated alternative adaptations to a range of environments, periodic movements, meetings, etc.

Some form of group culture was with us from the beginning, and its natural presence probably served to stimulate further, precondition and constrain the further evolution of our human trait complex. That group culture cross-sectioned in the small family unit, or band, in a mosaic environment of perpetual fright and competition and warfare with neighbors. Adaptation to our particular cultural arrangements favored the survival and selective advantage not of brute, direct strength but of indirect, sometimes brutal cunning. Not of emotional postures and gesticulations of ferocity and anger, but of the verbal communication of subtlety and convincing sounds.

It favored our increased sociability and ability to get along well with others, as well as a deeply ingrained fear and distrust of instinctually unpredictable strangers. It favored the development of tools or other artifices that could be carried with us to new contexts that allowed us to bring our functional adaptability in new environments with us. It favored the kinds of designs of general adaptability that precluded natural selection and biological adaptation.

It favored planning, predicting, producing, promising and protecting strategies. It favored cooperative, coordinated group activity, but also allowed for periodic individual separation and isolation. Finally, it favored its own transmission and elaboration, along with the reproductive transmission and evolutionary elaboration of the trait complex.

From this standpoint the early gene-culture co-evolution produced first and second order feedback mechanisms within a species wide cybernetic system that promoted both the evolution of the natural trait complex described above and the development of the kind of culture around that and upon that this trait complex was focused.

This evolving system had a great general stability in both the sense that it occurred upon margins away from competition with other life forms better biologically adapted to more specific habitats, and itself promoted a generalizing orientation in the further integration of the trait complex.

It is this general stability of the evolutionary conditions of the emergence of humankind that has gone unrecognized, a stability in a marginal, intermediate range of mosaic of different settings that allowed humankind to consistently evade direct confrontation and competition with other, better adapted species, and thus to eventually, indirectly, out-evolve such species.

At some stage in this systemic evolution of both natural and human culture and the associated trait complex, there occurred a dramatic turning point at that period, probably relatively recent in human prehistory.

Cultural development began to take off on its own trajectory more independently of further evolution of the human trait complex that essentially halted with the elimination of the neutral selective forces that had been at work in creating this complex.

Human beings were, in opening to their world, created thus a new world, and thus in turn have through these new worlds they created, opened up more and more independently of evolution. Human cultural development preempted these selective forces and essentially brought a significant shift to human biological evolution in the directions that led to the development of human culture in the first place.

It can be intuitively guessed this occurred about the time of early domestication of plants and animals and the beginnings just before agriculture. This may have been at the stage at that the current racial differences had appeared in different regions of the earth. Human evolution has continued steadily, but not in the same manner as the process that happened before that led to the development of the basic trait complex.

It can be expected that gradual human population increase occurred over the long-term until movement became more or less constrained in most regions. People began to settle down at this point, and with this settling down, a base was soon created for the rapid expansion of human population around settlement centers. Settlement sizes gradually increased in size and representation of the human population until it eventuated in the formation of chiefdoms and even early proto-state development.

Settling down conferred a new kind of cultural stability for humankind. It allowed humankind to increasingly manipulate and exploit the surrounding environment, to create safety margins from natural environmental hazards. On the other hand, it was the enhanced exploitation of natural environments that allowed human populations to settle down in a certain focal area on a year round basis.

It is at this point that cultural development of human civilization took off on its own trajectory less and less constrained by the inter-linkages of natural selective pressures and forces of evolution. Human development became its own feedback system with the exploitation of the environment at its base, and human interchange and network patterns as a system of expanding the horizons imposed by any single environment. Systems of symbolization, socialization and signification emerged as well to confer a sense of universal unity of experience and to allow the integration of differences encountered in the world.

Human cultural development gained its own historical momentum and acquired a life of its own relatively independently of the actions and lives of its participants and enactors. It came to replace and gradually substitute the natural environments in that human evolution originally happened by ever growing regions of cultural environments in that human beings came to increasing define their own lives and experience.

As human cultural development increased and expanded, the natural environments of human evolution were reduced and their horizons receded.

Human culture shifted from a natural function within natural environments of conferring selective advantage and survival against selective pressures, to an artificial function of reconfiguring and controlling natural habitats and of reducing the continued existence and survival of humankind. It proved so successful that it eventually brought natural evolution to a near global bottleneck.

As has been said, the rest is a matter of human history. But it was a matter of gradually exchanging increasingly culture historical processes of the pan-human development of civilization for the natural history of the evolution of humankind on earth. The sense of historical processes and patterns became increasingly different, and the kind of structural dynamics underlying these processes also are different.

Evidence today suggests that human evolution has not slowed down, but may have perhaps increased speed as exponential population growth.

While human biological evolution and its natural history on earth had been driven by the forces and pressures of natural selection within an evolving environmental context, human culture historical development has occurred increasingly driven by divergent social processes and practices, within environmental contexts that were increasingly man made or regulated by human involvement. Furthermore the dynamics underlying culture historical development were dialectical and occurred at three levels simultaneously.

1. The symbolic level of unfolding Mind, the social level of human organization and interrelation, and is the environmental-ecological level of human adaptation and experiential adjustment of physical environments are important facets of human systems integration.

2. The stratification of human historical reality into these three levels of simultaneous coexistence and involvement has imposed on human reality the historical problem of dialectical reintegration of these levels.

3. The patterning that has subsequently for human culture historical development has been a kind of complex dialectic occurring between these levels such that no single level can be considered primary or derived, but form a feedback system in their inter-functioning that has evinced and explains the development of human civilization.

It can be said that the extremes of the dialectic—human symbolization and mind, and the infra-structural base of techno-environmental material adaptation, are neither a priori or primary in the development of the dialectic, but occur always relative to a dialectical center of human social relations whose primary existential problems are those of social order, transmission and reproduction.

Whatever the contradictions between the top and the bottom, or the mind and the body, these must tale place within a social context, be intermediated through social interrelations, and must effect or be effected by reverberations and changes in the patterns of these interrelations.

Change can begin in the center of the social mass, and find its consequences in the change of this social mass. The relative contradiction or polarization, or alignment and convergence of the extremes, must always be measured in relation to the social center.

In a sense, this alternative social dialectics of human culture historical development turns Marx, Hegel, and Marvin Harris all inside out and sees the historical error of stipulating or presupposing either extreme as primary and a prior in importance in understanding the dialectical dynamics of human historical change.

Human evolution and culture historical development was always preeminently a social phenomenon. Social patterning was never just a consequence of human history, but always also a cause in human history. Social environments exert a constraining influence on human adaptations and become reflected by and directed by human systems of symbolization.

We need a new, revised model of human social dynamics and process that sees this as central and preconditioning in the understanding of human history. Social relation, order, transmission and reproduction always present humankind with problems of maintaining patterned organization, systemic functioning and directive change through time, whether this is the natural time of evolution or the artificial time of culture.

In unwinding time for humankind, it becomes apparent that the clockwork of human culture history has been different from the clockwork of human natural history, and that the development of human civilization has been on a different time schedule than that of natural human evolution. Furthermore, it has proven difficult and dangerous to get these two general frames of time mixed up or confused in our understanding if human reality and the history of this reality.

The growth of human population on earth is in a fundamental sense a measure of our success, both as a species of natural evolution and as a human civilization. It is perhaps an inevitable, natural and unavoidable outcome of the success of human history. It is in terms of the social body of humankind, in its relative state of growth and development, that we can see the long convergence and inter-function of the two different kinds of clockwork.

It has been reiterated that human population growth is outstripping our every resource and the advancement of our culture historical capacity to effectively deal and cope with it. It has been estimated that we are rapidly approaching a developmental climax that will represent the zenith of the development of human civilization and that will comprehend and exhaust the carrying capacity of our world. What lies beyond this horizon we can only guess.

There is a sense of inevitability and irreversibility in the unwinding of historical time for humankind. We cannot wisely regress backwards to earlier states of development or evolution, and we cannot historically recover or even reconstruct the detail and complexity of interrelations that made previous life full and complete in the world.

There is a sense that we are bound within our different frames of time, and are carried inexorably forward in its unwinding. There is a grand sense that the biological clocks are ticking within us, slowly, unstoppably. We cannot stop this ticking, or replace these clocks with our artificial clockwork.

The most we can accomplish perhaps is to accelerate the processes of their unwinding, and to hasten that process forward to their historical and natural conclusion. There is a sense that no matter which way we go, what course of action we presume, the net consequences will now be generally the same.

Perhaps the most we can accomplish in the world, is a slowing down of their rhythm and the rate of their changing, such that we can allow ourselves a little longer time in the world to figure it all out before we too must change.

PART III: EARTH STATE
How Green is Your Grass?

It has not been uncommon in contemporary American culture for homeowners to become obsessively preoccupied with the state of their yards, and especially with the green and even condition of their front lawns.

Their local community status in the neighborhood is often linked to how green and neat they are able to maintain their lawns, and it is always possible to tell a household that is having management problems when weeds begin to take over and the lawn becomes browner and browner over the years.

A nice yard and a deep green lawn is often a deep source of pride and relative status for the home owner, and it is not unusual for individuals or neighbors to gossip about the relative merits of Joe and Jane So and So based on the current state of greenery of their lawns.

It has become a norm in many busy suburbs to have a gardener to regularly come and give the lawn a haircut and trim and to dump a few pounds of ammonia or phosphates over the yard to maintain its healthy green coloring.

It is more prestigious to have in some places a Japanese gardener who really knows his lawns, uses urea and cuts the lawn in alternating complex patterns. Individuals are always keeping a eye on each others yards, and worrying about keeping up with the Joneses next door.

In order to maintain to what amounts to a flat, even few hundred or thousand square feet of thin turf in a perennial state of green many avid homeowners will spare no expense, or go to any expense, even if they themselves or anyone else rarely if ever even walk upon it in such a way that they might enjoy the lawn of a local park, of a baseball diamond or football field, or of a golf course, or even a backyard barbecue.

These homeowners will make the seasonal sales of the local nurseries or gardening departments of bigger merchandise stores, and upon the advise of the resident expert, buy such and such kind of fertilizer, herbicide, insecticide, soil condition, at so many pounds per square feet, so many dollars per pound, rent or buy to own mechanical spreaders and self driving cutters, and commence to spread regular doses of chemicals over their browning, dying lawns in order to maintain them in a perennial state of green rejuvenation.

They will also spare no expense to install complex, self-timing, multiple scheduled sprinkler systems in their yards to maintain its constant state of greenness. Homeowners will frequently invest large amounts of time, energy and money into the establishment and maintenance of green front lawns.

If the old lawn falls into a state of exhaustion, they will hire a crew to come in, spray it down, cover it with plastic, and eventually scrape it off and roll out a new living carpet of fresh, green hybrid grass. Or they may be more motivated at attempt to do it themselves renting from the local rental yard a rototiller, churning up the earth, buying a few cubic yards of manure, and spreading their own grass seed, frequently with quite mixed results.

Beyond picking up a few tricks of the gardening trade, a few rules of green thumb, a limited folk knowledge of ethno-botany, and a few trade and technical names of plants and chemical products, and perhaps a few details gleaned from the local library or the gardening section of a book store, from <u>Sunset</u> magazine, or <u>Better Homes and Gardens</u> or the *Home* supplement of their Sunday newspaper, the understanding and awareness of the larger realities and connections with the wider world that the possession and maintenance of nice green lawn entails, usually ends at the cashier of the store they buy their gardening supplies from.

And the authoritative sources of their gardening knowledge and supplies cannot really be relied upon to better inform the green consumer of where the fertilizers ultimately come from, what the wholesale mark up really is, what ingredients are in their chemical sprays and amendments and what the ecological or physiological health hazards might really be, for such information, in the hands of the consumer, might threaten their profit margins and prove in the long run bad for their business.

And broader ecological awareness of the current state of the Earth often does more harm than good in the hands of the contemporary minded consumer. The Ecology industry has become a fashionable way of being with it in the world, and often leads to the consumption of expensive plastic components or of synthetic organic products that promote the very industries pushing ecological awareness for their own private profit.

People install expensive and fancy drip irrigation systems to save money, time and to conserve water, in their yards, gardens and patios, often to the point of substituting plastic process with what they used to do by hand with a sprinkling can. People Xeriscape their beds with expensive mulches made from timber of trees or mulch their gardens with large sheets of thick, non-biodegradable plastics.

People buy expensive, synthetic soil amendments with the name organic upon the label to improve the natural loam of their ground. These amendments typically come packaged in non-biodegradable plastic containers and typically contain unnatural and perhaps unhealthy soil additives.

The maintenance of perennially green lawns in North America continues unabated in spite of the fact that such cultural practices are probably some of the least ecologically adaptive and efficient possible.

The net cost in terms of fossil fuels, phosphates, nitrates, production of synthetic chemicals and substances that do not rapidly deteriorate in the environment, and the human energy, both physical and psychological, and the human time required for such upkeep far exceeds the net return of mulching grass clippings back into the earth.

The money, time, energy, and resources consumed in this activity of keeping American lawns green could be better spent on more ecologically adapted activities that benefit a far greater world besides that of private homeowners.

The fertilizers that Americans normally dumps on their lawns could be better used for the production of food in needy third world nations. The fossil fuel consumed in their manufacture and distribution could be better conserved for the next pending oil crises.

<u>Earthbound Perspectives</u>

The time spent in buying, deciding and spreading them could instead be spent reading interesting books, building rock and cactus gardens, or in therapy. The money that is consumed in support of such industry might be better spent in support of ecological programs to save natural habitats, protect wild species from further human predation and depredation or put into savings account for children's future education.

But the case of the greening of America's front lawns is illustrative of virtually every other aspect of modern American culture that is based upon materialism, consumerism, fossil fuels, third world exploitation, multi national industry and the maintenance of widespread obsessive-compulsive neurotic disorders.

America's answer to the natural problems of its frontier has always been to build a more modern shopping mall and a huge asphalt and concrete parking lot around it. It has been a part of our mass material oriented approach of capitalistic culture in virtually every aspect of modern existence—media, education, eating, recreation, work, business, war, trade, charity, even our artistic expression and our religious rituals.

There is no grander spectacle than to behold the story of the nativity in the Crystal Cathedral during Christmas time, just down the street from Disneyland with the huge paper maché mountain of the Matterhorn rising above the treetops and freeway overpasses.

America supports a sophisticated modern civilization based upon mass consumption that has become the paragon of power and status among all the rest in the world. It, and a handful of other overdeveloped first world nations, occupy the top of the apex of the global consumption hierarchy, and it maintains its privileged predominance through the world wide deployment of a vast, extremely expensive and extremely effective military organization that it has somewhat euphemistically called the Department of Defense.

The vast resources consumed in the process of developing and deploying this massive military machine, of building ever better arsenals of nuclear Armageddon, of ever more accurate missiles, ever more protective armor, ever more sophisticated systems of detection and communication, are vast resources that have long since been irretrievably wasted upon mass consumption activities that produce nothing of benefit or lasting consequence in the world except perhaps an illusive sense of security based upon a narrow definition of power as fear of destructive force and threat of violence, long contradicted by the lessons of our history.

The amount of national debt incurred in making war in Southeast Asia against the phantom of communism, and now in the Middle East to establish our presence and power of influence over the primary fossil fuel producing region of the world, to protect our own guaranteed supply of black blood has been money that could instead have gone to the alleviation of a great deal of needless suffering in the world, both domestically and internationally—malnutrition, starvation, disease, poverty, lack of education—all due to a general lack of money in a world dominated by its money market economy.

Ecocide of the environments can be defined as occurring at any point of the human development process that disrupts or destroys the ecosystems of the earth beyond these systems' capacity to recoup or restore their evolutionary equilibrium. The points of no return, of irreversibility, of development, are impossible to predetermine or predict.

No one really knows what the healing capacity of nature might be, what the finite limits of the earth's resources really are, or how much our science can continue to discover or invent means of alleviating the destructiveness inherent to our development or render it more intensively efficient without making it extensively expressed. Beyond such points, there is ecocide because its lost potential becomes irrecoverable, irreplaceable, and, its power to restore itself, irreparable.

This kind of definition for ecocide is problematic because it renders it relative to the process of development and to interpretive definition as to what the limits of nature might be, what the limits of development should be and what directions are negative while others are neutral. This makes relative the definition of ecocide susceptible to manipulation and distortion—to compromise by interests that wish to continue with systematic programs of ecocide.

<u>Earthbound Perspectives</u>

A preferable definition of ecocide is one that claims that ecocide occurs whenever there is mechanical manipulation and arbitrary alteration of the natural environment. In this definition, all development, especially extensively oriented development, is intrinsically and inexorably eco-cidal. It becomes a question then of the relative irreversibility, range of extensiveness, degrees of damage and destructiveness, long-term consequences, costs versus rewards, risks versus benefits.

Definition of what the acceptable limits to ecocide may be still subject to interpretation and hence negotiation, compromise and potential corruption, but it tends to set minimal limits to development and to predefine standards of what is humanly necessary and what is relatively unnecessary and disposable.

We can neither allow development to have a free charter to go whatever direction it chooses, nor can we so limit and constrain it that we frustrate its potential progress in directions that are less rather than more destructive: i.e., more beneficial at less cost to the environment.

Development should be promoted to some point that it meets minimal standards of human health, rights and freedoms but beyond this it needs to be restricted and regulated such that its further pursuit does not continue to damage the Global Ecology of the Earth.

In this sense we can say that bombs and guns are more intrinsically eco-cidal than are rubber balls and running shoes. Similarly, bicycles and buses are better than sports cars and limousines.

A small nature reserve is less eco-cidal than a shopping mall or strip center. A passenger train driven by steam is less eco-cidal than a super sonic transport, a space shuttle or jumbo jet run on jet propulsion fuel. Chicken and beans are less eco-cidal than beef, pork and fish.

The history of ecocide of the earth has been a history of unintended consequences of progressively directed human development. No one suspected that a dammed up stream would reduce the flooding and fertilization of the riverine plains downstream and reduce the estuarine siltation at the mouth.

No one suspected that spray cans, air conditioners and charcoal lighter fluid would rapidly erode the ozone layer of earth. Countless examples of the essential blindness and myopia of development designs that either backfire or produce a whole plethora of environmental reverberations that no one planned upon.

No one in the fifties counting on the miracle fuel of nuclear fission/fusion and design aircraft to be powered by nuclear reactors, expected a Chernobyl or Three Mile Island. No one driving new gas-guzzling cadillacs and sports cars in the late sixties anticipated a sudden oil crises and embargo in the early seventies.

Ecocide is largely a function of the ecological interconnectedness and interdependency of the entire web of life on earth. Cutting down forests in Southeast Asia or in South America might be indirectly related to the production of carbon dioxide by the fossil fuel driven economies of the industrialized first world.

No one guessed early on that a gradual green house effect would occur and with global warming glaciers would retreat at unprecedented rates, winters would be unusually warm and summers unusually unseasonable, or that the sea levels would eventually start rising again to swamp all the developed coastal regions on earth.

No one expected that wasteful over consumption and careless contamination of groundwater tables, mechanical desertification of agricultural areas, coupled with paving over core regions with concrete and asphalt, would interrupt the basic water cycles of many regions and result in unrelieved drought and the increasing cost of portable drinking water.

And yet oil continues to be spilled over the ocean, contaminates continue to wash downstream, lead continues to settle in Greenland ice, and manmade mountains of wasted plastic continue to grow. Food prices will continue to rise, as will oil prices and energy costs. Forests will continue to fall until few tress are left standing. Skylines will continue to rise, deserts expand, and the basic mineral resources will become more and more depleted.

<u>Earthbound Perspectives</u>

The human proto-history of Easter Island is an exemplary model, and ecological paradigm, for the future Post history of the earth. There the Polynesians eventually cut down the all the trees of the island until no more existed.

In the mania of *Mana* they carved out huge stone heads to capture and revitalize the forces of nature for the productivity of limited land and reproduction of the population. The people, ruining their inescapable and fragile habitat, were left without a means of escape or of adaptation on a barren island world.

Ecocide does not just entail the irreversible disruption and destruction of the earth's ecology and natural environments. It also has entailed the destruction and disruption of the whole process of biological evolution of life on earth, and in a deeper and more profound sense, this is a much greater and potentially devastating loss than the kind of environmental/ecological devastation that is occurring everywhere at different rates.

Every extinction of a species, directly or indirectly related to human development, entails an irretrievably loss of biological genetic information and of evolutionary potential that required millions of years to create.

As more and more species become endangered or threatened, they lose not only important genetic, reproductive potential and flexibility, but the natural cultures of their group ecology in the natural environments are irretrievably lost, becoming irreplaceable.

As we deteriorate or erode the life support systems, and the life systems of different species in the web of life on earth, we deteriorate and erode the entire fabric of life on earth, as well as the evolutionary potential of life as a living environment on earth to respond adaptively and evolutionarily to changes on earth.

We have, via the promotion of progressive development, virtually brought the whole evolution of life on earth to a standstill, and we are now attacking the very foundations for selection and survival in the natural world. Life on earth cannot be healthy, adaptive or long-lived if it becomes institutionally restricted and dependent upon zoos and human goodwill.

Ecocide is the term coined to describe what has been happening to the natural environments of the earth every time human beings pursue the progressive promise of technological development. It was what happened in Vietnam with our Roman ploughs, five hundred pounds bombs, napalm and herbicides. It happens every time we level a hillside to build condominiums, clear an empty field to put in a corner strip center, or dump cancerous herbicide on weeds in order to plant new lawns.

It is happening in the torching of oil refineries in the Persian Gulf, and in the spilling of oil into the ocean from oil tankers or platforms. It happens when we cut down the trees of the forests of the world to make lumber for everything from Japanese chopsticks to two-by-six redwood planks for our decks.

We commit ecocide every time we explode another atomic bomb on earth, whether in the sea, in the desert sands or in the frigid wastelands of Siberia. It happens every time we ignite our charcoal briquettes with lighter fluid, use a can of spray paint, turn over the ignition of our cars and trucks, or launch another rocket into space.

Ecocide describes our destruction of the natural ecology of the earth's environments for the sake of the development of our civilization, and it is a term for the artificial death of life on earth and for the planet earth itself as a living, evolving entity.

We continue to commit ecocide, and if we individually become disillusioned and seek to step off our merry go round of modernizing development, then there are many more others who will gladly, madly take our place on the ride. We are constrained to share in the perpetuation of ecocide because successful adaptation and adjustment to a modern, civilized world demands such participation.

To do otherwise is to suffer self-abnegation, social death, ostracism, isolation, marginalization, alienation and virtual annihilation in the world. Our refusal to participate is construed as a sign and symptom of abnormality in a world that has become normally and morally mad. It is to risk and suffer the consequences of rejection in a world that is moving forward at all costs, in spite of the consequences.

<u>Earthbound Perspectives</u>

And there are also great incentives for successful adjustment and participation in ecocide—the material amenities, the level of consumption and waste, the illusion of power and security, can be overwhelming to the sensibilities of most people.

But the apparent worldwide normality of participation in ecocide is itself a measure and symptom of the degree to that our civilization has become unnaturally diseased and destructive.

The fact that for all its sophistication, individualization, and enlightenment, modern civilization offer little latitude and few other legitimate alternatives other than such participation in ecocide, becomes the primary indication of how evolutionarily maladaptive and inflexible our human global society has really become.

This explains a generally pervasive mass psychology that is driving modern humankind forward. It is a fear motivated psychology, a hoarding panic to get what one can before the last of the supply runs out, to scramble viciously against others in the world to get ahead of them and to climb to the top of the material mountain, to do almost anything necessary, to compromise virtually any and every moral sanction, in order to make it larger in the sterile world.

It is a collective archosis of humankind that has come to the realization that the world is finite and that time is quickly running out—to get all you can while the going lasts. People also now know that to lose the race now, to fail out of the System, is virtually irreversible.

If they opt out of participation within a basically eco-cidal system, then they will become systematically eliminated from the reward structure of the system, and will not likely be allowed to reenter, especially at previous levels of engagement or opportunity potential.

This psychology is also characterized by a fundamental sense of mistrust, insecurity and existential uncertainty about the world that entails the inordinate needs for the hypocritical illusions of trust, security and certainty in the world.

The system is loaded with bobby traps by which, if we are not careful and wise in our forward steps, we then can easily become victimized. Social relations are becoming increasingly spurious and based upon convenience and advantage—such spuriousness of social relation is increasingly built in to the structure of modern living and so is unavoidable and unpreventable.

Accompanied by all this, is a fundamental sense of social and existential alienation and anomie of the individual personality—of being isolated and alone in an over crowded, busy, and impersonal world running on illusion, hypocritical values and pretentious imagery.

Getting hooked on the main line of mass media consumerism is the only way left for coping with participation in an eco-cidal world system. Daily doses of mass media consumption provide us the temporary, transitory hypes that allow us to get through the boredom and essential meaninglessness of the day.

The sublimation and mythological symbolization process of the mass media, combined with its distortion and selection of information about the world, is a powerful mechanism of the system for maintaining conformity and reinforcing consumption values within the system.

While the rhinoceros is being poached into extinction before our very own eyes, we can watch ten-year-old nature programs glorifying the natural habitats and beauty of the rhinoceros, and in the process accept the illusion that we are actually doing something to save the species forever.

It is important that the representatives of the system promote the status quo of power and inequality in the world, and that they continue to convince us that there is indeed no other way for the system except through ecocide.

If we come to accept what they want us to believe, that we are absolutely alone, powerless and helpless to prevent ecocide from happening in the world, and that our only personal and social salvation is through participation and perpetuation of such ecocide, then that makes their jobs of administering life and death that much simpler and more morally unproblematic.

If the whole world can become convinced that continuing development of world civilization is the best possible and inevitable future, whatever the costs and sacrifices, that science can solve any problem, even the problems of ecocide, then this will seal the deal and the final fate of humankind and of the earth forever as unpreventable and unalterable from its present direction of development.

To refer to earth states emphasizes the point of view that while their way may be in a general sense a single state of the earth. The current condition of the global ecology or status of the world system or the organizational structure of world order, there are also actually and more accurately different multiple and overlapping states of earth that may be inter-functioning and interdependent to some extent, and also relatively separate.

As such earth states may refer either to the differing ecological states of the earth's atmosphere, hydrosphere, biosphere or of differing geopolitical nation states, international alliances, or of different socio economic states of the First World, Second World, Third World, etc., or of differing regional states of economic, socio cultural, historical integration.

To segment the earth into different kinds of states is a way of cross-examining these differing states in relation to one another, and to understand how these different parts and partitions must fit back together to form alternative states of the possible earth as a potential whole.

Our world is understood in terms of its participation and subdivisions. The whole has long been defined by the interrelations between its parts. To the extent that certain single parts or elements have come to predominate in the world, they have come to stand for and define the whole in place of the other parts.

We come to think of the whole in certain specific terms instead of other possible ways, and we come to act in relation to the world as if the primary part were the whole world in disregard of the rest of the parts.

One particular aspect of contemporary American cultural consciousness is the mono-linguistic, culturally monolithic worldview that it maintains in relation to the whole, and the relative lack of awareness, multi-cultural literacy, and geographic ignorance it has about the rest of the world.

American cultural consciousness is surprisingly inbound and this in-boundness of our conceptuality about the world is a reflection of our attitudes about our own cultural superiority—that the world was meant to become like us, that all difference is the degree of distance from our own way of life, that our predominance in the world is legitimized by our natural birth right, that the closer different cultures are to our own, the more civilized they must be, that America which is in the long run a global enterprise, in that Washington D.C. is the hub of the global wheel, and that the rest of the world will become like us, democratic and capitalistic, if given enough time to eventually work out their own internal differences and problems.

We are witnessing not only the progressive unfolding of global ecocide in the name of world development. We are also experiencing socio-economic polarization of the world by private capitalistic interest groups, socio-political-economic bureaucratic encapsulation, and cultural homogenization within a single global system of shared values of mass consumption/production.

These processes are going on simultaneously, more or less, in every region and part of the world, and they are stimulating contradictory processes of the balkanization of the world into competing ethno-national splinter groups under the umbrella of structural integration of the nation states, such that different identities, solidarities, and motivations increasingly cross-cut the traditional monothetic boundaries of states and undermine the previous order of national unity and stability based upon the balance of power in the globalization of the international arena.

In the broader sense, these global processes render the recent pro-American involvement in the Persian Gulf, as the principal arbiter and enforcer of international justices and world peace, albeit *Pax Americana* style, and its continuing conservative federalism and republicanism, something of a maladaptive anachronism a world in that iron and bamboo curtains no longer exist, the Berlin wall has been torn down by the very people whom it repressed, and ethno-national communities everywhere have international contingents and foreign colonies.

Our own forward posturing of military might in the world has suddenly come to appear quite morally awkward when the very enemy upon that its powerful presence was predicated has suddenly dissolved in front of our eyes, while new kinds of enemies emerged from the global woodwork.

Most Americans have been left with a deep seated gap in their conceptualization and evaluation of the world, such that they intuitive sense that something is not right, but their own systems of rationalization and mythology preclude bringing it out and coming face to face with the key issues.

In the name of patriotism, national solidarity, national strength, even in the name of democracy, the so called leaders have secretly sold American economic interests out to foreign competitors for their own private and personal aggrandizement, in the name of prosperity and progress, and have in the process emptied American coiffures into their own pockets and into the hands of international state and non-state business interests.

America voted Reagan two terms as President not because of his inherent leadership abilities, that he did not have, nor his competence, but because he was preeminently an actor and a media figure. In him, Americans voted for a symbol, an empty voice, a figurehead of big business and powerful private interests. They voted not for leadership, but to acknowledge the vacuum of leadership, to renege responsibility and forfeit independence in true leadership to yield to partisan private interest and party interference.

People voted for a false sense of security in a big, impersonal system. It was a silent, unconscious acknowledgment that no one was in control, that no one should be responsible, that what was leftover was for everyone to take all that they could get while the going was still good. In him, America acquiesced and capitulated to values of the higher authority and impersonal power of the system.

Americans have been slow to catch on in the Post-Reagan reconstruction period that their corporate public interests have been short changed in a bad deal with international interests, and slow to grasp that in the new world there is no more national leadership that can be relied upon. Bush has been making war here and there to divert public attention from this basic fact.

Congressmen make glorious speeches about the general good and then silently vote in favor of private interests. Americans have been slow to realize that in the contemporary world, there is no more national leadership that makes any relevance or sense, if there was ever such a grand illusion. Now there are only special private or state and non-state interests promoting their own success at someone else's expense.

Without another public enemy upon which to declare war and to mobilize public attention and interest, America too must begin dissolve as a political unity into many different, competing with self-serving splinter groups. The Washington puppet show cannot long maintain the illusion of cleanliness and sacred authority.

The rest of the world has never really suffered the real world naiveté of American culture in all its virtue. Their world has always been a world of vice and corruption, and virtue exists not because of it, or in reaction to it, but in spite of it and in disregard of its influence, America, as a culture, is coming of age in an old world of humankind.

The entire earth has changed rapidly right before all of us, and our old divisions, boundaries, and partitions of its spaces and regions are no longer adequate for the human understanding or relating to the world in an adaptive manner.

As we carry our old, outmoded differences with us into our new earthbound environments, we are experiencing what Alvin Toffler long ago referred to as "future shock." Our previous frames and schemas no longer fit our new sets of experiences, and we become disoriented and at a loss to figure out so quickly what has changed about our ways of seeing the world.

As long as the world continues to pursue collectively a policy of global development with its concomitant ecocide of the earth, then a sense of crises, helplessness, dependency, existential emptiness, anomie, and impending climatic doom must continue to unconsciously undermine our collective illusions and to contextually overshadow our collective horizon.

It will continue to accelerate in its changing in social and structural ways that we are less and less in control to direct or prevent. They will continue to happen ever more rapidly in spite of what we do, both because of what we do as well as in negation of what we do.

<u>Earthbound Perspectives</u>

The changes happening in our world are tending to skew obliquely our traditional and common sense categories and conventional ways of seeing the world, such that the world no longer seems to make sense given the inadequacy of our framework for understanding it.

This skewing effect means that new experiences are transacting our previous lines of experience in ways that we can no longer clearly define and that create a sense of radical discontinuity and disorientation between past and present.

Our previous interests and intentionality structures no longer make as much sense given this skewing effect of our new global experiences. There is a divergence and conflict of interests and intentions between those interests rooted to the past and those oriented toward the future.

With the skewing of interest and intentionality, comes as well a shifting of basic identity and existential sense of meaning and purpose in the world. With changing identities and loyalties, with shifting involvements and commitments, our values and relations with the world become reoriented about a new and different kinds of "glocal and lobal" foci.

Our goals, expectations, beliefs, representations, are also becoming altered and reinterpreted in the confrontation with our new experiences. We elicit old frames of understanding only to have them be consistently disrupted and defeated, entailing that we need then to somehow reevaluate these frames or else replace them with new ones that makes better sense of the world and work for us in the world. The general feeling is one of losing a sense of balance, or a centeredness of being in the world, that we find vulnerable and threatened by strange new environments.

We often seek new maze-ways of our collective world and often flock to whatever false prophets who claim to have the answers.

The tension produced within current earth states is largely the consequence of differential distribution of resources, knowledge, expertise, money, power, material goods, food, etc.

Such resources become concentrated in some regions and relatively scarce in others, and this unevenness of the structural landscape of earth leads to social imbalances and stresses in its systemic functioning.

The inequalities produced by this overall unevenness and the differentials of distribution and availability are becoming more pronounced and extreme as development continues comparatively in the way it has mostly been pursued.

There is something fundamental about the competitive values of Capitalism that leads eventually to monopolism and a hierarchy of resource consumption/production. Successful competitors eventually drive out and displace unsuccessful ones, and big companies tend to swallow up or destroy smaller, weaker ones.

A utilitarian philosophy premised upon the greatest good for the greatest number of people leads to an historical patterning of extreme polarization between the relatively few haves and the huge mass majority of have-nots.

Such a worldview is also premised upon a world of unlimited good. In order to increasingly maximize profits, producers must manufacture infinite numbers of widgets that are sold to infinite numbers of consumers. Such production requires that there be corresponding infinite numbers of widget components and infinite amounts of basic resources from that such components are made.

Furthermore, the principle of profit maximization means driving out competitors by underbidding them, minimizing costs of basic resources by maintaining monopolistic control over their acquisition, and by "exploitation" of the basic labor requirements involved in the semi-integrated processes of their production.

Given the real world efficacy of such a worldview, certain kinds of things in the world make sense. First, social evolution dictates that economic competition is a process of social selectionism in that the best survives.

This selectionism underlies the principle of progress that is central to development in the world. It also then becomes understandable to link up social selection as a logical extension of natural selectionism, and to claim that only the fittest survive and the weakest must perish.

<u>Earthbound Perspectives</u>

It becomes of primary importance then to establish a scientific orientation that clearly and unequivocally demonstrates the casual linkages between nature and culture, between biology and behavior, genetics and social history. It is also sometimes forgivable if the System sometimes becomes "fascist" in its extreme orientation and premises that those who survive must be the fittest because they survived, and that those who perish must not be fit to survive anyway.

Therefore poor people are people somehow genetically miss-endowed and the biologically maladapted to success within the social system. The social system must also create bureaucratic mechanisms that reinforce this process by systematically excluding the poor, weak, failed from access to resources that would otherwise hinder progressive development and survival of the fittest. Thus social institutions of structural poverty, weakness, and dependence are created to recapitulate the core values of such a worldview.

The flip side of this doctrine is that those who have become successful within the system must be the socially and biologically fittest to survive, and they must therefore be the chosen ones who are privileged to reproduce above all the rest.

Symbolic systems should reinforce this moral universe by extolling the beautiful people as the embodiment of natural virtues and as being inherently incapable of doing wrong, no matter how narcissistic such people may really be. If they sometimes do err in their ways then their mistakes are quickly euphemized away and they are conveniently let off the hook.

Another somewhat contradictory consequence of this is that to insure market maximization, a potentially unbounded market of consumers, then birth control programs should not be reinforced. It is no coincidence that both Presidents Reagan and Bush have demoted the support of family planning in third world nations that suffer extreme problems of over population, and have also been sideline champions of 'right to life' movements.

Over population is seen in this case not as a global problem and a global responsibility, but as a local problem and a local level responsibility. Several corollaries come from this attitude towards the plight of the poor. The rich were meant to get richer, and the poor were meant to get more children.

This assures that the wealthy will stay wealthy and the poor will increase in numbers and in proportion. It is the realization of the capitalist hierarchy in reverse. Also, rich people are encouraged to have more children, as this is construed eugenically as beneficial to the future of humankind—the reproduction of greatness.

Also, though the poor are not prevented from getting pregnant, they are from the beginning chastised for the problem of poverty and population. If one child dies of malnutrition or lack of appropriate prenatal care or medical attention, then the parents can be expected to soon have another one anyway. It can be expected that the poor are good reproducers anyway.

They need proportionately fewer Cesarean sections and have higher rates of infant-mother mortality. A young girl who has her first child by eighteen, will be expected to have at least four or five more by the time she is thirty years old. If the young teenage daughter of the wealthy becomes accidentally pregnant, she can always be flown away to a different town, city, state or country to have the necessary operation.

The poor get no vacations; the rich just take another vacation. Similarly, third world nations saddled with the social burden of over population are conveniently kept subordinate upon the global hierarchy by these attitudes and policies. By maintaining overpopulation, they can be kept in a position of poverty and dependency, readily exploitable for their cheap labor, resources and recreational environments.

Overpopulation and a lack of birth control policies effectively reinforces and recapitulates the attitude that these nations were meant to be exploited—that their peoples are racially inferior and culturally backward, and must be looked after by the wealthier nations for their own best interests. By maintaining over population and poverty, these nations also form zones in that inferior products can be tested, experimented with, and consumed at least cost to the system.

Another related value of this worldview is the basic principle of social/natural hierarchy, that is reflected in taxonomic classifications of things in nature as well as of the social world that is rank ordered along a scheme of pyramidal hierarchy of an infra-structural base, a structural middle class and an ideological superstructure, or along the lines of a Great Chain of Being in that things higher on the totem pole are higher on the evolutionary scale of progress. Thus chance can become more idealistically abstract and thus more can be fooled."

From this perspective the third world nations can be seen as representing effectively the infra-structural base that is seen as the resource pool supporting the upper structures. The values of social hierarchy reinforce values of social conformism and authority, especially the authority of wealth and private property, as well as sumptuary privileges that inevitably follow.

Social hierarchy becomes reflected domestically in capitalistically organized societies in terms of a three-tiered class/caste structure organized in the same manner as the world capitalistic system has become organized.

The history of competition is held to determine who should get ahead and who shall fall behind in the struggle to get on top of the social heap. Those who are on top, or who at least appear upwardly mobile, must be naturally endowed with the right stuff for success. Those at the bottom, or suffering downward mobility, must be cursed with the wrong stuff that prevents them from climbing up the ladder.

These values and their reflected attitudes can be referred to as social racism in the sense that it is a kind of biological determinism of class/caste boundaries that is somewhat skewed along the natural boundaries of race. It is not so much a matter of white or black, but of wealthy white and poor white oe wealthy black and poor black.

Another value that is a corollary of the capitalistic worldview is that money makes right and money is a sign of sacredness. This value is very basic to the capitalist worldview and goes back to the Protestant (Calvinist) notion of one's calling and of whether one is chosen or selected for admission into Heaven.

The fear of death, or of what happens in death, and the lack of certitude about who is predetermined for heaven or hell, creates a fundamental sense of existential anxiety and cognitive dissonance that leads to the emphasis of the egotism of non-being—of becoming obsessively preoccupied with behaving as if one were selected for admission into Heaven instead of Hell.

It becomes vitally important then to one's personal sense of security in life that one adopt the attitudes, symbolisms and rewards of success in one's calling, make lots of money, own lots of property, become a father like authority figure, and embody in one's everyday being the principles and values of hierarchy, superiority and privilege.

This close association between wealth and righteousness, not to mention cleanliness and virtue that is found in capitalism, is not too different from the kind of hierarchy that is expressed in Hindu India under the Brahmanic tradition. Status symbolisms of wealth, showing off one's status, as predetermined and select, becomes a focal preoccupation of culture to the point at that a dowry is more important than the bride that comes attached with the dowry—hence suttee.

From this standpoint, the three tiered capitalistic caste system, the traditional Hindu caste system, and the ideology of racism and the Great Chain of Being, in that Whites, then Yellows, Browns and Blacks are ranked, are similar kinds of systems that prescribe rules of endogamy or hyper-gamy and of occupational exclusion or separation.

Such a system is reinforced by an ideological and symbolic system of collective representation and belief, incorporating values of hierarchy, authority, the legitimacy and legitimating function of wealth, sumptuary status symbols and the monolithic, materialistic and hedonistic amassing of private property.

It is possible to speak of a global market economy that is becoming increasingly characterized by a diagonally stratified class/caste system—in that vertical class boundaries are becoming skewed by overlapping, horizontally stratified caste hierarchies.

In such a system, individual allegiance and identity gained within a national culture is contradicted by and compromised by competing allegiances and identity with ethno-national groupings that have characteristics of both classes and castes within a global market framework.

Promoting ethno-national identity and solidarity entails reinforcing internal class hierarchy and externally oriented caste boundaries in relation to other competing class caste groupings. These groupings become similar to Hindu "*Jats*" that tend to be localized and occupationally specialized and that juggle and struggle for position within a larger caste stratified society.

The ethno-national, class caste sub-groupings of humankind working within a capitalistic world system can be stratified and divided along the lines of a number of different distinguishing traits—religious affiliation, political orientation, racial identity, sex, age, socio-economic status, location on the political spectrum, ethno-cultural heritage or identity, geographical homeland, psycho-geographic identity, and birthplace, status role identity or occupational specialization.

An Irish American Catholic Democrat whose family hails from Boston might be very different from an Irish American Republican whose interests are centered in Southern California.

Characteristic of this kind of componential or conglomerated status identity is its sociological "interposition" of status position becomes correlated with multiple overlapping hierarchies with the correlated social psychological phenomena of increased levels of social confusion of identity, cognitive dissonance, the stress and strain of differential tensions, loyalties, cross-cutting commitments upon an individual, feelings of relative deprivation in comparison to other groupings or identities, feelings of frustration in blocked social mobility within one or more hierarchy of social status.

This creates a pervasive and fundamental crisis of identity within a larger system that is inherently competitive, alienating and disenfranchising anyway. A lack of upward mobility is tantamount to relative downward mobility—going nowhere is a falling backward from progress. There is a pervasive need to keep up, to acquire the latest edition, the newest model of car, the most current design or fashion of clothing.

Within such a diagonal social structure of the world system, the psychology of Nonbeing becomes the social psychological phenomena of a collective archosis of a culture dedicated to the values and orientation of nonbeing in the larger world.

Personal and social identity is no longer ideography—the cult of individuality is but a superficial irrelevance. Identity becomes preeminently nomothetic within multiple classificatory hierarchies and taxonomies on the world.

Within such a world culture and social structure, there is a pervasive, almost paranoid, mass psychology that the "grass is always greener" on the other side. We need human categories upon which to externalize, project and objectify as if real our own deep-seated feelings of inferiority and fear of failure in the world.

We need to see our social world in such a way that our values of hierarchy, authority, status, make objective sense in the larger world. We need to always feel like or at least appear as if we are getting ahead, upwardly mobile, going somewhere. We need to associate with the right kind of people, evince the right attitudes, and adopt the right behaviors.

Within a competitive framework, success of other counter reference groups could and should be one's own. What things of value others may have are potentially one's own possession, and what one does have one deserves, no matter at whose expense it might have been by.

Within such a world, the values and orientations of equality and egalitarianism are largely an ideological fiction, a falsehood, a sense of false consciousness, and, when embodied by certain representatives within the system, a matter of fundamental hypocrisy of identity.

Equality and egalitarianism become 'anti-structural' values that can only exist marginally, counter culturally, separately, or in ritually outlined contexts of ceremonial Communitas, liminality and rites of reversal.

Social hierarchy has been a near universal principle of social organization of humankind, except perhaps at the level of the band on which level almost all relations are face-to-face and interpersonal and everyone knows everyone else within one's cultural universe.

But this is a relative equality perhaps—elders still have some measure of influence over juniors and the group as a whole still constrains the behavior of the individual in ways that set the interests of the group above those interests of a single person.

It is entirely likely that the values of social equality are inherently unrealizable and unrealistic, and that values of social hierarchy are perhaps necessary and ineradicable in the world.

Even in democratic North America, where all people are constitutionally created equal and endowed by their creator with certain inalienable rights, still it goes without saying that within its long standing system of common law and justice, some people are more equal than others, and rights protected under the law become relative to one's social worth and the amount of property one owns.

The legal system protects the rights of private property over and above the personal rights of people such that the latter inevitably become alienable and compromised by the former when the two sets of interests they represent come into conflict. No society can be created that does not reinforce hierarchy and entail inequality to some minimal extent and still work well in the world as a corporate social entity.

But both equality and hierarchy are socially relative matters—hierarchy can be more or less extreme or emphasized. Its values can be stressed or left unmarked or be basically devalued and dysphemized. Equality, too, though never absolute, can be relatively realized as a reduction of hierarchy and a general evening out of differentials of uneven distribution or unfair access to resources.

The gradient between the top and the bottom does not need to be so steep or extreme, and the hierarchy can be leveled or flattened out such that the differences between those at the top and those at the bottom are not so disproportionate. This would concomitantly increase social mobility in the world and reduce the possibility of evil that comes from the emphasis and exaggeration of hierarchy, inequality and authority.

Such leveling out entails certain fundamental changes in our capitalistic way of doing things. We need a blanket socialism of basic services that guarantees the protection of human rights as well as interests and basic freedoms from exploitation and violation.

We need a global reign of peace rather than of terror and threat, such that the values leading toward equality, of tolerance, respect, and nonviolence can be cultivated in the world while the insecurities that nonbeing depends upon might be reduced.

It requires as well that we put a handle and a brake upon development and slow it down from the speed of a hare to the pace of a snail. We must stop further ecocide and allow nature enough time to heal some of its wounds, if it is not too late already.

Our basic sense of social identity would go from being one stressing class caste status to one of multiculturalism and pan humanism along a single integrated multi-cultural continuum. Boundaries will still be there to negotiate, but they will be more like passageways and thresholds for passing between different states of reality than like gateways or fences preventing and hindering such cross movement.

There has been nothing actually necessary or inevitable about the recent events and developmental states of the earth that our own failure to face the facts, to confront reality with courage instead of cowardice, to direct change in alternative ways than what has actually happened, have not made it so.

The problems that the world is now facing were recognized long-ago by enough people, that things could have been done to forestall and prevent many unfortunate consequences. Development has been what we've decided to make it, and will continue to make it.

The United States had the vision and the reason twenty years ago in its first oil crises to adopt policies leading to an alternative fuel economy. Now, much of the economic stagflation and recession, the growing polarization and deficit, have been due to the continuing and increasing dependence of the American economy and development upon fossil fuels derived primarily from the Middle East.

It is not an accident that twenty years ago the Pentagon and CIA shifted its long-term strategic objectives from the halting of communist revolution in Southeast Asia to the securing of America's oil reserve in the Middle East, and it then began laying the basic tactical and strategic designs that culminated in the recent war with Iraq.

Saddam Hussein was a very convenient and not entirely coincidental scapegoat for our own aggressive political policies and military posturing there to protect our vital national interests. An unrestricted supply of oil to the US may be vital to its national strategic interests, but it has never been absolutely necessary. We had options, and alternative avenues to development, and we failed to take them in a timely manner.

Now we are struggling to survive under the spell of the continuing delusion of the given, taken for granted necessity of our system and its way of life. It has been our grand illusion that we have failed to confront and come to terms within its entirety.

The system under which we struggle to survive is similar to the ecological system of the entire earth in that many things are functionally interconnected to many other things. Changes in one aspect reverberate and have consequences in many other aspects of the system.

Professors can in their insularity and immunity berate and derogate people like Ronald Reagan or George Bush, and yet turn around and promote ideologies of socio biology that uphold and legitimate basically social racist orientations of the system, or in other ways of funded or endowed research, promote the existing interests of the system.

An educated engineer can be against war in the Gulf and yet his/her lifestyle will continue to depend upon his/her design of ever more accurate guidance systems for military missiles. Similarly, in the name of anti-communism, we may participate in the systematic destruction of the rain forest, and its inhabitants, as in Vietnam. A public housing developer may genuinely deplore the destruction of the forests on earth, and yet wipe out whole natural habitats of flora and fauna in the course of building a project.

It is relatively easy to look out in a general way to see the broader outlines of the problems of the world, but it becomes an entirely different matter to focus in on the specific interconnections between these problems and our own personal existential predicaments and dilemmas. It is to see how and in what exact ways development and ecocide become our own reasons for being in the world and sense of purpose for the world.

We are living within a system that is increasingly embedding itself into our awareness and our unconsciousness, into our environments and our experiences. We are living in a world that is becoming increasingly bureaucratic and administratively top heavy, with an increasingly polarized class structure and increasingly inflexibility and frozenness of social mobility.

It is happening within the span of a single lifetime, of a single generation. We are increasingly engaged in expected role performances and in enacting our parts within the system without reflecting on the consequences or existential realities in that our actions are situated and over-determined.

We increasingly take for granted as given and necessary a great deal of social inequality and noise that is not necessary or a priori to our own construction of it within our social existential realities.

The range of choices available to us today, the degrees of freedom open to us now, are much more restricted than they were twenty years ago. They will quickly become even more restricted, and alternatives increasingly more effectively impossible the longer we procrastinate and perseverate in our old, tried and true ways of doing things.

The solutions and alternatives available to us twenty years ago are no longer available to us, and our ability to do anything about the developmental direction we are following will continue to diminish past the point of ultimate no return.

Today we are creating boundaries, differences, social divisions between people when none need occur. We are reinforcing such boundaries and differences, and creating greater social distances between people in an increasingly over crowded and shrinking social world, when we could be bridging these distances and diminishing these differences.

To continue emphasize and promote divisions, difference and distance in a social world of diminishing space, resources, alternatives, must eventuate in explosive consequences for all of us.

When we speak of the greening of the earth we are not talking about putting more fertilizer on front lawns of American homes, or about moving to where the grass is greener. We are talking about promoting ecologically minded, environmentally protective and conservative, and evolutionarily adaptive strategies of living on earth with ourselves, and among ourselves, in ways that do not lead to developmental destruction or ecocide.

It entails a basic existential realization about the extrinsic and intrinsic limits of our lives and of the system we live within—in spite of how we were raised, we cannot have our earth cakes and eat them too, we cannot continue to have everything for virtually nothing, and we cannot expect to achieve and develop unreal worlds at other people's expense.

It entails an acceptance of our own personal responsibility for participation in the development, or underdevelopment of the system on earth.

It entails a way of seeing and relating within and in spite of the system such that we can become more aware of the net, long-term consequences of our own and others actions on earth, and of the alternative possibilities for acting and reacting upon earth, both naturally and socially.

More specifically we associate the green movement with a radical group of ecological extremists who blockade nuclear tests and sabotage environmentally destructive development projects.

But as a ground swell social movement, greening of the earth entails a more pervasive and powerful sense of public awareness and involvement in the issues of ecocide and the future directions that development will take.

There is more voting power than in periodic elections in the daily decisions made in the market place by the average American consumer to create changes, to boycott environmentally or socially destructive products or practices, to become better, more realistically informed and disillusioned with the system.

In this sense, to declare an international holiday—to give the earth a day off, to take a one day break in the whole process, and to slow development by a single day, to go sit under trees and to celebrate nature, would be better than to promote development even one more day.

Where we are headed, globally, locally, and personally, we should not be in too big of a hurry to get there. We cannot go too slowly forward, and we cannot afford to be in too much of a hurry. We should not have to feel constrained to do anything socially significant tomorrow except take the day off.

PART IV: POPULATION BOMBS
Many Millions of Malthusian Miracles

Real numbers too large to count, millions or billions, are really beyond our ability to realistically conceptualize or even imagine in terms of powers of ten or as so many zeros following one. They are numbers far too great to even remotely comprehend or clearly conceptualize in any but the most abstract way.

Now, if we multiply these numbers by the kind of complexity that even a single human life time presents us with, then we have some vague sense of the enormity of the anthropological problem in trying to embrace a realistic notion of a pan human reality in the world.

We can only handle such a problem by gross over simplifications or mass generalizations in terms of national character stereotypes or in terms of a standardized inventory of cultural traits in a large, cross cultural sample or survey.

Though it is rarely acknowledged as such, it is the shear enormity and vastness of this human reality that renders cross-cultural studies and panhuman theories in Anthropological research most difficult and problematic.

The necessary reductions, simplifications, reifications, that are inherent in any such task usually goes unmentioned and unquestioned in anthropological literature, because if these problematic issues of scale were opened up, it would most likely make anthropology seem like so much singing in the wind— interesting perhaps, but too narrow and limited in scope to necessarily reflect human reality or the challenges of the contemporary world in any but the most hypothetical way.

Statistical surveys involving a few hundred, or a few thousand subjects are of enormous logistical and methodological difficulty—much less hundreds of thousands, millions or billions. No one really has a good idea of the whole picture of human reality as it is unfolding before us, or as it has unfolded during the past.

We can only risk our credibility on gross estimates based upon theoretical conclusions, intuitive insights, a great deal of ignorance, a few leaps of faith and some wild inferences and wonderful guesswork.

The Renaissance Genius was supposed to live in a world that was comprehensive in its intellectual totality. The world then was supposedly much smaller, simpler and perhaps less sophisticated that it is presumed now to be.

Now, it is held, the contemporary conceptual world is too specialized, too complex, and too compartmentalized, to be comprehended by any single mind or even any group of intellectuals. Today, it is held that there can be no more Renaissance Genius who knew of everything.

We live in a world that no one has a bottom line in, in that no one has a complete picture of the whole, or even understands most of it. Today, the most we can hope for is partial, fragmentary, and rough comprehension of the world—seen in outline form only from a great, estranging distance. Then we can only half trust that the bigger picture maybe big enough.

We must learn to swallow what it has been that we've been doing with our anthropology of the world with a great grain of salt. For every world that becomes recorded ethnographically, there are many more that have vanished forever from human memory. For every reality that becomes enlightened ethnologically, there are multiple alternative realities that have remained undiscovered.

We must learn to accept with some disillusionment that we have not actually been doing quite what it was that we believed we were doing, and then seek to better understand what it is we have actually done in relation to the world. The world, and its realities, remains larger than life, intransigent to our investigations and probes, and aloof from our approximations.

What we have been doing is more on the order of careful speculation based upon a limited amount of information, rendering generalizations from quite fragmentary evidence that push us toward a sense of universal awareness. The success of such an approach depends upon our careful, painstaking attention to minor detail and careful analysis before then leaping to conclusions.

We have been more like detectives on a forensic case, sorting out and piercing together a few clues to try to figure out what actually happened at the scene of the crime. We frequently depend upon witnesses whose credibility and reliability and actual experience may be no greater than our own, and frequently much less.

From an accumulating number of such studies, we range over the literature of previous and current work being done, and add our two cents worth, and try to pull out from it a more complete comprehension than before.

We have been reconstructing a patchwork anthropological version of the real world—more of a collage or mosaic of roughly interconnected accounts and momentary pictures—particular instantiations frozen forever for scientific exhibition. And in a sense, this piecework collage of Anthropology which has been is more important to active anthropologists than is the real world upon which it is hypothetically, presumably based.

The real world of people is only a source, a background, a reservoir, the field where one gets one's information. Once having obtained the interesting or important or significant data, a sort of extraction process resembling strip mining or panning for gold, then the anthropologists is free to discard the informants, disregard the rest of the world, return to his/her office in the Ivory Tower, and begin weaving a new part of the tapestry.

The real world becomes rapidly left behind after the first few phases of research, the researcher achieving enough authority on his/her area of study to no longer be dependent upon the ultimate source of their information, being able to put the real world upon a shelf, to collect dust until further need arises.

What seems most missing and lost in this process of ethnographic extraction of anthropological information, is the preliminary question of the real world relevance of subsequent work, of what happens to this knowledge and information once it leaves the field for the office, the distancing of surplus value as the substitutes for reality sit upon the bookshelves of the library collecting dust until some fresh new naïve researcher rediscovers it again.

It is readily apparent that the products of anthropological research and work, that stand as symbolic substitutes and representations for the portions of reality that they authoritatively subsume, become in the process of annealing the real world material into ever longer and thinner and more tenuous connections, more anthropologically significant and relevant than the actual real world itself. After all, these are supposedly the things that will make or break an anthropologists professional career, and the real world be damned.

More often than any anthropologists would like to admit, real world relevance becomes subsumed away under the guise of subsequent academic authority, lost between the pages of the mountain of literate understanding.

The specialist observer becomes the official spokesperson for her/his special people in the world, no matter whether that voice or understanding may really know these people's personal names or actually witness even a small portion of their actual, lived experiences in the real world.

The naïve, simplistic sense of realism in its thin veil of written words is really all that anthropology can depend upon for its credibility and relevance in the world. This is too often a poor substitute for the actual experiential realities that it disguises and displaces in the imagination of its readership. It is indeed only a thin line separating this anthropological imagination about reality and the uncharted ocean of anonymous ignorance upon which it floats.

It is in reaction to this irreconcilable difficulty of doing anthropology that makes the anthropologist want to believe that they are extracting not only the essence from the experiential material of the real world, sorting out the critically important from the chaotic trivia, separating the relevant, more meaningful information, from the static nonsensical noise; selecting out the key elements from the hodgepodge admixture of many different shapes and colors.

It is not enough for the anthropologist to be a Sherlock Holmes, adducing whole worlds from grains of sand, but the anthropologist must also be a physical scientist—a chemist who in a natural laboratory is figuring out the principles of material relations and reactions in the world—fine tuning the extraction process on the basis of empirically demonstrable, cross culturally and statistically verifiable, principles and laws of social interaction and human belief and behavior.

But it is not quite certain whether the alleged chemistry of the anthropological investigator, as scientist in a white lab coat, is not always by some sleight of hand performing a feat of alchemical magic and trickery. A performer before an audience creating fostering an illusion of the transmutation of real worlds into the paper bound reality of anthropology.

In spite of this fundamental limitation of the horizon of anthropological awareness, and in spite of the criticisms against the reality of its enterprise, anthropology, has achieved remarkable success in representing the world in a realistic and naturalistic manner that remains literally interesting and scientifically intriguing.

It may be mostly illusion, but it remains perhaps a necessary world of illusion—an antidote to what could otherwise prove to be a very monochromatic and monotonous ideological world order.

Given the limited range of our own senses and sensibilities, it is perhaps the best we can do in representing the world realistically and naturalistically, and it has thereby enlarged our world by its presence and participation within it. Our worlds are not the less for it.

In our valuation of its science, anthropology claims to be mainly neutral in its relation with the world. It is supposed to be neither philanthropic nor misanthropic as an enterprise. If it takes from the world in one way that might seem to diminish or desecrate the private lives of the people it studies and whose lives it reifies on paper, then it also gives back to the world in other ways that can make peoples public lives more complete and fulfilled. As an enterprise, its directional development has been relatively harmless in the world when compared to other kinds of developmental activities.

If anthropology's products are sometimes misused by other people beyond the capacity of anthropologists to control, then this is perhaps true of any kind of information about reality that is subject to manipulation and distortion by people who have deliberate purposes in deception, distortion, and manipulation in other forms of directive development in the world.

If it sometimes misrepresents the real world, then it mostly does so unintentionally and by accident, and this act of misrepresentation in the world is also a part of its own developmental history.

Perhaps being the best we can do in the world, and lacking any better means for going about it, we can learn to make the most of its limits, to live and work and perhaps even prosper within them.

There is a sense that we too are natural living species of the world, and that even our culture, its artificiality and development itself, is a product and function of the larger natural world from which it originated and within which it works. In this sense, the ecocide of development becomes our own ecocide as well—as we work to destroy nature in the world around s we are also acting to destroy the world of nature that exists within ourselves as well.

In this sense, we must reconsider the possible eco-cidal consequences of our own anthropological developments in the world—the ways in that our own predominant directions of human development might possibly be affecting our adaptation in the larger world and hurting our own special ecology in that world.

When we refer to the history of development, we are also implying the natural and cultural histories of human development—of the ways we have become changed, biologically, psychologically, and socially as a consequence of our development in the world.

We must seek to understand the ways that anthropology, in its own development, have contributed deliberately or unwittingly to these human developments in the world, whether eufunctional or dysfunctional, whether philanthropically or misanthropically.

To the extent that anthropological development has been rooted in a tradition of enlightenment that implies a notion of progress towards some perfect state, and some form of directive change over past, imperfect states then anthropology must share some of the responsibility in the creation of modern utopias and dystopias in the world.

The prolonged history of human development in the world has been a history of distinctively mixed results. It has been carved out with a double edged sword that has in the process of distributing its fine sense of justice to the world, also created in its wake gross inequalities and violent injustices in the world. It has mostly been a delayed history of two steps forward and one step backward.

By and large, human development has so far benefited mostly a few in the world, just as anthropological attention has so far mostly focused on only a few in the world, and it has by far done nothing for, or perhaps even detracted from the development of any more in the world whose faces have since passed by unnoticed, whose unwritten names have been forgotten, lives unrecorded passed away, and whose voices have been lost in the background silences of the libraries and reading rooms of the interior, intensive worlds of anthropology.

We cannot recover so much that has been lost in the process of constructing and reconstructing our own histories from the past, but we can remind ourselves of our own hubris of our anthropological intellectuality and the great need for human humility and humbleness in our development.

Hung up by its own problems of its authority, and authoritativeness, in the world, anthropology has suffered from a perennial crisis of its professional identity. This crisis has been particularly acute during the last decade and is becoming more extreme in its divisive consequences upon the world of anthropology.

It has long been a crises of ego-identity—of ego reality testing, ego rationalization, ego definition, ego defense mechanisms designed to protect its very relative sense of consistency, coherence and continuity in a rapidly changing world, thus designed to give some overarching sense of symbolic unity to the diversity and frequently disruptive and discordant experiences of reality.

It is, more importantly, designed to protect and promote the efficacy and illusion of its own nonbeing in the world—its fundamental symbolic vicariousness that allows its own somewhat oversimplified and abstruse representations to stand for so much else actually in the world.

It has sought to substitute its fundamental nonbeing in the world for the experiential realities of being in the world—being that works to continually undermine its own collective representations and to historically relativize its knowledge and understandings of the world, however implicit or explicit in form or function.

This anthropological nonbeing in the world comprises its own ideological false consciousness, the primary purpose of which is the denial of its own natural history, and an evasion of the fundamental existential dilemma of death in the world. Its worlds are dying before its lens, if not eyes, and it becomes history faster than it can be recorded, researched and reconstructed as past, ever-present, frozen reality.

Failure to confront the natural processes of the dying world of which it is a part, of people, culture, civilizations, and of histories inexorably changing and passing away without any ethnographic epitaph, and to come to terms with its own historicity and relational context in the world, leaves the anthropological enterprise, and the anthropological ego-identity that is the other part of this enterprise, in a permanent, fixed state of loss and disorientation, that it must then somehow seeks to recover and repair.

Humpty Dumpty has fallen from its fence, and all the king's men and all the king's horses can't put him back together again.

There is an important connection, though, between this acute crises of professional identity that anthropology is suffering from, both personally as an individual ethos of belief and behavior, and paradigmatically as a collective nomos and as a corporate enterprise with its own directions of development and its own sense of social solidarity and its own connectedness to the world.

This connection is that the crises inflicting anthropology internally is as much a reflection and representation of a larger external crises in the world as it is a problem instrinsic to the world of anthropology.

The eco-cidal change in the real world, the acceleration of its historical movements and irreversibility of many of its linear transitions, has been causing major symbolic and experiential reverberations in the interior domains of anthropology.

The crises of identity infecting the average anthropologist is part of a larger world wide crises of identity affecting most of humanity as it struggles and seeks to define itself in a rapidly changing world. Old labels, definitions, references, interpretations, no longer fit new situations, people, environments, in which older frames of reference no longer work.

If the world had remained relatively static and its changing relatively steady and stable, then the anthropology would most likely have reflected this steady state of the world in its own relative harmony and paradigmatic stability.

History would still be happening to both, but not in quite as unsettling and discordant ways. What now is a crises, would then perhaps have seemed more like a minor stare of tension in regard to difference in the world—more of a soothing, background noise than a loud, disrupting explosion.

It is no wonder that the last decade in which such tensions have become increasingly acute, that anthropologists have become increasingly reflexive about their own status and relation in reality—increasingly aware of tho fact that as the world changes all around anthropology, anthropology is also changed by the world.

As the certainty and stability of their own sense of situation, of their own positions and stances in relation to the world becomes increasingly relativized by the rapidity and unpredictability of so much transition in the real world, anthropologist become increasingly introverted and introspective through their own lens, questioning the very ground and whole raison-d'être, sense of purpose, objectivity and intentionality and historicity of their enterprise and professional calling in relation to the wider, truer world.

It is not just that empire has returned home and that Humpty Dumpty is unreconstructively shattered, but the rise of reflexiveness with anthropology represents as well in very real terms anthropology's return of the repressed.

It is the sense of difference that in a younger, fresher world it could project outwardly upon the other in the world with immunity and relative impunity if the consequences, were in fact differences waiting to be discovered within ourselves that we had conveniently, perhaps necessarily, repressed in order to be sense of symbolic unity of anthropological world view.

Anthropology's own past, its own relationship with the world, are coming back as ghosts to haunt us in the present, and anthropologists must conduct their own intra-departmental witch hunts to discover the sources and causes of its own differences. In catching up with the changing world, the changing world has caught up more and more with anthropology.

The reason of the repressed and its own introspective reflexivity points up an intrinsic contradiction in the world and praxis of anthropology. In its ritual praxis, and academic embedding, anthropology has always actually been more intensively oriented towards its own academic interiors, caught up in the pathways of paradigmatic power, than it has been really extensively oriented towards the exterior world.

In this sense, going to the field has been more of an anti-structural rite of passage in the professionalization of the Academia bound anthropologist—and the realities of its empiricism and ostensible extensiveness of orientation has been more of a veil of Maya than the actual structural determinants of successful adaptation within academic anthropology.

What remained repressed was the public recognition of this intensiveness and interiority if anthropological realities as the primary basis of its authorial authority in the world.

What anthropology has long failed to face is the illusion and intensiveness of its own source of power in the world—of the dependence of its power upon academic insulation and separation from the real world as so many symbolic fictions and collective representations of reality, and also the actual marginality and relative powerlessness in its extensive orientation in the world.

Its extensiveness in the world is as the professional stranger and the marginal observer whose real world orientation is defined betwixt and between different worlds in a world of differences.

But what mattered was the intensive orientation of the insider's position within the academic status role hierarchy—the list of publications behind the professor's title, the number of citations in the literature, the relative position within insider networks that opened or closed doors and that provided windows upon the external realities of the world, the number and amount of research grants earned, the number of graduate students lined up outside the door waiting to be let in, and the degree to which one became a mentor in a father/mother role model.

Now anthropology is facing a world that is simultaneously exploding in its extensiveness and imploding in its intensiveness. The academic boundaries and borders have been invaded and cracked wide open, and the larger than life, really real realities have come rushing into its quiet, dimly lit interior world. The barbarians are at the gate, and are demanding to be let in with their battering ram.

It really should be no surprise that anthropology is in a state of crises, which is growing worse each year. It should come as no surprise, and with little sadness and regret, if anthropology will never, ever again be able to look out upon the world with innocent, rose colored glasses, or any extended telescopic view.

The mirror of Humankind is more than cracked. It has shattered like the Humpty Dumpty it long reflected. Anthropology will be left with just the pieces with that to reconstruct its worlds. In its maddening celebration of Dionysian difference, Apollonian reunification and order will never be again be restored.

All this is a prerequisite pretext by which to frame the anthropological problem of global over-population and its consequences for the future of human development in the world.

It is as if each of us were wearing our own watch or timepiece that we could not take off. It is as if in each of us there are a separate and different biological clock that is ticking away minute-by-minute. We attempt to synchronize our watches and clocks with as many people in the world as possible, such that our schedules can run smoothly and on time in as coordinated a manner as possible.

But there are just too many people with too many different senses and sets of time, that the possibility of their coordination and synchronization in the larger world is lost to the chaos of different schedules, conflicting routines, alternate rates of change.

It becomes even more problematic that for each of us, our clocks were wired up to an internal device—a time bomb or a mechanism set to trigger into activity at any possible moment, possibly leading to self-destruction after some lapse of time.

We continue walking, interacting and living in a world with many other people, always aware of or reminded of our own time that ties us into the larger scheme of organization, but never sure of when or how the devices within us will trigger, or of what may then happen.

Within such an anthropological world of humankind, we are always being controlled, never sure of our control, and never knowing when and if we may suddenly lose control altogether.

As we become preoccupied more obsessively and compulsively with control in the world, the changes in the world are getting more and more out of control.

In order to cope with the scope and extraordinary dimensionality of the global problem of population, anthropology must adopt an orientation of greater extensiveness than it has ever had in its past.

This is not an easy feat for anthropologists, as it would entail reorienting their praxis and "betweenness" in a world of difference. It must learn to cope with not so much relativity in the world itself, but its own relativity of anthropological praxis within the world.

We cannot be of the center, or be created in relation to the center, and adopt a genuinely de-centered framework that is outside of the center. Anthropology cannot expect itself to maintain a central intensive orientation about its own very restricted base of power in the world, and expect to achieve an orientation of extensiveness that would be diametrically opposed to such an intensive centeredness of orientation.

We are defined by the context that situates us and our perspective and praxis in relation to the world cannot but be expected to reflect our basic position and orientation in the world.

In becoming more extensively oriented, anthropology must begin taking greater account of its own historicity and of the general problems posed by coming to terms with human historical patterns.

As such, it must adopt a genuinely diachronic approach that embraces its own synchronic analysis of reality in terms of the synchronicity of events in the world, and the independent co-occurrence of similar events.

As such, it must give up a search for essential structures and fundamental structural homogeneity underlying the spatial pattern of relations in human reality, and its synchronic perspective of diachronic events as multiple overlapping time frames, as causal or correlational, sequentially arranged events in time.

Shifting from an intensive and space like orientation, to a more inclusive, extensive and time like orientation, requires that anthropology give up certain of its time honored practices and associations with physical sciences, that it disinvest itself with the search for first and ultimate causes and hidden last laws underlying the behavior of human developmental history.

Though basic extensiveness and history of being are core elements of its ethnographic praxis, anthropology does not know really how to deal with these aspects of its reality in an unbounded, unframed, non-intensive way, in a way that can preserve the historiographical and ethnographic context of its realistic and representational work, and yet spare the larger world some of its more general verbiage about unifying structures, underlying principles, and universal patterns, etc.

The virtue of anthropology is its empirical ground in a world of difference, in difference to the world. For an extensive orientation, difference is enough in itself. It explains itself in its experiential definition of reality, of what it means to become and remain uniquely and distinctively human in an increasingly human world.

The anthropological problem with global population begins with counting people. No one knows exactly how many people there are in the world now, or have been in the world in the past. The rate is increasing so fast now that the current global estimate of five billion is likely to double within the next four generations, or just over one hundred years.

The carrying capacity of the earth had been estimated to be just around 7.5 billion that will be reached within two generations (about 2010, this originally written in 1992, about a generation and a half earlier.)

If we start trying to directly count every person alive, and to keep track of all births and deaths, by the time we are finished we would still have to start all over again, or we might be unlikely to finish our counting as the population would be increasing at a rate faster than we could keep up with. Besides, people have the intransigent habits of slipping through the cracks in the system uncounted, or of moving here and there and so missing the census altogether or else of being counted more than once.

Complicating this simple task of directly counting people, are the problems presented by the differential rates of population increase in different areas of the world, as well as the corresponding birth and death rates.

Some nations have populations that are increasing very rapidly, such as Nigeria, while other nations have maintained near zero or even negative population increase (Japan, for instance).

Hence, the problem of population is more acute in certain regions, especially undeveloped third world regions, than in others, notably the most developed first world countries (with notable exceptions in Mainland China and India. It also is a problem if gross inequality in the world between the wealthy and the poor.

We must look at global population increase in terms of the patterning for human development that it entails. The age structure and social dynamics of the global population will change considerably over the next three generations—but we are not exactly sure how it will change.

The population is estimated to stabilize within four generations if the current rates of growth are brought under control, but this is a big if, and it is possible that the global population will develop its own mechanisms of population control whether we are effective with family planning or not.

As the age structure of the world population changes with each advancing year, the social environment of the earth will also develop in related ways proportionate to this changing age structure.

It can be predicted without much uncertainty that the natural environments of the earth will only become increasingly strained and eroded under the pressure of this massive increase, but it is the issue of social circumscription that such numbers must entail which are more problematic.

Each passing generation will grow up and learn to live in a world fundamentally different from the ones before, and the sense of reality predominant or apparent today may not necessarily be the same, or even similar to the realities actual or apparent tomorrow or the day after.

Any previous experience of our history will not quite prepare us for what we and our children and grand children will begin soon to encounter in ever increasing capacity.

Our children and their children may even become socialized at a very basic level in environments and realities considerably different from any that had come before—their whole worldview shaped critically by increasing data literacy and electronic data literacy, from any that has come before.

Their whole worldview, way of experiencing and sense of being in the world may be different than what it was for us now or had been for our ancestors at any time previously. Furthermore, our children and grand children will come of age in a world that offers very different challenges, opportunities, problems and complexities than we are now aware of.

With each advancing year, the growth rate of the population will creep forward and higher up the age levels of world society.

Now, and for the next generation, the effects of global population increase will be mostly felt at the lower levels as most of the population will be disproportionately younger than they are older.

Consequently, nurseries, day care centers, pediatricians, elementary schools worldwide should be expected to first start feeling the effects of this increase, not to mention the tired, over worked, underpaid, frustrated parents of these children.

The effects will increasingly creep up the ladder of socialization to affect high schools, colleges, universities, and the job and employment structure.

The kinds of demands made upon the system will be expected to change accordingly—basic necessities, jobs, money, food, even water, will become increasing in demand and shortage, rendered more expensive, as the larger population grows older into adulthood and begins to have their own children.

With the arrival of our grandchildren, there will be a well-developed vicious cycle of human developments occurring on earth. Most of the social Systems of the earth will be strained beyond their capacity, and ever increasing numbers will soon be on their way.

We can speak safely of a progressive deterioration of services available to meet human needs. Areas that focus directly with the concern of human growth, health and development will be especially hard hit—schools, medical facilities, social service agencies.

The vicious cycle of human under development will be one of generally decreasing quality of life for more and more people and aspect of sparse quantity of living, and lower average standard of living levels worldwide.

Death rates must begin increasing, after a brief period of delay, and with perhaps unanticipated patterns. Infant mortality rates must increase, as well as mother mortality rate. More people will begin dying younger and the average age of longevity for the world's population must begin to gradually decrease.

While average longevities are increasing around the world, death rates by disease, malnutrition, by Helminthic infection, by accidental trauma, by old age, by war and disaster, by violence and by suicide, must all be expected to eventually increase in time with deteriorating social environments. It may become a very real problem of how to dispose of all the corpses when few people have enough money to pay for a funeral.

With the development of such a grand, vicious cycle, we can anticipate rather explosive reverberations when the functional structure of the World System suddenly breaks down under the cumulative weight of overpopulation.

Global overpopulation may be a time bomb that has a very slow, delayed fuse. It is not so much that exponential increase in population growth doesn't have its fullest impacts until the last few moments of its natural history of development, but that as the younger grow older, they will make increasingly unmet demands upon the system to fulfill even basic needs and expectations, and in the face of extreme inequality, these people can be expected to finally do something about it.

Certain patterns presuming a kind of ego-logic of environmental determinism can be expected to emerge in the near future. Birth control measures and abortion represent more cost efficient means of controlling population, than say childhood starvation or systematic elimination from the social system.

There has been a greater proportion of resource investment in a mature, exploitable, adult than in a young child just starting out in life. A mother can afford to give up a young baby to prevent herself from starving—better to save the reproductive mechanism rather than its primary products. She will soon likely have another new baby anyway.

As resources grow tighter and scarcer, as with scenarios of local over population, strategies of resource diversification, of hoarding, and patterns of social atomization, panic, migration, and perhaps even warfare as a population control mechanism, can be expected to occur.

The problem with global over population as compared to local overpopulation is that there will be fewer and fewer places to escape to and fewer and fewer alternative resources to find in the shrinking earthbound environment.

It can be expected that unexpected and unintended patterns will happen in different directions of human development. Science may create new wonder drugs, miracle foods, and healing therapies to alleviate much of the human suffering in the near future.

Science may also be relied upon to devise new mechanisms of human annihilation that may effectively remove sizable portions of the human population from resource consumption and selective social competition. Models earlier in this century are already available.

Perhaps many people will decide not to have any children, nor any kind of professional career. Programs of eugenics and dysgenics might become inaugurated and socially sanctioned or reinforced—programs of sterilization or forced abortion for poor people, or of selective privileged reproduction for wealthy people. The television industry will sure be to boom, along with the pharmaceutical industry.

The near future of our earth may not be all doom and gloom. People may really decide after all that on lifeboat Earth there is always room for a few more, and learn how to adjust and tolerate the ever deteriorating social conditions.

Global carrying capacity may be really dependent upon sustainable infrastructural development. Population globally will be expected to reach over 9 billion by 2050, while beginning to level off around 11-12 billion by the 22nd Century.

Maybe, amidst all the suffering and death, more people will learn to appreciate and respect the essential dignity and potentiality of human life on earth, and act in a more concerted and determined fashion to foster equality and equivalence on earth.

Maybe we will eventually give up our bombs and our guns, and instead devote our lives to helping those most in need of help rather than to continue hurting them any further. Perhaps we will wake up soon and realize what human development is all about anyway, and that none of us are that different in the world after all.

The problem of over population in the larger world will become expressed as ever increasing numbers of people having their basic needs for survival being met less and less within the World System. This will become especially apparent in the need for nutrition.

The world will see an increasing incidence of widespread protein calorie malnutrition, childhood nutritional diseases of Marasmus and Kwashiorkor, greater amounts of utter starvation from lack of anything to eat.

Food prices are guaranteed to rise above the ability of increasing numbers of people to afford quality or adequate amounts to eat nutritionally healthy diets.

Protein calorie malnutrition is a relative form of deprivation of essential amino acids, that are irreplaceable in the body, and of 'balanced proteins' that provide the full complement of protein in the body for its maintenance.

The body can adjust itself to lowered levels of protein intake, and of caloric intake as well, but not without cost to the orgasmic functioning of the body, its deterioration, and increased susceptibility to diseases and illness, and the lowered level of efficiency and energy.

The availability of certain important vitamins and minerals, especially calcium and potassium may become strained or scarce in certain regions of the world, even though these are relatively easy to replace artificially in the diet.

Given widespread malnutrition, multinational institutions like McDonalds and Kentucky Fried Chicken are likely to become curious and especially profane, tokens of a bygone era of fast convenience foods.

In the long run, feeding of lower levels of the trophic chain of life will become more and more necessary in the human world of greater and greater need—cereal, grains, cabbage, chicken and eggs will become more efficient means of feeding the population than cows, milk, sugar and potato chips.

Fresh drinking water can also be expected to become of ever-greater demand and ever-decreasing supply. Contamination and pollution, desertification and desiccation, wastage of ground water and the concrete watersheds of the core regions, will insure that more water will have to be treated, filtered, processed and bottled to be assured of being portable, and that fewer and fewer people will be able to consistently afford to buy such necessary but luxurious commodities.

More and more people will end up having to rely upon water not fit for human consumption, and thus will become more and more susceptible to bacterial infection, mineral poisoning, etc. as a consequence.

Draught will affect not only human habits of water consumption, but the availability of fresh foods, patterns of preserving and storing foods, and the amount of arable, soil rich land available for cultivation. Cleanliness may become not so much a virtue as a sumptuary privilege of those who can afford to fill the bathtub with fresh water.

Energy resources will become increasingly in demand, decreasingly in limited supply, and more and more expensive and unaffordable for more and more people. People will not be able to afford the cost of boiling water to make it safe to drink, or of cooking foods or meats to free them from parasites. Energy costs in packing, procuring and distributing food, water, etc. will cause the costs of food, water and energy to increase even more.

While these problems will increasingly have traumatizing affects upon the poor, and will tend to make more and more people poorer and poorer, the rich people will remain relatively unaffected by these changes.

They may have to restrict their budgets a little bit, but the percentage that the increasing costs of basic necessities affect the overall income will be well within their means, and have less overall impact upon their lives.

But even they too, will eventually have to adjust. They will be able to eat steak and lobster only once a week instead of every night, and they may end up having to lay off their cooks, housekeepers, and servants.

It can be expected that local economies and food getting patterns will emerge in response to local needs and demands for good, cheap and clean sources of food, water and energy. A good example of this is the kind of hawker economy prevalent throughout Southeast Asia in that a single cook, at a single charcoal burning stove, can feed fifty or a hundred people or more in a day, and in that it is cheaper, better and often more enjoyable to eat at such stalls than to go to the markets, buy the charcoal and cook oneself.

Development oriented governments will try to restrict and limit such activities as part of an underground economy by health regulations, licensing and taxation, or by safety and building regulations, but the only alternative will become homeless missions, soup kitchens and true Thanksgiving and Christmas turkey dinners.

People must eat and drink if they are to survive, and it requires energy to enable people to eat and drink. Hungry people are generally not very happy people, nor very productive. This will be the bottom line in the World System attempting to cope under the strain of global over population. People who are slowly starving to death have absolutely nothing to lose in the world by seeing the system changed.

Bureaucracy has been a great social innovation of human civilization. It is the Grand Achievement of the system designed to keep people in their appropriate institutionalized places within the hierarchy of social relations, and to internally reinforce the structural functioning of the system as a corporate enterprise.

Bureaucracy of the Big Brother variety can only be expected to grow and proliferate in direct proportion to the increase of global population and increasing hunger in the world. There will be increasing numbers of regulations to violate, forms to fill out, faces to interface, doors to close and lock, and lines to wait in.

The person behind the window, or on the other side of the counter, will not be too much better off than those standing in line—the only difference will be they do not have to stand in line for their food, with the only service at the front of the line.

The question of conformity to the power of the system will become more and more naked—"Do you want to eat?" The price people will have to pay for such naked conformity will be their own humanism and the freedom of their own souls, chained as they become behind desks, windows and counters.

Bureaucracy itself tends to grow, following Parkinson's Law, in size, top-heaviness and increasing inefficiency, or in bureaucratic self-sufficiency without necessary external stimuli. Once bureaucracy becomes officially institutionalized, it becomes more difficult to remove or control.

The chains of authority grow longer and longer, more interconnected and more impersonal. Responsibility becomes more diffuse and negative and subject to double standards.

Bureaucracy creates designs that shunt excessive people into loops and maze-ways and reservoirs in endless waiting—always with the deceitful promise that their file, form or case is being processed in some pile upon some other bureaucrat's desk.

Behind bureaucracy is a whole threat of persecution, punishment and violent force—a legal justice system, a police force, a military organization, ready at a moments notice to step in and reinforce coercively the dictates of the bureaucratic system—this is called mobilization.

Once such mobilization is set in motion, the great inertia of bureaucracy creates a tremendous momentum that makes it hard to manage or stop again. It tends to create its own historical trajectory.

A world that becomes increasingly burdened by bureaucratic inertia will become increasingly unable to meet the needs of the masses, and will become maladaptive and increasingly inflexible to change. People will become increasingly anonymous and alienated within the System, and the System will increasingly malfunction and make more and more 'mistakes' that will victimize more people but will not be the responsibility of bureaucracy to correct.

Populations and subgroups will seek paralegal alternatives outside the institutional aegis that may better serve their needs.

The bureaucratic system will become increasingly susceptible to corruption and amoralism, and will come to hide greater and greater circles of deceit that go on behind closed doors to advantage people within the system and increasingly disadvantage those without.

Bureaucracy will more erect and more effective screens of obfuscation and delusion that are designed to trick and fool the masses that something is being done to help them, if only they continue to cooperate and wait their turns ever patiently in line.

Bureaucracy represents the ultimate form of reification of the human being—of alienating humans from their own natures, from their own needs, from their own rights. Bureaucracy, more than any other social institution, besides war, turns people into things that can then be destroyed or conformed for exploitation.

We can measure the complexity and development of our civilization by the sophistication and scale of its bureaucracy and its functional purposiveness.

It seems to be Parkinson's paradox, that the only way to serve and guarantee the protection of people's basic needs and rights is through socialization of the government institutions designed for these purposes, and that therefore inevitably entails the growth of bureaucracy, that in turn results in the systematic obfuscation, delimitation, corruption or denial of people's rights and needs.

Another way of looking at this is to see that government organization will be always challenged by serving two contraposed sets of needs of the private interests of special groups and the public interests of many different people. While organizations may be set up ostensibly for service to the community, its functioning is often undermined by increasing, cross-cutting sets of demands and influence from private, special interest groups.

To fail to meet the second set of interests may result in conflict or resistance to public policies and in interference with the proper functioning of the institution in service to the people. Either way, it is usually the needs and rights of the people whom the bureaucracy is designed, at least ostensibly, to serve that becomes compromised, that then tend to become secondary in the system's sets of interests marked by institutional deformations and global displacement linked to social-behavioral deviance.

We must anticipate with the growth of population, the growth of bureaucracy to manage the problem of this population, and with this growth, its continued compartmentalization and specialization in dealing with certain precise aspects of the problem of the people.

Those specialized compartments will be staffed by professional need experts who carry the institutional knowledge and authority for manage the social needs associated with their particular domains of authority. It an be expected that increasing human needs will become increasingly appropriated, sanctioned, and defined in context to the system, and the power to meet these needs increasingly usurped or co-opted by the system for other sets of privileged interests.

In relation to the system, the problem of population may affect it simultaneously and differentially at several levels of socialization. Increasing failure or problems with primary socialization associated with the rise of poverty and its social problems will tend to undermine the ability for the system to achieve effective secondary socialization resulting in social deviance.

Also, increasing differentiation and specialization of the system creates greater internal contradictions and discrepant possibilities for such secondary socialization to occur, tending to render it incomplete and problematic.

The effects of such general failure of socialization to occur is that people's basic identity will conform less and less, and become increasingly intractable to the established constraints of the system, whether these constraints are direct and explicit or indirect, contextual and mostly implicit.

Given such a downgrading or deterioration of its overall effectiveness, the system itself must become increasingly inefficient and ineffective in its function of its own corporate reiteration and in its transmission and reconstitution of its structural nomos, ethos and pathos in succeeding generations of humankind.

The system may be expected to respond in several different but interrelated ways. First it must adopt techniques leading to the intensification and enhancement of its socialization and resocialization processes.

<u>Earthbound Perspectives</u>

When before it demanded commitment and dedication, now it involves sycophancy, mindless devotion, fanaticism, and personality conversion. Where before it was a nine to five routine, now it becomes a round the clock ritual process.

One strategy will be the creation of a Brave New World Utopia in which social engineers and technocratic psychologists will create Alpha, Beta, Delta, Epsilon, categories into which people become slotted from birth, by that consistency stressing environments indirectly reinforce behavior modification such that there is a basic sense of ritual conformity, complacency, expectation and satisfaction with one's lot and position within the system.

It is a world in which enough compensatory mechanisms provide the continuous levels of gratification that keep people existentially benumbed and subdued.

In such an order, ethno national groupings will become the target of such rank order hierarchical classifications that define one's class caste position in relation to the whole—defining one's values, the level of one's access to resources, to rights, one's status role identity, and occupational profile, and whom one can and cannot marry and reproduce with.

Another strategy, not mutually exclusive with the first, but perhaps quite complimentary with it, and applied more effectively to the lower echelons of the system, is more of a Big Brother dystopia based upon a minimizing kind of military social structure in maximizing control and conformity.

Uniformity, lack of individuality, denial of subjectivity, of humanity, and sexuality, among the Proles rather than elaborative, and techniques of behavior modification and brain washing, threat and fear-based scapegoating, cartoonish stereotypes targeting in zoomorphic forms members of listed out-groups, will favor more negative reinforcement and punishment and the threat of violent force than the kind of 'kinder, gentler, world order' for the higher echelons. The people of these lower echelons will be socialized for supervision, for obedience, and for destruction.

It can be expected that the upper echelons will be maintained in a state of perennial routine operational normality—a relaxed steady state of functioning, while the lower echelons will be maintained in a perpetual manner of repetitious state of recurrent crises, or else chronic mass mobilization in that reactionary regimes and regimens within the system will continuously, incessantly assert their righteousness and exercise their regal-institutional authority and power.

The system can be expected to work in several ways to reinforce its plausibility structures and where these are no longer possible, given the potential for discrepancy between the real and the make believe, the said and the done, the official and the actual, then it will resort to other means, namely brute force, by that to constrain the human masses into passive submission.

Without a doubt, advertising specialists, social psychologists, news agencies and industrial and management sociologists are working right now on ways to further perfect the system's means of subliminally inducing socialization, of symbolic persuasion, identity conversion and mass delusion.

A great influence in favor of the system's self-maintenance is just its embedding and overarching context of its everyday enactment by so many people caught up within its grips.

People the world over proceed in their daily routines in relation to the system as if this were the normal, expected and basically unquestionable mode of reality—as objective seeming and common sense appearing as the rising of the sun every morning.

The fact that this system is becoming increasingly monolithic in the world order, increasingly coherent and non-contradictory, increasingly predominant in social structural, political economic sense, and increasingly culturally hegemonic in its basic value orientation and focus, confers upon the system a tremendous massiveness of its self-evident credibility. It seems to work quite well when all we have to do is to look around and find the proof of its scientific efficacy in our everyday lives.

In a way, global overpopulation can be seen as a way of nature catching back up with human development of its technological civilization, through its own natural history of human development.

Global overpopulation will soon be outstripping development, in the sense that the improvement and changes brought about by new development in the ideological name of progressive betterment of humankind, will soon no longer be able to stay ahead of or keep up with the growth and size of the human population.

It will not bring about the kind of scientific and technological paradise for humankind that it has so long promised.

In another sense, it will be at that point that human evolution will begin again, so long slowed in suspended animation of human culture-histories progressive march towards civilization and power.

With widespread, uncontrolled disease, hunger, malnutrition, violence, and with people again responding to environments in basic ways in relation to basic needs, selective pressures will become set in motion that might lead to the evolution of a new kind of person better adapted to future environment of contamination, pollution, and ecocide, but it may not be the kind of people we either want or expect to become.

It is at this point to that system fractures and breakdowns of the functioning of the system in surprising and sudden, and catastrophic ways, can be expected to occur with increasing frequency.

With such breakdowns, the system can be expected to lapse into a long-term cycle of degeneration of systemic functioning, a kind of self-destruction of the entire order in a process of negative cybernetics. One set of detrimental effects will trigger off a chain of other detrimental effects that will indirectly rebound back to further deteriorate what had already become detrimental.

In the process, it can also be expected that a great many people will perish before the system, or what left of the state of the earth, achieve some kind of lower order global developmental equilibrium and long-term stability.

Global population may actually begin decreasing substantially in such a dying off of humankind, but in the process selection pressures for human evolution may be re-inaugurated in some evolutionarily directive way. This kind of scenario is too reminiscent of the holocaust and of the Nazi superman ideology and its programs of systematic genocide. Perhaps there is an unknown history of such events in the human past.

Given the irreversible structure of change in the Universe, the overarching principles of randomization and entropy, and given the histories of unintended consequences that have plagued the past of human development, there is no reason to presume or believe that our reality will become anything but increasingly different as never before, that we will ever achieve a more stable or steady state of affairs on earth, or that things will eventually get back to normal in the many ways we've learned to expect them to be or become.

Nor is there any reason to believe that our realities should follow our science in its progress towards greater coherence and consistency and unity of understanding in the world—relativity and diversity is in the upswing, and is here in the world to stay.

There is no reason for believing that our realities will not become increasingly divisive and different, and that any previous sense of order will ever be able to comprehend such potential difference. The pattern of human history could be becoming less predictable, stable, steady and self-determining than before, rather than more.

It is of deep and great importance that we learn how to see the unique realities of the individual not as expendable, but as necessary and invaluably precious, not as exploitable but as potentially possible, not as things within the system, but as people who will bring the system into power in managing the changes yet to happen.

It is vitally and profoundly important that we learn to look at all people, and at the whole population of humankind, not as so many mistakes of Malthusian world states, but as ephemeral miracles of nature in need of nurturance and freedom of expression. The Malthusian world may shrink infinitely, relatively speaking, but there will always be room enough on it for a few more people.

We begin looking around to decide who should finally get off the lifeboat earth, then we must first look to ourselves. The world does not necessarily need greater energy power, but it does have greater people power that has so far gone mostly untapped and wasted. This is the true wellspring of human development that cannot be counted in a census or measured in sophisticated statistical estimates.

It is logical that the system should find passive indirection, non-participation and non-violence fundamentally threatening to its sense of order in the world and to its continuing functioning in control of the World.

It would be logical if it tried to annihilate, effectively exclude and taboo and punish people for such practices, especially if they try to create effective alternative plausibility structures for such practices within, and yet separate from, the dictates of the system.

The issue has always long been one of self-determination in confrontation with the world, except that very few people have ever realized this enough to put it into practice, and if so doing, then it is likely they become annihilated in the process.

Many good Christians were fed to the lions in Rome long before Rome became the capital of Christianity. The greatest potential for determination remains in the non-determination of people's possibilities.

PART V: GLOBAL SYSTEMS, INC.
Multinational Human Dynamics

The short history of the recent, brief war in the Gulf is a text book example in anthropological history of how the world system functions in a concerted manner to annihilate a threat to its structural status quo and sense of order in the world.

The characters all played their parts so superbly and convincingly in this grand, global stage production: it unfolded with so much socio-historical dramaturgical effect. For a brief spell, it swept up everyone's attention and focused it in a single direction of the unfolding developments within the system. The props were all in place, caricatures well presented.

The scud rockets reminiscent of Hitler's V-2 rockets, the threat of poisonous gas and plastic masks over babies' heads. The little satellite colony of New York was being threatened once again. The vindication of modern American technology in the Patriot missiles, that seemed to effectively prevent the destructive landing of the scuds.

The war itself—the air war, the countless number of daily sorties and raids and missions, huge self-guiding explosive bombs falling from afar down chimneys, through windows, into doors— exploding out whole bunkers filled with who's who and who knows what. The torched oil fields of Kuwait, glowing on the satellite land sat maps. The huge black clouds like a perennial darkness.

The whole show had a surreal quality about it that was reminiscent of the devastation of Vietnam—of the most sophisticated technology mobilized in concerted action, to systematically reduce the military structure of an entire nation to so much twisted and broken rubble.

The landscapes of burned out of tanks and armored vehicles, smoking in silent stillness. The maps, generals, soldiers, the newscasters, the public reactions, the President's speeches and prayers all populate that strange mindscape

<u>Earthbound Perspectives</u>

The war in the Gulf has provided us with a clear paradigmatic example of how systemic development functions in relation to the environment, in social interrelations, in its overwhelming magnitude and massiveness, in its international mobilization of resources and technologies, in its huge cost.

It is not irrelevant that more Americans died accidentally in the preparation and persecution of the war effort than as casualties of enemy fire. The war may have unfolded in a less clean way, it may not even have been necessary, and many other people in the world continued to go hungry in spite of it.

What exactly is the world system, and how precisely is its development affecting the general human condition on earth? The world system has certain distinctive characteristics serving to distinguish it, and that explain its style and pattern of development on earth, and that entail certain decisive consequences for humankind's condition on earth.

First, it is a function of scientific and technological civilization. Second, it entails industrial development of certain core regions that rely upon resource exploitation and the "underdevelopment" of surrounding peripheral regions.

Third, this differential of its development entails as well asymmetrical social relationships between people of the core and of the periphery. These asymmetrical relations become reflected by and reflective of its internal hierarchical social stratification into separate tiers of class caste, in the formation of labor requirements in service of the system.

Fifth, the world system has a history rooted in a capitalist political economy. Its defining features are that of free market capitalism, whether it is protected or controlled or regulated by the state.

We deal with the challenges of Internationalism and border bound geo-politics and the challenges of ethno-national integration. As a predominantly capitalistic enterprise, the world system can be seen as a corporate social organization in that its functioning and structure extend beyond the purview of any individual constituent of the system.

It is big and impersonal, and like a nation, exists on its own identity separate from any or all of the identities of the people who compose it.

As such, it has an ideological, politico-military superstructure, a techno-econo-environmental infrastructure and a social structure that exist in a dialectical relationship to one another.

It has a general worldview and a general cultural orientation associated with it wherever it takes hold, but this worldview and cultural orientation are not shared equally or completely by all the people who comprise the system.

It exhibits an increasing degree of social integration and organization based on organic solidarity and professional specialization, mass production, labor management practices, and extreme division of labor. It tends to functionally define and integrate most or even all social institutions in relation to its center and to annihilate any form of social resistance toward its own promotion.

In order to promote and reinforce its hegemony in the world, it relies heavily upon techniques of mass dissemination through the media, and with the increased effectiveness of techniques of persuasive manipulation and thought distortion, this reliance upon the media as a controlling device has increased with its development.

Historically, the development of the capitalist world system has had certain consistently evident consequences upon the human condition. First, it tends to disrupt local economies and cultural ecologies, supplanting these and tying them into international relations of dependence based upon commodity production, procurement and access to money, markets and business frameworks.

It has, wherever it has grown, entailed a rearrangement of interpersonal relationships, or family organization and life, and of cultural orientation around its own predominant ethos and existential dictates. Third, it has tended to generate a surplus of underemployed labor, supplanted by technological developments, that has tended to generate a large reservoir of readily exploitable labor supply.

<u>Earthbound Perspectives</u>

It seems to have erected bureaucratic screens that tend to systematically exclude this surplus labor reserve from full participation within the market system. It has tended to equate rights and freedoms within the system with property ownership or legal title, and to systematically deny rights and freedoms and access to resources to those dispossessed of property ownership or legal status. Its development has long been based upon unregulated exploitation, of both human and nonhuman resources, and thus has always depended upon the relative availability and accessibility of these resources.

Often overlooked in political economic studies of the world system is the important relationship that the political side of control has played in the promotion and development of the economic market system.

In this sense, some form of administrative colonialism and military imperialism has always accompanied economic expansion and exploitation, and industrial forces of development have always depended upon the control established by basically fascist military forces to enforce the system's dictates.

The connection between fascism and capitalism, capitalistic communisms and statism, imperialism and development, and colonialism and exploitation, has often been overlooked in historical studies of the rise of the capitalist world system.

It is time to set the historical record straight, and to take each of these aspects of the World System in turn and see where they lead us in our inquiry into the recent history of human development. Finally, it is necessary to consider the functioning of the system as a corporate whole that is leading humankind down its own pathway of development regardless of the long-term consequences.

Human culture historical development on earth has appeared similar to natural evolutionary history. Separate cultural groupings of humanity can be seen as separate species evolving under different selective pressures.

The difference is critical though. While the genetic information carried by a species remains unable to be transmitted between species, the elements composing any culture can and have been readily transmitted with and between cultures.

While elements or even combinations or aspects of a culture are transmittable, the culture historical patterns of a whole group remains more or less non-transmittable, unless groups engage in patterns of inter-state aggression and military-economic imperialism.

We may hypothesize that some features, aspects or elements of a culture are more readily detachable and transferable than other characteristics that are closer to the center of the core of the culture.

The cultural core is focal to the culture history of a group and remains relatively resistant to change and relatively conservative in its orientation, even though it is at the core that the greatest amount of elaboration and endogenous development of a culture will occur.

It is also this core of a culture that will be fairly prototypical in the culture historical representation of the group. It will provide the templates of understandings by which experience will become modified and group identity and social life will be shaped by events and by structural and acculturative influence.

The relatively non-focal aspects of a culture that are more independent of the culture's distinctive identity, and thus of more neutral and unmarked valuation within the culture, will be more readily detachable and movable to other areas.

The transmission of such traits is not unlike the transmission of disease agents carried by vectors that move between cultures. It follows the typical s-curve of epidemiological patterning of disease, from introduction, to mass infection, to a leveling off.

Civilization can be described as an inter-cultural and pan-human, transcultural and acculturation phenomenon of historical development. Its possibility arises from the transmission of elements between cultural groupings, and the interactions between different people that lead to socio-structural changes.

It is similar to the evolution of life in the sense that it represents an evolving environment and ecosystem within that speciation events take place, and yet its rate of growth is much more rapid and its patterning is much more flexible, hence unpredictable, than what evolutionary changes bring.

<u>Earthbound Perspectives</u>

Civilizations arise form the transmission and interrelations established between culture historical groupings, in that one group may become assimilated, amalgamated, or integrated within another, either partially or as a whole. Such process usually result in either the destruction of the original focal center of a culture, or at least in its critical shift in relation to a new, predominant focus presented by its relations within another cultural area of influence.

Cultures may be quite selective in what they incorporate into their sphere, and transmission may depend as much upon the selectivity of the receiving culture as it depends upon the fact of transmissibility or of availability of features itself.

In this sense, there are endogenous, intensive factors of cultural change at work, primarily within a cultural focal center, and exogenous and extensive factors of change, occurring in the relations of transmission established between groupings.

Endogenous and exogenous factors form mutually constraining limits that work in an historical dialectic in the development of civilization. Whole cultural groupings, center and all, can be forcibly incorporated into another cultural sphere of influence, and its unique pattern thus becoming critically altered or even obliterated, while its endogenous elements become swallowed up and reintegrated within the historical pattern of the receiving culture.

The development of human civilizations has largely been an irreversible process leading to greater levels of socio-structural integration and to greater intensification of elements. But it has also been a process of cycles and aperiodic uncertainties.

This has been the result of primarily exogenous forces overwhelming the more naturally evolutionary processes of endogenous development and gradual speciation between cultural groupings, evidenced in the dialectical differentiation of a language into mutually unintelligible languages over time.

The gradual rise of civilization has lead to a reversal of this process as supra-cultural entities arise from the structure of exogenous relations and changes. Separate groupings are brought together under a single sphere or umbrella of historically stable and corporate relations that tend to persist as a structure of the long run.

This development has a cyclical periodicity and a cyclic patterning of growth, death, decay and rebirth in that periodically the natural endogenous tendencies toward differentiation tends to overwhelm the supra cultural structure and to break it down, as so many barbarian forces of entropy. But in the process of a civilization's demise and disintegration, the seeds are sown into more fertile soil for the rise of new civilizations that encompasses and transcend the old.

It is a paradox that while exogenous factors lead to the rise and collapse of historical structures of civilization, the possibility for such patterning depends upon its incorporation of endogenous cultural elements of change, and upon its primarily endogenous orientation towards its development.

Thus, civilizations, like the cultural groupings that they incorporate, are primarily intensively focused and exhibit characteristic, proto-typical core style patterns that are in an historical sense relative and particular to its own provenience, and that, as a whole, cannot be transmitted.

The dialectic between the natural development of cultural groupings, tends to be endogenous yet extensively oriented, and the historical development of intercultural civilization, tends to be exogenous yet intensively oriented, from the historical parameters by that to frame a culture historical understanding of the rise and development of the present World System in that we live.

All civilization, and our current World System, can be said to be predominantly "intensively" oriented in its structure and functioning in the world, in a way that it impacts and orients our lives about its center of power, turning us "inwardly" rather than outwardly in the world.

Development of civilization occurred upon three levels of social integration—the material techno environmental level, the social institutional level, which is the interactive and reproductive level, and the symbolic, ideological and cognitive levels.

No one level has been causally pre-determinative or independent of the other levels, and together they form a complex dialectic of development, such that basic changes in any one level may entail concomitant changes in the other levels.

The rise of civilization has been represented by the differentiation and dialectical interrelations between these three levels of development.

Elements comprising each level, whether these are tools, agricultural techniques, or ritual practices or institutional arrangements or ideas or symbolisms, become transmitted between cultural groupings, or from civilizations to civilization, and become reconfigured into new patterns of the development of historical civilization..

It is the individual, distinctive elements that are the substance of civilization that become carried and transmitted between people, reconstructed and utilized.

Factors that determine why some elements of civilization become selected out while other elements become selected for in the process of civilized development are probably multiply-determined, but there are some general principles of this selection.

First, the design of elements themselves tend to become elaborated and streamlined over time as they become reproduced and reworked and continuously modified to fit new environmental arrangements. New elements are created to replace old elements that better fit into new environmental arrangements.

The design, selection and displacement of elements is determined by both form and function of these elements. They may work better than previous elements, or their overall design may be aesthetically more pleasing or more in harmony with the prevalent patterning that the elements may take.

In general, there has been an overall tendency for elements to be selected for that allows a directional pattern of development towards greater intensification of civilization and toward the realization of power that such intensification entails.

A particular element of culture may work, where previous elements may no longer fit adequately. It is not enough for such elements to be merely different, or to differentiate in an extensively random fashion. Such elements must change, but in a more integrative, intensive direction.

In this manner, we can see the advantages that cultures had who had the bow and arrow over those without, who had the conception of zero, or of the wheel, or of gun powder, or of a single God, versus those with many animistic spirits, or those who devised a republican assembly, or a court system, or stratification or bureaucracy, over those that remained lead by chiefs or big men.

Once such elements were created, their self-evident value in cultural integration and intensification lead to their easy recognition and transmission across cultures.

The silk worm was a secret that the xenophobic China at the far eastern supply end of the Silk Road, safeguarded surely by the Great Wall to screen populations passing by for many years, as well as the art of making fine porcelain.

Keeping an element secret confers advantage of one cultural grouping over another, but once the secret gets out, the advantages of its being kept secret become counterbalanced by the exogenous developments that its transmission and reiteration, and subsequent modification, leads to.

There are those anthropologists who would privilege material and technological developments over other kinds of elements, as pre-determining of the general directionality of civilized development of humankind.

But this is more an arbitrary preference for material artifacts and "objects" with a substantial, easily recognizable identity as so many "artifacts." But there is no way to prove that the domestication of a wild plant for cultivation necessarily had greater impact upon a civilization than the formulation of the idea of a single God, or the creation of middle level managers or a Mandarinate to run the affairs of a large state upon a local or regional level.

<u>Earthbound Perspectives</u>

Any given element of civilization can be defined by its paradigmatic proto-typicality in subsuming a range of possible alternative patterns in what change can occur. No single element is purely technological, or purely symbolic or purely social. Each element has symbolic, social, and technological aspects and consequences in its reality.

A tool or a weapon is never just a device for mechanical alteration, but also carries certain, particular set of symbolic and social value and function. The conception of God is never purely disembodied or abstract, that it does not somehow become represented or substantiated through social ritual process or material symbolic forms.

Such elements become arranged in regular syntagmatic patterns within a given cultural context that allows them to function and make sense of the world. Such elements can be said to constrain human experience and behavior, and to be contextually constrained within a tradition and history of a cultural sphere, and allow the mediation of environmental change.

The syntagmatic arrangements or patterns of elements are based upon the objectifications of their intentionality structures and their pragmatic, functional purposes as well as their symbolic embodiment and design.

Syntagmatic and paradigmatic relations are temporal-spatial dimensions of the on-going instantiation of the historical patterning of human reality. They dialectically precondition one another such that syntagmatic order of recursive structure determines the selection of paradigmatic alternatives, and syntagmatic ordering are determined by the selection of overarching paradigmatic categories.

The only a priori rule governing these arrangements are that they make sense given the contextual environment of relations in which they occur.

This environment itself is changing and developing in certain directions and the rise of the proper set of circumstances can precondition the invention or innovation of new elements to fill in the gaps created by the changing contexts. In this way, we get independent simultaneous inventions when conditions become ripe for their creation or fruition to take place.

The developmental patterning of human civilization, that has been seen as progressive has been the long-term epiphenomenal consequences of fundamental human symbolic behavior and creative capacity.

It is the individual human creativity to invent and produce new and different elementary forms or to innovate or purposefully alter forms to fit new functions.

Elements are preeminently symbolic, whether they are tools, social roles or identities, or ideas, and it is this symbolic capacity of these elements that allows their mediation of environments, their functional integration and intensification and their selective elaboration, alteration or streamlining.

The functional constraints occurring in the articulation and instantiation of symbolic elements are based ultimately upon the basic range of human needs, experiences, relations occurring within a cultural context, and the existential entailments involved in the fulfillment of these needs.

Any element is unlikely to be retained for very long in an untransformed state if its own existence interferes with the adaptive functioning and interests of the people carrying it. There really is no way of demonstrating the a priori existence of a basic structure underlying such constraints beyond that functional structure dictated by the limits of these basic needs.

The elements and contexts conditioning their expression become recursive and reiterative in its perpetuation of basic patterns or structures. The number of elements manageable within any delimited or bounded system must always be finite. Systems composed of too many elements, too many choices, too many relational possibilities, too little constraint, become clumsy and incoherent in their patterning over time.

Such systems become noisy and cluttered. There does seem to be natural organic limits to inherent, unaided human information processing and symbolization that to some extent predetermines how many elements or possible combinations or ordering of elements, or event or the basic kinds of elements involved.

Once begun, the self-organizing patterning of such systems become to some extent preconditioned by the environments of their own total history of relations within the system.

The robustness of the systems whole environment and historical patterning functions to condition and constrain the possible alterations of its elements—their space, their function, their capacity and potentiality for development within the system.

Once invented, elaborated or widely diffused, elements are not simply eliminated or eradicated. There tends to be a gradual accumulation of elements over time. Rules governing selection, survival elaboration and development of particular elements are determined by their on-going functionality and usefulness in the mediation of change within the system.

Elements fall into disuse if they serve no objective sense of purpose, and tend to become displaced by a more objective sense of or active elements. Elements can be stored in pools or reservoirs, tool kits, armories, treasuries, libraries, dictionaries, oral traditions, customs, rituals, to be indefinitely preserved or safely stored until they are recalled, reinvented, or revitalized. If no such system of their storage and stockpiling exists, than these symbols must become forgotten and lost and irretrievable to the system. Storage enhances the flexibility of the system.

Such means protects and preserves the symbolic knowledge based on the socio-cultural organization of social relations.

With the development of civilization, needs redefined socially in social environments, as derivative or secondary socialization and institutionalization, become developed with the possibilities for the perversion or prevarication, such that elements may be promoted or elaborated within the system that may interfere with the needs of some people, or occur at their expense, while augmenting the fulfillment of inflated needs of other people.

With the rise of intensification and integration, differential relations of power in the expression and articulation of elements arise. Some elements may become 'emphasized' and elaborately inordinately or disproportionately, while other elements may become de-emphasized or devalued. Differential topographies of civilization arise, such that there occurs different culture historical patterns of elementary salience, interest, and functioning.

The development of elements in civilizations has seen the emergence of multiplex functions or relations between elements, increasing integration between elements. There has occurred as well increased stratification between elements, stratification of elements within elements, embedding of elements into experience and everyday life, as well as increased domestication, internalization, and interiorizing of human social environments in that these elements are articulated.

The process continues today. These are consequences of such systems of elements hyper-compartmentalizing into discrete or highly abstract functions, partly as a form of storage, and the development of the systems capacity to deal with more elements in a more efficient manner. Such processes continue today, and their innovation and design too were elementary creations of the development of the system.

There has been a certain amount of shortsightedness and narrowness of view in the development of human civilization. Humans may be creative, but rarely are they exceptionally so. They seem much better innovators and modifiers of preexisting elements than they are originators of brand new forms with new functions. Once an idea is invented or discovered it tends to eventually catch on and spread rapidly, becoming soon elaborated and refined during the subsequent fake history of its development.

There are countless examples of such development. Early man may have stumbled across naturally occurring fire many times before anyone figured out actually how to make fire happen, but once learning how, almost everyone on the scene soon became a master fire maker.

Similarly, human flight was long believed to be impossible until the Wright brothers demonstrated its possibility in defiance of common sense. Then it was only a matter of a few years before humankind was flying to the moon and back, and the possibility of global flight became an everyday human reality.

The original creation of new basic elements opens up new ranges of possibility for developmental patterning that did not previously exist before, and creates revolutionary reverberations in the development of the whole environment of civilization itself.

Their potentiality may have been circumstantially evident or else maybe suggested a long time before anyone hit upon the way to make it happen. But once started, there is usually no turning back the clocks of historical development.

In this sense, the development of a secular science based upon the understanding and manipulation of natural ordering principles of the universe, was an inevitable outcome if the development of civilization, as were the development of alphabets, of mathematics, of literacy, printing, of computer manipulation, storage and transfer of electronic media.

All perhaps had to await the prior development of previous, preconditioning elements, but it would only become a matter of time before it would have been realized objectively in history, once the circumstances for their development occurred.

The development of human civilization to its present state was not mandated by natural law, nor is there anything intrinsic or principled about this development that made it a predetermined outcome.

Also, its historical processes and patterns are not unlike or unrelated to those occurring in the development of other civilizations in the past. It was the cumulative outcome of many people interacting, and the gradual buildup of a civilized context that preconditioned the possibility of certain kinds of contributions—especially of science, and its technologies.

Science and modern achievements if civilization were always possibilities waiting to become realized by human invention, or discovered by human learning, but it had to await the historical development of appropriate contexts and preconditions that would render its discovery and invention likely.

When we refer to the world system today, we are referring to something a bit more than just its science, technology and industrial production, but we are also implying a social, cultural, and ideological orientation that has a particular capitalist spirit and ethos.

It has become a predominant patterning in the world, so that all other alternative orientations are becoming subordinate and refocused to the world system's core center.

When we speak of the world system, we are also referring to the human dynamics of being and nonbeing, of interrelationship and experiencing of the environment, and how these have been altered in adaptive response to the changing conditions under the system.

It is important in these regards to understand that from a psychosocial and psycho geographical standpoint the success of the system always depended upon the political and economic and social organization and mobilization of a grouping of people distinctively defined vis-à-vis other groupings or marginal out groups that were seen to be either competitive or in conflict with the group or else subservient, complementary or dominant to the group.

The system has always depended upon the maintenance of its boundary identification and thus upon internal hierarchy of authority to reinforce its conformity, as well as in-group/out-group projection and symbolic behavioral externalization. It is the structure and the pattern of these groupings that have been changing within the system, and are still changing, remaking and reshaping the structural boundaries of the world in the process.

The developmental changes in the system have had ineradicable and irreversible consequences, the patterning of the whole system has had an historical momentum of its change in the face of which individuals, groups or corporate organizations can do little to stop or prevent. Part of its momentum of directionality and irreversibility is due to its great contextual inertia, that, once set in motion, becomes much more difficult to stop.

Also it is due to its diminishing degrees of freedom. Once having chosen a certain pathway of development, it becomes increasingly constrained in the kinds of subsequent options and alternative patterns that remain available to it.

Being all that we are basically left with, people find they have little choice but to go along with it or to become annihilated by it.

Too, it has meant mixed blessings, and many of its negative consequences have been unintended side effects and unforeseen possibilities of the long run, but its short term and narrow range of benefits continues to motivate and drive most people to seek it out and to promote its further development.

The System itself has been founded upon the fundamental notion of its own self-sustaining growth and development that is seen to be potentially unlimited. Its growth orientation renders it a mass oriented system, such that greater mass production, mass marketing, mass organization, has always worked against the interests of the individual and the small entrepreneur, and for the promotion of large-scale organization and corporate big business.

Mass capital and the property ownership has meant greater profits, that in turn has meant increased growth within the system, and all attempts at its control lead to strategies of diversification and at circumvention of control that in the long run backfires by rendering the system more and more out of direct control.

Though the system continues to grow upon its margins in an extensive manner, always enlarging its compass of involvement and horizon of activity, it leads to greater degrees of intensification as it tends to pull more and more elements, environments and people within its network and entrap and entangle these in ever greater degrees.

Loosening of direct control leads to stronger attempts at directive control, often creating a negative feedback cycle leading to greater loss of direct control as well as to goal substitution of more aggressive policies and threats.

This objective of unlimited growth is based upon a presumption and a requirement of free access to an unlimited reserve of basic resources of its commodity production, whether these are human resources of labor and know how, or they are natural resources of energy, minerals, food, land, flora and fauna.

In its growth, it tends to gobble up resources in an unrestrictive manner, without regard to the long-term recycling or replacement of these resources once they have been used up.

In other words, the system has always been founded upon one of resource exploitation—of getting something for nothing, or more for less—whether this exploitation has been human, energy, material or environmental. But its growth always leads eventually to a more for less cycle.

Sometimes it is claimed that its increasing efficiency has resulted in better use of resources, but this must be seen within a larger context that the process of exploitation itself has become increasingly efficient, and its contribution to the system's growth has in the net balance of the long run lead to increased exploitation of resources at a faster rate.

In regard to human resources, it has used people exploitatively for its own growth interests when and where it has seen fit, and has otherwise neglected or discarded people as inefficient burdens to its own growth, or has tried to redefine the human identity within the system from that of basic person based consumer to that of mass producer consumer.

It will seek to exploit people at one end of its teleological-technological chain or the other—one way or another alienating people from their own basic interests and needs in the service of the system.

Whether it exploits people as mass producers or mass consumers, its net consequences for most people are those of any form of exploitation—that of depriving people of their own basic rights, freedoms, and rendering access to basic resources and meeting of basic needs conditional and contingent upon the degree of status role identity and achievement within the system.

Though it is implicitly loaded as a value orientation, there is nothing religiously moral or ethical about this survival imperative it tends to impose upon all people differentially. It is completely secular, and works implicitly at the every day level of common sense.

We may summarize this extended discourse thus:

- Exploitation of resources leads to depletion and deprivation.

- Exploitation of natural environments leads to their degradation and pollution and eventual destruction.

- Exploitation of people leads to increasing alienation and basic dependency upon the System.

Systems of social or behavioral exploitation of people increase competitiveness between people, leading to escalation to conflict.

The world wide pursuit of development has lead to its rapid intrusion upon many cultural life ways, and an inevitable upsetting of these life ways in ways that serve the interests of the system but that lead to increasingly exploitation, alienation, and dependency of the local cultural orientation.

It has also intruded more and more into the existential life world of the individual caught within its grips, such that it comes to embed its as if an internal controlling and orienting mechanism within the unconscious of the individual psyche.

It comes to be externally reinforced in ever-greater ways in the everyday environments of the individual. Psycho-geographic identity of the individual comes to depend upon its presence in the life world, and the sense of consistency, and continuity and security that this presence presents to the individual.

The individual's basic nexus of social interrelations, the cultural nucleus of the primary family, and the local spheres of identity and sociality becomes reorganized and reoriented in relation to the focusing power of the dictates of the system.

Differential distribution of critical knowledge, of money, of cash earning resources, leads to the disruption of traditional patterns and the introduction of new salience and values within inter-human relationships.

It comes to reorganize people into relatively regimented life styles in rather rank-order, class stratified social units. All other activities and interests become subordinate and subsidiary to the primary interests and activities of structural service to the system's interests.

Individual identity becomes primarily based upon its status role identity within the system's socio-economic and political economic context. The individual exists within social spheres of influence and plausibility structures that either come to reinforce and constrict or else to deny or annihilate this identity.

Though the development of the system tends to be totalizing and totalistic in influence, and tends to necessitate a socio-centric kind of totalitarianism of control over the individual's life and livelihood, its not total in its control or influence upon human reality.

There remain many gaps in its spheres and areas of influence in people's lives, and other subsystems and underground systems tend to fill in those areas of human life and need that the system tends to leave vacant, underserved, and unfilled.

Individuals and sub-groupings within the system persist in counter reaction and counter valuation to the dictates or influence of the system, and many still resist its encroachments into their lives and relations in the world.

But more and more, even these kinds of responses to the increasing influence of systemic development within the lives of people tend to become, and be construed as, merely counter reactions to the system, or as regressive nativist movements, or as deviance from the implicit normative standards of the system, than as anything that is merely separate from or independently different than the system. But this sets thee stage for transformative, revolutionary change as well as for rebellion.

Difference and variation thus become allowed only within the broader or narrower constraints of the system, and becomes contextually defined by interrelations within the system. Attitudes, worldview, beliefs, collective representations, values, increasingly incorporate these constraints indirectly and in an implicit way, such that it becomes increasingly less easy or possible to easily entertain or even imagine the possibility of social difference or altercation outside of these constraints.

The system, wherever it flourishes, promotes difference and differential access to resources, values of hierarchy and its own systemic authority, and leads to structural inequalities between people, where none before may have existed, and where none otherwise need to exist. It also leads to relationships of increasing interdependency and asymmetry within the larger world.

With increasing structural interdependencies, differentials, and asymmetry, the ranges of choice and of freedom of action, initiative and functioning of people independently of the constraints of the system becomes increasingly narrow constrained, channeled and circumscribed.

Such choice becomes increasingly problematic and complicated under such conditions, and people become more normatively and behaviorally incapacitated in exercising such choice or in bringing such freedom to realization, emphasizing instead blind and empty ritualism.

In this, the system does not help, and even strives to hinder such alternative decision making as counter productive and resistant or inimical to the interests of the system, by educating and convincing people that they really have no choice at all but conformity to the system.

The system, as an entity, must be seen as completely impersonal and non-subjective in its functional orientation. Though there may be many representatives and voices of the system, and though some people may fair better within the system than many others, and though some may seem on top of it while others may seem to be at its bottom, and though most people may come to embody the system in their life worlds as if it were vital and human, still, it is completely super-organic and ultimately impersonal and inhuman in orientation.

It is a corporate affair whose systemic interests encompass and encircle any and all individual interests or group interests. Its long-term interests exist beyond the life span or life world of any of its composite people or sub-groupings. Though some people may appear in greater control of the system than others, and while there may be managers and the managed, the system as a whole, corporate human enterprise remains basically beyond anyone's control, running on its own strange structural functional autopilot.

In the last analysis, the interests of the system and the long-term objectives of its own structure and functioning are not even in the interests of people or of its human components. Its reason for being is epiphenomenal as an historical patterning, existing for its own sake, than for the sake of the people who've made it happen.

Though its promotion has generally benefited many people in many ways, its negative downside cannot be denied as well.

It is claimed that its long-term development has lead to an improved condition of humankind globally and historically, such that people now are more absolutely prosperous, materially wealthy and productive, and medically healthy, and that life within the system has been sounder and more secure than life before or beyond its influence. These arguments and claims are undeniable.

But these side effects of the system's functioning were not necessarily the reason for being of the system in the first place, that were primarily power and profit oriented, nor does its continued development directly or absolutely benefit all of humankind, but rather only incidentally and relatively.

The system exists for the sake of the system, its interests are other than those of basic human interests, except to the extent that people make its interests their own, mostly as "false consciousness" and people are sustained and rewarded within the system in the way and to the extent that they serve its own interests, and promote its development. Development occurs for development's sake, and only incidentally for human development.

As such, this development has tended to favor increasing social organization over less, increasing conventional conformism as well as deviance versus adoptions of adaptive strategies, increasing mobilization and exploitation of resources, human and nonhuman, rather than rationing or conservation of these resources.

It favors greater degrees of human involvement and constrain, rather than constrained involvement and wider margins of freedom and unconstraint, and thus has tended to demand more conformity rather than allow more difference.

Within relationships that are becoming increasingly interdependent, asymmetrical and differential, it can be expected that in general social relations should become more strained and difficult.

Under such strain, there is greater likelihood for the fission and breaking up of such webs of interrelations, as they come to reverberate and resonate in greater tension the competitive stresses and structural strains that they incorporate.

It can be expected that with such increasing normal tension of inter-human relationships, human social relations will become increasingly marked by competitiveness, impersonalness, spuriousness and mutual mistrust, and affective distance and estrangement.

It can be expected that face-to-face, discursive events between people will become increasingly conflicting and concerned with the paradigmatic problem of control management in such events.

Finally, it can also be expected that individuals will come to bear within their own private lives a great deal of the tension, stress and strain experienced in their social relations, and this internalization will come to have negative consequences for further human developments within the system.

The illusion that the development of the system promotes human development must be maintained, even in the face of contradictory evidence or conflicting experience. The necessity of maintaining such an illusion is rooted in the human need to cope with stress by maintaining an experiential continuity and identity of perceptions, projected into the indefinite and highly uncertain future.

It would become increasingly problematic to simply redesign one's existence and hand over one life to the dictates and service of a system that comes to be increasingly at cross purposes to those fundamental needs of human development.

In the face of mounting counter evidence suggesting the contrary, it will become for many increasingly necessary to uphold and reinforce the illusion of the personal and humanness of the system at any and all costs, even if this entails the flagrant violation of basic human rights and a total denial of the place of human subjectivity in the world.

Within social circles that serve to foster and create such mass illusion, people who might otherwise be quite skeptical and human, will be led to believe and behave in basically contradictory ways, and will be in their symbolic justifications of their experiences and rationalization of action, make up the difference.

Many people, caught within the influence of power and conformity, will come to believe and behave in ways that they may not, in a larger context, realize they are behaving. Identity within the group, within the system, will increasingly become an issue of personal and social survival, as well as existential crises, the ante for success within the System will keep going up, and the risks of failure become heavier and heavier.

The horizon of one's objectiveness in life for advancement or promotion within the system, will keep receding from one's reach. Others will seem to be getting ahead in the directions one is constantly running towards, but always falling ever more behind.

Within such a social environment, there will be less and less resistance to as well as great susceptibility to the influence of insider's networks and circles of deceit that serve to foster the preferred interests of the select few to the disadvantage of others within the system. This will become the principal strategy for mobility and mobilization of resources within the system, and will become the predominant structuring principle of social order and organization.

PART VI. HIDDEN FACTORS
Human Stress and Response

What is the power of human imagination to create alternative worlds and different realities that it can then bring to realization, and what is the influence of our mythology that allows us to enact our myths and in the process, foretell our future.

There is something strangely fascinating about many sciences fiction films that were created during the Cold War Era. They depict in terms of realistic settings and scenarios possible futures of our scientific quest for power in the world. They have an uncanny power to illustrate for us our own pre-selective interests, intentions and objectives in the enactment of our alternative futures.

In the futuristic world of scientific discovery, research and development, nothing that is imaginable is impossible. Thus we have before us in living animated color alternative visions of our own possible future—in cannibalistic, flesh eating zombies; in the invasion and taking over of the world by plant like body snatchers; in the rise of gigantic man-eating insects from the irradiated dust of nuclear testing; in Dr. Strangelove's and failed Fail Safes; or in Cyborg Worlds in which biology and technology, metal and soul, flesh and plastic, become fused into new forms of automated life and living automatons.

The frightening, life like fascination of these Sci-fi visions are in their illustration of the possibilities of our own future development and becoming in the world. They stand as animated metaphors for our own scientific destiny and technological fate. The monsters that they bring to life before our very eyes—the Godzillas and King Kongs, are the allegorical monsters of our own possible becoming that we normally keep hidden and locked away from sight. They open the Pandora's Box of human reality.

It is no accident that interest has shifted from repressed dreams of Frankensteins, Mummies, Draculas, Creatures of the Black Lagoon and Hunchbacks of Notre Dame and Phantom's of the Opera—from the repressed Victorian visions of an Edgar Allan

Poe, or Robert Louis Stevenson or Oscar Wilde, toward more life like and normally appearing human monsters of Freddie Krugers, Night Stalkers, Serial Killers, Chain Saw murderers, Zodiacs and the Son of Sam. We have gone from Jack the Ripper and Dr. Jeckyll/Mr. Hyde, to Edward Scissorhands and Heavy Metal.

In many of these stories there is a recurrent meta-theme of 'death oriented' science gone wrong, creating in the laboratory monstrous side effects that stalk and plague the city skyline. There is also a recurrent theme of a psychopathic killer and a social menace. In these themes we can recognize the return of the repressed and the retributive vengeance that becomes wrought upon the world in increasing destructiveness.

There is in such symbolic enactment the expression of violence and animal aggression that is normally bottled up or kept hidden and secret, chained up in the dungeon of the deep unconscious. The unconscious is not just personal and psychological, but even more importantly, collective and mass oriented. The monsters are importantly mass murderers and serial killers who nonetheless constitute the worst possible nightmare for each of its tormented victims.

In all this human darkness and shadows lurks more than a few grains of truth about our possible future development. There is a very real sense in that those things that we cast out of our world with violence that we repress into oblivion, may return in future generations to haunt and plague and victimize our world.

We can in these sci-fi visions get a glimpse at the nature of some things that we have tried to cast out the gates of our paradise, or else imprison away within its very depths. We can see the real unintended monstrosities of life created by a science gone wrong in its experiments, or the transformation of nature and of the natural human into a composite machine of living tissue, electronic circuitry and plastic organs. Otherwise it remains difficult to think beyond global holocaust.

In this regard, death itself as the ultimate state of nonbeing and of becoming represents symbolically the ultimate source of fear, terror, retreat, evasion, hiding, and attempted escape that we sometimes unconsciously use our science and our social worlds for solutions.

Whether death comes by accident, or as an unintentional consequence, or an experimental error, or by deliberate violence, or by incarnate evil, it comes inevitably nevertheless.

When we try and cast death from the Garden of Eden, we create the inevitability of its revisitation in some future time. All our science and progress will not cure the disease of death or solve its mysterious and dark dilemma of our own nonbeing and nothingness in the world.

It always comes back to haunt our illusions and dreams, and even if we face it in all our weakness, fragility and even courage, it remains the source of fear, anxiety, uncertainty and irreconcilable paradox of understanding in our world. Not being able to live without death, we are confronted with the challenge of learning to live well with it.

There is another sense of intuitive understanding in that history is said to repeat itself. There is an inexorable circularity and cycling of historical pattern that states that if something happened before, especially recurrently, then it can possibly, even likely, happen again, in ever-greater presence than before.

Thus if we have a First World War and then a Second, we are logically persuaded by the patterning of our history to expect yet a Third and even a Fourth. And when we survey the military record of the human species as far back as we can discover, we find irrefutable evidence of the recurrence and increasing intensity of warfare.

Similarly, we get a repetitive patterning and cycling in the rise and fall of historical civilizations. Empires come and go, wax and wane, and in their wake seeds are sown for greater climaxes of culture historical development.

If we have had an end to a *Pax Egyptiana*, *Pax Romana*, *Pax Britannica*, then we can also expect an eventual demise of a *Pax Americana*. In the future we may even expect a new *Pax Nippona* or a *Pax Sinitica*, but who can really tell where the next centers of major civilization will really take place. Perhaps even somewhere out in space.

Similarly, if archaeological evidence suggests that what happened on Easter Island may have happened in other contexts as well, and if paleontological evidence suggests that life on earth has gone through not one, but several episodes of biotic climax and mass extinction, then we must become suspicious that it could happen to us sometime in our future, and we must pay heed to possible warning signs of its occurrence.

In the whole of the human past, there may not have been one "Dark Age" but several, or even many. The dawn of human civilization was an emergence from a primordial Dark Age of the human condition.

So it should not be unexpected that the experience of a Dark Age is something unusual or strange to the range and continuum of human experience on earth. It may merely represent a transition to a new mode of living and doing things, the passing away of an older way of life, and a re-fertilization in its ashes of the earth from that it was derived in the first place.

There is a maxim that comes from the human experience of its own past. Those who do not learn from their mistakes are bound to repeat them. There is a wide question now whether we have learned enough in our valuation of the modern and the present, from our own rather spotted and bloody record of the past.

It always remains a strong possibility that what we believe we are learning from the past is but the values of the present that we symbolically retroject upon a past that can no longer speak for itself.

We may actually be rewriting our pasts in histories to suit our own future needs, and in the process of such historical revisionism for ideological intentions, we may actually be forgetting or necessarily have already forgotten, the real lessons of our past.

The start of every fresh war we hear that this is the War to end all wars, and we celebrate its victorious completion with the assumption that there is now widespread, future peace in the world, that then becomes our interest and future duty to protect.

But wars may not actually solve all the tensions on which they were founded, and may in their historical enactment, sow the seeds of even greater tensions and animosities down the road. War actually seems to solve very little in the world, except who gets to keep the sacred scepter of civilization until the next war breaks out.

World War II and Vietnam were two very different kinds of war for the American people. Though we won one and lost the other, the lessons we seemed to learn from both we seem to have either forgotten or been unable to forget.

In the first, our worst enemy became our best ally, and in the other, we made our best possible allies our own worst enemy. It is evident that the lessons that are clearly there to be learned in the history of both wars, of their basic lack of necessity, tyranny, and inherent evil, as well as the escalation of their intrinsic destructiveness, we have consistently failed to learn, or systematically forgotten these lessons.

In the most recent war in the Gulf, we had a model of World War II clearly in command, and we all claimed that this was not another Vietnam. But the war lacked the sense of necessity, involved the inevitably tyranny and evil, and evoked the frightening specter of the totalization of the lethality and destructiveness of modern warfare.

Given the expectation that the increasing tensions and straining forces within the development of the system will be felt in social relationships, it is fitting to look for symptoms and signs of such stress and strain in embodied terms of the way people come to incorporate within their own being and behavior, or learn to cope with or adjust to such increasing levels of social environmental tension. It can be expected that definite long-term patterns of typical human responses will become evinced as these tensions gradually increase their pressure and slowly take their toll.

Such stresses can be expected to have certain definite and permanent influences upon the human character. They will leave their imprint upon the personal and collective being of humankind, and this in turn will become transmitted to subsequent generations as certain enduring problems. The system as well will be expected to devise schemes and develop ways of further exploiting these patterns in directions that will further promote its own developmental interests.

The principle psychological and sociological problem that humankind will have to face and deal with effectively over the next few generations are the psychological and physiological responses and reactions to pandemic, widespread, and unrelieved stress and tension in social relations.

Whereas in the past of the development of the human system the central problem has been increasingly a preoccupation with the problem of control and the realization of power, this can be expected to continue except that the problem of control will become differently defined and will become increasingly a problem of not getting out of control.

The problem of the realization of power will be in terms of the usurpation of personal, independent forms of power, and in increasing methods and mechanisms of persuasion and conversion to the dictates, practices and ways of the system's development.

The individual psyche and life-world will increasingly become the locus of central control and the focus of interest in power, and this will be accomplished mainly through modern technology and mass media.

The grand paradox of this will be that human beings will become increasingly erratic and uncontrollable in their responses to stress and adaptation to alienating environments. Control and power will increasingly become a problem of human control and human power and of self-control and self-empowerment within the framework of the system.

In human response to stress, the system will have reached its human horizon to its own maddening pursuit of development. Upon the margins of this horizon, the development of this system will become increasingly less intensively orienting and increasingly more extensively oriented in its dealing with the globally randomizing forces that these human limitations will impose upon the development.

These patterns of human stress and response, through expressed in local ways, will be quite pandemic and generalized within the whole system. Everyone will suffer, though not equally and in the same way. For many it will be a living nightmare, for others it will merely be a life long neurosis and desperation. Even the few wealthy controllers of the system may not be spared the effects of this suffering.

The social environment will become increasingly threatening and chaotic for the individual. The threatening and chaotic nature of this predominant social environment will overshadow virtually every aspect of human existence.

Patterns of avoidance, of fear reaction and projection, of over compensation, and uncontrolled frustration and aggression will become increasingly frequent facets of normal, everyday life.

In this regard, perhaps, it is necessary to separate out the consequence from the experience of short-term, but perhaps traumatically intense forms of stress, from death and separation to the witnessing of violence, from the consequences of long-term stress that may be less intense but more widespread, subtle in its expression and yet nonetheless lasting and profound in its human alterations.

Both forms of stress and response will increase, and there will be much overlap in the effects and symptoms between the two, but in their extreme they may produce distinctively different and perhaps opposite but equal kinds of human reactions.

But whatever form it takes, neither the stress nor its results will easily go away, nor will people be able to ever escape from their clutches. They will carry it around with them wherever they go, like a yoke around their necks.

These patterns of stress and response create a degenerative cycle of cybernetics, both for the individual adaptation to his/her life world, and for the collective adaptation to changing world environments.

This negative feed back cycle will be a vicious one from which no one shall escape, nor the system. It will work to minimize its losses rather than to maximize its own gains, and in the process of switching from an intensive or an extensive orientation, will inadvertently come back into alignment with basic human interests in survival and health.

The vicious cycle of stress and response is such that decreasing adaptation and increasing maladaptation fosters a proclivity towards greater experience of environmental stress that in turn begets even less adaptive response.

The last consequence of this vicious cycle of de-development of both the System and of human participants within it is either natural death, by one means or another, or else a kind of symbolic social death of the individual's autonomous human identity.

This has been referred to as desymbolization, and whether it leads to sycophancy or sociopathy, all it really eventuates in is the transformation of the person into a zombie—the living, unfeeling, dead.

Part of the grand paradox of this human horizon, vanishing point and singularity of our shared global civilization, of the development of the system will be that though it further intensifies, domesticates and interiorizes human existence, this will not be found in the realization of greater internal privacy of the individual, but in the internalization of the collective into the internal, interior spaces of the individual psyche.

Interiors will become increasingly collective interiors rather than private interiors, and such social interiors will become increasingly crowded and will in the process crowd out personal private space more and more.

People will seek escape, even at the risk of death, from such crowded interiors, for the fresh air of being outside, in an extensive environment, however polluted, corrupted, and barren such a wasteland may become.

The interiorizing of development can be seen in its circumscription of natural environments, such as national parks, nature preserves, zoos, gardens, ostensibly to protect such environments from the degradation and depredation of extensive developments, but in their artificial in bounding such natural environments inevitably become fictitious, false and corrupted by the subsequent crowding of human traffic.

For people, it will become an increasing existential dilemma and decision as to whether they wish to live an unnatural social death in an impersonal and alienating interior environment, or else to die a more natural life in the loneliness of an empty, barren desert.

<u>Earthbound Perspectives</u>

It can be expected that increasingly the symptoms of stress will be experienced and expressed in psychosocial terms in the incidence of group archosis—the transferring of the psychological conflicts of the individual upon the social relations and collective orientations of the group.

Such archosis may provide a temporary environment of therapeutic relief for the suffering of its constituency, but itself must lead to boundary activity between such groups that will eventuate in conflict and the creation of more stress between people.

It can also be expected that alternative, counter groups or revitalization movements will arise as normal reactions to such stress, and that these movements will attempt to create alternative exterior spaces outside of the stressful influence of the system, and in adaptation to new extensive environments that offer little except relative normative freedom from the constraints of the system. The stress will remain, but will become refocused as an existential problem of environmental adaptation and survival.

It is part of the grand paradox of development and its consequential redevelopment that the system will, upon its extensive horizons of human stress and response, become redeveloped and reconditioned as an instrumentality of human control and personal empowerment.

Instead of reforming the individual to serve the dictates of the developmental imperative of the system, the survival imperative of the system itself will become increasingly rehabilitated upon its margins in its increasing service to human development.

When this begins to occur with increasing frequency and rapidity, there will then become a shift and rebalancing of dialectical tension within the development of the system, and in the historical development of human civilization in general, between the people and regions of the core and the people and remaining resources of the margins that will eventuate in struggle, a state of world civil war for determination of the future of human and Systemic development in the world.

This will be a global civil war of worldwide proportions, and of lasting consequence, because it will not only split brother against brother, but will internally divide the individual between being and nonbeing of becoming, between the dying life and the living dead.

The battle will become increasingly one for control over basic resources, spaces, and for the collective mind of humankind. It will become waged between the sycophants and sociopaths of the core who seek in ever more reactionary and conservative, fascist fashion, to maintain order and control over the peripheries, and internal hierarchy, and the marginal escapees and existential excludes of the system who will work to disturb, hinder and re-appropriate access to basic resources for their own survival interests.

Part of what may occur is the re-inauguration of basic evolutionary selective pressures of humankind, such that there emerges upon the margins of civilization a new kind of Homo adaptor who is better adapted to deal with the stresses and tensions of existential survival in wastelands and perhaps a modified form of *Homo civilitrix* who becomes increasingly inbound and alienated from their own basic needs in survival.

It can be expected that while the former variety will suffer many short term setbacks and losses, it will become in the long run a more adaptive survivor and generalized progenitor, while the latter civilized form will in its over specialization to absurd interior, intensive environments, go soon the way of the dinosaur and the dodo.

Perhaps Homo adaptor will hunt Homo *civilitrix* doing in a last struggle of genocidal extermination. But it is more likely that Homo adaptor will not need to do so, and will also recognize the moral need not to do so, and will benignly allow Homo *adaptor* or *civilitrix* to commit its own racial suicide.

In the future contest for survival, the aggressors of today will become the inbound defenders of civilization tomorrow, and the barbarian hordes will be banging upon the gates of our posterity.

Cut-off from access to their basic resources, these defenders will quickly deplete their stockpiles and reserves before they must perish or else surrender to the chaos that knocks upon their door. Some may open the doors to their paradise in the vain offer of reconciliation and renunciation of their power and control.

<u>Earthbound Perspectives</u>

The future will bring a new dark age for the entire earth, whether or not there is an actual dark ages from nuclear holocaust. This dark ages will be one during which nature will recuperate and recover much of its own regenerative powers in the beginning of a new evolutionary epoch of life on earth.

Humankind too will slowly rehabilitate itself in a renewed sense of revitalization and of extensive being in the world in evolutionary harmony with natural forces of selection. Chaos will not become so much of a threat to an old way of existence but a renewed way of life.

The new dark ages of humankind will also witness the widespread birth of a new religious, pan human light that was born from the previous suffering.

This new light will be formed on the basis of the near universal condition of suffering and stress of humankind in its previous state of degenerate existence, that will bring humankind to a collective understanding and empathy of the problem of human suffering by having it implanted beneath their skin and thus will become normatively and morally immunized against the kinds of disease agents that caused this suffering in the first place.

When everyone comes to suffer the same disease of stress and maladaptive response in interiorized environments, they will become similarly aware of the possibility of this suffering in others, and from this widespread awareness will be born a newly developed sense of human identity that is contingent upon the rehabilitation and removal of the causes of this suffering.

In a strange twist of fate, the development of the System, in its redevelopment, will create the very ground for its own rehabilitation and resolution of the systemic consequences for human development.

But the carriers and those embodied of the old tradition of civilization will sadly come to a realization of this after it is too late for their own recuperation or rehabilitation. They will come to know and understand the difference, but they will no longer be able to incorporate the difference into their style of life and development.

It will become the new mission of Homo adaptor, primitive, marginal, unspecialized, like a mongrel or a mutt instead of a hybrid breed, to incorporate and embody this new, alternative civilizing mission of human civilization. Greening and Green Peace of the World System will inevitably come, but more indirectly and at greater human sacrifice than anyone now would believe.

The future world of humankind and nature will not be a paradise. A new kind of civilization will arise from the ashes of this one with many of the old templates and problems of the previous civilization. It will represent a new syncretism of many old elements along new thematic lines.

But it can be expected that Homo adaptor will no longer be capable or culpable of perpetrating certain kinds of evils that it has been our human condition to suffer from. They will perhaps have a new set of dilemmas and evils to contend with, and they may once again set the development of their civilization on a renewed collision course with the natural environment of the earth. But it will not be in the same way that we have done so today, and it may yet be a long time in coming.

Many of the old stresses and tensions may remain or become renewed in the redevelopment of human civilization. But what may be of lasting importance is that the psychosocial topography of this new civilization will be essentially different and altered in terms of its relative salience and depths of its textured human fabric, in terms of the differential contrasts and tonal scales of being in the world.

There may still be cores and peripheries within a world system of structural integration, but who controls what will become rebalanced, and the old differentials and asymmetries of power and control will be realigned in a more manner of more even and fair distribution between core and periphery.

In the realignment of old loyalties, what was once national identity that is becoming increasingly ethno national class caste identity, will in the future become increasingly panhuman ego identity reaffirming the position and importance, and independent power of the individual in the social world. It will become increasingly an anthropo-graphic human identity the landscape of which is focused upon and focused by the position of the interacting human being in a wide nexus of inter-human social networks.

In this can be revitalized some old, outcast stereotypes of the peasant family bound within a village cultural tradition, and of an alternative fringe or petite cottage industry is that stressing economic self-sufficiency, handicraft production, barter and reciprocity of exchange.

These stereotypes may have always been only stereotypes—the peasant inbound in her village world was never genuinely or completely independent of the larger political sphere in that her context situated her.

Taxes still had to be paid, conscription still took place, larger cash markets still promised greater rewards and opportunities. But there remains something basic and genuine about such a way of life, something commons and unadorned that is of immense value in human adjustments and predicaments.

Within such contexts, humans were more jack-of-all-trades, master of few, rather than hyper-compartmentalized, over specialized organizational people. There is something to be said for the myth of five acres and independence, for grass roots self sufficiency, local control and familial responsibility.

With the approach of the human horizon at the margins if systemic development, with the individual becoming more and more the locus of control and the focus of power within the system, there can be expected to occur a process of re-humanization within the system and of the system's basic orientation.

This can be seen reflected in the historical movement of social structure from earlier periods of socio-religious identity and kingship, to national patriotism and geo-political interest groups, to ethnization of the world and the rise of ethno-cultural and ethno-racial consciousness, or identity, towards what can be seen as the rise of an individually, anthropo-graphic focus and a pan-human collective identity within the system.

The other social difference will remain in the world as a basis of reference and inequality, but these will become structurally subsumed within larger, more embracing orientations in which human identity becomes increasingly realized within the structural definitions of the system.

In the personal and social atomization of humankind, people will discover in learning how to cope with the absoluteness of their own relative aloneness and existential loneliness in an over crowded world.

It forms the ground for a renewed sense of human identity that learns how to transcend such alienating aloneness through inter-human relationship.

When such conditions are pushed to the extreme, people will seek out an empty desert to fill with their aloneness rather than suffer the suffocating and stifling pressures of the social masses in which their greatest fears and feelings of loneliness become most acute and expressed.

People will learn to revalue certain aspects of previous lives, and to reinvigorate their secular civilization with a sense of lived tradition that in its secular, modern era is all but absent in the prioritization of the new and replacement of the old.

The globe may indeed become a new global village that is electronically intermediated. It may have some of the affinities of the old tradition bound village, but lack the localness and immediacy of its scale and presence in everyday life.

It will be a human bound village, rather than a culture bound village. If it becomes a global village, it is likely as well to become a global open-air marketplace where the networks are long, the action is fast, the people are many and diverse. People may be expected to be seen once again haggling over the prices or relative worth of some item or service, without a fixed price tag or sticker and an unhelpful salesperson.

In such a future for development, two kinds of ritual religious orientations can be developed. Her first, extensive kind of orientation harkens back to a long and commonplace culture historical tradition—a long stream of little traditions—that dealt with the ritual celebration and symbolic expression of death as a rite of passage and as a rite of separation and reintegration.

This kind of ritual elaboration of death, associated today exclusively with commercialized Halloween and funeral parlors, has become largely outmoded in the secular age of science. Its renewal and revitalization in human redevelopment will provide a culture and symbolic context by which to bring 'death' back out into the open, and provide a social means for dealing with the separation.

The second tradition, associated with great traditions, is the Dionysian celebration of life and the Apollonian reinstatement of order and organization in life following episodes that threaten chaos and disorder. This kind of ritual can be found in the Roman forum or coliseum where gladiators, Christians and lions copiously shed blood to the delight and pacification of the masses.

It is found today in modern sporting events, the Olympics, football and soccer games, wrestling and boxing matches, in that there is usually a great deal of betting going on and not infrequent episodes of mass hysteria and riotous violence.

It can be found in popular concerts and at peace-ins. It existed in medieval tournaments and during military parades. In Brazil, it is the basis of the annual carnival celebrations and dance competitions that go on in spite of the perennial persistence of suffering, poverty and everyday death. This kind of ritual process reinforces the system through its anti-structure, and is based upon the heightening of the illusion of nonbeing and becoming.

The former kind of ritual process, that is becoming less frequent and less a part of normal, everyday life, is one that is rooted in an extensive orientation towards Being in the world, that entails a symbolic coming to terms with death as both natural, and supernatural process.

The second kind of ritual process is intensively oriented towards the reinforcement of nonbeing and of becoming, involving the implicit denial of death or its projection upon the loser or displacement from the winner, during the competition.

The former, extensive ritual orientation focusing upon death and separation, can be said to be a mechanism for dealing with short term traumatic experiences of death or separation episodes, that may be brief in duration, but uncommonly salient or important in its radical disjunction with everyday life.

Such ritual provides a means of ameliorating and therapeutically rehabilitating the effects of this radical disjunction, and its disorienting influence, in everyday life. It frames the exceptional and makes it usual.

The latter, intense ritual orientation focuses upon the celebration of the everyday experience of life, as a mechanism for reinforcing and coping with the long-term endurance of many everyday, pervasive, and sometimes cumulatively overwhelming stresses and tensions of existence, deprivation, frustration, denial. These rituals provide a release of the built up tensions and a focus for aggressive and impulsive drives.

The association with impulse control disorders, with gambling and physical violence, and with sadomasochistic role reversals, becomes a way of highlighting and framing the everyday inequities and makes them exceptional in their symbolic anti-structure and projection onto the abnormal.

The two kinds of ritual process can be seen as complementary in everyday life, and as revealing, depending upon their relative emphasis, of the relative extensive or intensive orientations of the historical patterning in which they occur. The style of elaboration of either kind if ritual process can also be revealing of the underlying values and symbolic topography in which they occur.

The patterns of human response to stress will be variable, but they can be expected to follow certain overall directions of development. First, there is an occurrence of 'delayed stress' reaction in that there is a predisposition to re-experience the emotionality of such trauma triggered by minor environmental stimuli.

There is associated a kind of symbolic dissociation and passive cognitive withdrawal from normal, everyday involvement. There is a lowering of thresholds of tolerance for suffering, frustration, stress that triggers inordinate and uncontrolled reactions.

There is paradoxically an increased tolerance to the experience of pain, suffering and stress—a kind of desensitization of its experience as an everyday event. Avoidance personality patterns, adaptive response disorders, withdrawal from everyday, normal participation, disorientation and depression, and borderline character traits are the consequence of such stress. It could be that long-term stress leads to the development of certain kinds of impulse control disorders, such as explosive aggression, repetition compulsion, gambling and substance abuse.

Somatization of disorders, hysteria and conversion reactions can be expected, as well as a shallowness of affective cathexis and transference with others. Other long-term consequences that could be involved are forms of disorder of sexual expression, psychotic disintegration and withdrawal from reality and patterns of social codependency and interpersonal abuse.

Such patterns are associated with downward social mobility and with low self-esteem and low achievement motivation. Low self esteem creates its own self fulfilling prophecy in that failure, setting oneself up for failure and finding friends who reinforce one's sense of failure, all tend to reinforce low self esteem and the actualization of failure in life.

There is in this the potential for a vicious, degenerative cycle of de-development in that withdrawal from stressful situations, fascination and compulsion to stress, and patterns of maladaptation and failure beget ever greater stresses in life that lead to ever greater withdrawal and adaptive malfunctioning.

Attitudes, affective expressions, behavior and belief patterns associated with this kind of vicious cycle become transferred from one generation to the next in early childhood socialization, in lack of strong role models, in miss-education and socialization for failure, in the transfer of low self esteem from the parent to the child, and in the acquisition as primary socialization in bad habits.

When such patterns become embodied and embedded at the level of primary socialization, they become much more deeply ingrained in character, much more natural seeming, and much more difficult to eradicate by subsequent reconversion or alternation. In such a way, the sins of our parents can visit upon us and upon our own children in unseen ways.

A whole poverty of culture orientation and a cultural orientation of learned failure, can become cultivated and transmitted through time in an infectious manner, even though the initial causes for such an orientation may be long since absent. In such a way, major traumatic events can come to have cultural and symbolic repercussions that extend through many generations.

When we speak of the kind of extensive ritual, we must see it as dealing with the primary process of death and separation at a level of primary socialization—alternation and reconversion.

When we are dealing with the more frequent, intensively oriented ritual process, we are dealing primarily with secondary socialization dealing with separation and death as secondary, symbolically derivative aspects of nonbeing and becoming. In the former process, death is dealt with more directly and basically as a primary process of being.

In a sense, incomplete primary socialization is a consequence of this vicious cycle of human de-development, and it leads as well to a failure of primary processes of ritual reinforcement. Secondary socialization and rituals associated with reinforcement of secondary process likewise become impaired in their performance.

Discrepancies between primary and secondary process can occur, and such discrepancies that may result can be due to or lead to impartial socialization or failure in the ineffectiveness of such ritual process.

It is possible that the consistent failure to perform rituals related to death at the time of its occurrence, could lead to later impairment of socialization, or to impairment of the effectiveness of such rituals later on.

It is understandable that secondary socialization process and secondary ritual process that aims at persuasion rather than at conversion, and at symbolic identification that is relatively abstract, impersonal, and distant, must be continuously reinforced or reenacted to be effective, while primary socialization, ritual and conversion, though occurring less frequently, tends to be a more longer lasting and permanent process. The former aims at reinforcement and enhancement of one's status identity, the latter leads to change or modification of this identity.

There is a sense that only by coming to know and coming to terms with our own heart of darkness, with the full range of possibilities of evil and difference within ourselves, that we are able to extend our empathy of human possibility of being and becoming to encompass a wider range of human difference, and to embrace and tolerate a wider range of human weakness in the world.

It is only by the recognition of such possibilities within ourselves, in our learning, that we can become our own most hated enemy or feared monster, that we can learn live with such hate and fear in a way that renders them harmless, and even helpful, in our world, instead of allowing this same feelings, by their unconscious projection, to become enactments in the world of our own hidden becoming and unconscious sense of nonbeing.

Such empathy does not excuse the perpetration and perpetuation of evil in the world, but it does, by its understanding, does ameliorate some of its more pernicious consequences of its suffering in our lives, such that we can learn to live in spite of it, rather than because of it or as a result of it.

Putting fear into its proper perspective, by facing those unknown things we fear and personalizing them within ourselves, and in coming to terms with the destructiveness of hate in our lives, allows us to escape the patterns of avoidance and dependency that leads to the vicious cycle of promotion of hate and fear in the larger world.

This cannot be accomplished in only or purely an intensive sense of secondary ritual performance or in interior contexts of relations. It must be carried out into the extensive world, and enacted upon the level of primary process of death and being in the world.

It is effective as a conversion or alternation experience affecting our whole being, or else it is not effective at all. Seeking such experience at the primary level in an extensive sense, and learning to live with what one discovers about oneself and the possibilities of humanity in such a quest, is not an easy or straight-forward thing.

It is risky and sometimes dangerous, but it is a necessary trial by fire that if not undertaken, cannot yield the kind or quality of experience that is necessary for the growth of the individual.

The System promotes a great deal of illusion and hypocrisy at the secondary level as a substitution process in place of things that should be sought for at a primary level in an extensive way. It is much simpler and safer to substitute words for deeds, and in the process convince only the foolish or the blind of one's own genuineness of being in the world. Thus a great deal of what passes for genuine experience in our world is actually derived experience in name only.

This is a basic difference between the global villager and the peasant villager of the past. One who never leaves the village to see the wider world or avails oneself of primary experiences in the world in existential relation with other people, must always suffer the fate of superficial existence and spurious experience—of nonbeing, and vicariousness of being in the world. On the other had, an intensively bound tourist can travel the world over, and never ever leave his/her own culture bound way of life.

Primary experience is waiting to be encountered in the world—but it must be actively sought out, and its acquisition is never smooth nor hazard free.

Only by accumulating a ground of such extensive experience in the world, can an individual build up a fund of understanding on which to test and validate related subsequent experiences, whether these experiences are intensive and derived or genuine and coming from the reality of another person.

To promote professors who have never left the classroom environment or who only have traveled as first class tourists in the world is to promote a derived intensive orientation in academia lacking any substantive ground in existential, experientially primary reality.

It is to construct a paper-thin version of reality that is lacking in its depth and in its breadth.

It is vital that in primary education we promote approaches that undue the effects of incomplete primary socialization, by providing healthy role models, environmental enrichment, a healthy sense of personal identity and of self-esteem for the individual child. It is also vitally important that in higher levels of secondary education we complete the process of socialization in an effective, multicultural, extensive and panhuman manner.

Teaching values and perspectives rooted in multiculturalism and pan humanism are neither impossible nor necessarily difficult to do, but this does entail that we undo the effects of the kind of secondary ritual that tends to reinforce in the individual identities that are tied to nonbeing and becoming in the world, and that are rooted in social difference and inequality between people in the world.

Education remains the most effective tool available for the transmission, socialization and enculturation of people. It is to the best interests of humankind that the goals of education be separated from the values, interests and dictates of the system, and that education works to promote human development rather than systemic development in the world.

The future remains to be realized by humankind. Human responses to increasing stress in the world may lead to some interesting surprises.

Human beings tend to be much more adaptable and flexible than our histories usually give us credit for. They survive and continue in spite of what happens to them in their history. Not all alterations and developments in our future will be expected, and there will be some good with the bad, and some bad with the good.

Perfection is not only an inhuman state, but it is an anti human state of affairs. The realistic aim of human development is not progress towards paradise, but it is the relative alleviation of human suffering in the world and the relative realization of human rights, equality and freedom for the whole world, as members of a single Hominid species and global guardians.

PART VII: FINAL SOLUTIONS
Lost Causes and Lasting Consequences

History has taught us a few important lessons. It is relatively easy to trick people into doing what is against their own best interests—all you must do is to lie to them in a consistent and convincing manner.

Nazi Germany's final solution to the Jewish problem was one of the few times in recorded history that a state's bureaucratic machinery set itself to the single minded purpose of actually annihilating another racially distinct group of people, though the systematic deceit involved was really nothing new.

What is frightening was its recentness and its massive scale of intent and its deliberate, large-scale, industrial-institutional implementation. Though it was not the first time that one group has destroyed another, it has probably been the worst case of such mass slaughter of human life.

But systematic bureaucratic exclusion of whole groups of people from even minimal access to resources or to screens of support or to political economic participation within the world system goes on everyday as a matter of business as usual policy. And though it may not be direct annihilation, its final consequences are often the same.

One of the lessons learned from the Nuremberg Trials was that knowledge creates responsibility. One could not claim ignorance and look the other way in the perpetration of crimes against humanity. It seems to be a lesson that our world system has since forgotten, or neglected to take to heart.

What is even more frightening to consider, is that what happened in Nazi Germany could have happened in virtually any modern nation state, even the most democratic and historically most liberal ones, if the 'wrong' group of people had ever gained control.

With all our massive bureaucratic machinery in place, knowledge is systematically, routinely obfuscated, responsibility is routinely passed on and ultimately diffused into the oblivion of the System, and, once mobilized, the massive inertia of bureaucracy makes it extremely difficult to reverse or redirect.

The history lesson of the holocaust is that it can very likely happen again, if we are not careful to see who comes to power in the world.

There are many lost causes in the modern world. Pursuing paradise or a developmental utopia on earth is proving to be a lost cause. Saving the ecology of the earth is also proving to be a lost cause.

Driving down the fast lane of Southern California's freeways trying to get ahead in life is also a lost cause—there is always someone faster who is ahead of you. Dressing lavishly on credit for the daily fashion parade and impression management is also a lost cause.

No matter how much you spend, there are many more spending more than you, and even more who do not care how much you spend. Getting a higher education in America is proving to be a lost, and expensive, cause.

Similarly, pursuing peace on the earth through the escalation of increased destructive force potential, the stockpiling of nuclear weapons, and the mass production of expensive modern military machines, is also a lost cause.

History has taught us that lasting peace has never been forthcoming from preparations for waging war. Consuming a limited supply of fossil fuels on earth is proving to be not only a lost cause but a bankrupting dead end in development as well.

There are many things people are doing on a regular, daily basis that, cumulatively, will have lasting consequences for future earth history. Building plastic mountains of disposable diapers is one. Spilling oil into oceans is another. Razing all remaining forests. Laying more reinforced concrete is yet another.

Exterminating the few remaining species of wild mammals on earth is yet another. Having more babies is yet another. Watching television instead of reading a book is another. Letting our children watch TV instead of reading a book to them is another.

Casting about for answers, it should be readily obvious that there are indeed few if any 'final solutions' to the predicaments that face humankind on earth. The pursuit of progress in the development of the System is one such solution that has been proposed and is widely promoted.

Human development is another, alternative, and perhaps more viable solution that nevertheless remains largely unheeded and neglected. Nazi Germany believed it had the Final Solution to all human problems in its eradication of inferior, non-Aryan races of people on earth.

Widespread interethnic discrimination, the world over, has been one systematic bureaucratic solution to the problems of development. Scientists will tell you that the only solution is in the progress of Science. Theologians of the world will tell you that the only solution is a religious one—mostly likely their own particular brand. Ecologists will tell you that the solution is the greening of the world and in purchasing a copy of <u>Gaia</u>.

The average Joe and Jane Doe on the street will tell you in a more common sense manner that the solution is in "more police protection," "stopping crime," "controlling drugs" or in kicking people on welfare off their arses. Politicians will tell you they have the solution, if only you vote for them, and the President's solution seems to be in developing mightier military machinery.

As we are running short on time, we must learn to be very careful in everything we do, that we are not pursuing lost causes, doing things that have lasting consequences, and promoting solutions to our problems that may be wrong.

The development of the System has been historically a process of ethno-schismogenesis in that boundaries and differentials have led to competitive drives and development in competition. This has occurred in the Arms race, the Space race, the race to carve up the third world pie. It occurs in market competition between businesses, leading to new and better strategies. It seems that national mobilization and focus in many countries depends upon this kind of productive ethno-schismogenesis by the competitive presence of another 'enemy' nation.

Such ethno-schismogenesis has conferred upon the history of such patterning of development a kind of evolutionary flavor and sense of inevitability of its progress. But it has also led to the recurrence of conflict and to the breaking down of the international relations that maintain the System.

There is a fundamental social psychology about such ethno-schismogenesis that entails certain characteristic consequences to its developmental cycle. It entails that people of the out-group become derogated as something less than fully human, or if human, then as something fundamentally different, and inferior, than the in-group. It also entails a kind of fascist solidarity of the in-group that can turn into some violent forms of social hysteria and that can be easily manipulated and directed.

There is a particular blindness about the ethno-schismogenic development if the system that means that it stumbles somewhat haphazardly down its pathway.

Perhaps it is a necessary blindness—the kind of Nietzsche illusion that is the prerequisite to social action. It is not the same kind of blindness that characterizes natural biological evolution, as it is in a sense a self-imposed and self-reinforcing blindness while evolutionary myopia is innate and does not need to be self-reinforcing. Selection will ensure removal of species that reach their own dead ends.

The kind of blindness characteristic of the ethno-schismogenesis of development is that we must see one another and ultimately ourselves, as something other than what we really are—as something less or more than fully, naturally human. It requires that we superimpose illusions of super humanness upon our selves and our system, and dehumanize others and their systems.

The blindness of ethno-schismogenesis requires that nonbeing and becoming must be reinforced and that the subjectivity and naturalness of being in the world be consistently denied. It requires that we superimpose upon the world, in the name of development, the system, our way of life, a kind of moral imperative and normative injunction as a model or paradigm for the Nonbeing and becoming of the entire world, for all of humanity.

The tragedy of the ideology of ethno-schismogenesis is that in the final analysis the development of the System is a totally inhuman one, and from the standpoint of human development, mostly unnecessary.

Anthropology can and ought to make a lasting contribution to the realistic understanding of where the development of recent earth history is leading us. Anthropology can contribute the kind of understanding that Nietzsche claimed killed social action, 'for action requires the veil of illusion.' Unmasking the monster of development and the system, we can see that it is not a strange, impersonal god, but that it has an all too human face in the mirror, blinded by its own imagination.

The proper point of departure for a development oriented Anthropology is not the systemic development of global civilization, but the problem of human development within the transforming environments of global civilization.

Such an understanding requires that anthropology no longer be so much a system's science or a synchronic, structure oriented analysis, but that it become preeminently an historical and culture historical science which means that we must also be dealing with an irreducible normative human science.

To see the development of civilization as an extension of natural evolutionary process is to mistake the general principles and lessons of human history with the laws and constraints of selection governing natural history, and in the process to implicitly ignore and even deny the arbitrariness, customariness, ideology and unpredictable consequences that characterize historical changes—it is to ignore the human contribution to the making of this history, and ultimately, to deny humanness of historical realities altogether.

It does not need to be reiterated that such system oriented, law searching, natural scientific and paradigmatic anthropologies are tethered to the structure and service of the system within which their own modes of information promotes and promulgates.

The crises of identity and definition that anthropology has been undergoing has in large part been a reflection of the larger world crises of change and history that it is internalizing and coming to be more and more reflective of its internalized world order.

It is a consequence of its own failure to embrace the more human oriented aspects of recent earth history—as a matter of human development, and thus, in its failure to make any lasting contribution to the illusion-deflating understanding of the realities of this history, it instead becomes blindly crippled and susceptible to the effects of this illusion.

Human history and civilization is running up against both internal and external constraints—what might be described as social/environmental circumscription. The System, given the finite delimitation of its basis for development, is reaching the zenith of its self-organizing, super-complex criticality.

The System is being forced into a double bind in that, its extreme hyper-development, must further develop in order to maintain its own Systemic order in the World. It must continue to create ways to push back or circumvent the constraints to its development, but in the process, it must also further augment the constraining effects of those limitations.

We have stepped outside of nature's evolutionary fold, and in the success of our development we have virtually brought evolutionary process to a standstill on earth. But evolutionary clocks are ticking away within us as well as around us in our earthbound environments. We cannot escape the inexorable unwinding of this natural clockwork. Evolution is rebounding upon our development not only around us, but also through us, in our own problem of human over population.

It is working through other ways to further stress and constrain our systemic development. As our development is leading to inexorable ecocide of the earth, we are inadvertently and blindly destroying with our technological development the very foundation for life on earth, our own included.

The social structure of the system is becoming historically transformed in unforeseeable directions, in spite of what or where we expect or wish it would go. It is leading to increased differentials in resource acquisition and availability and in greater social inequality in the process of development. Old identities are suffering the shock of the new as structural realignments necessitate psychosocial realignments. The predictable human response is the escape from reality back into a false sense of retrojected, revised history.

Further systemic development is running up against its own human horizon, as the stresses and strains and tensions of its super criticality become focused more and more upon the role and position, and tolerance of the individual within the system.

Further development is leading down the road to human de-development, but in this effect, the system exhausts itself at its own human horizon. It cannot continue without itself becoming realigned and reoriented in a more human way.

This may result in further, deeper ethno-schismogenesis that sunders the system into more than one part, into one that is more extensive and human oriented and one that remains rooted to the intensive development of the core, and the system oriented.

It is possible that an evolutionary regression and revitalization process could be inaugurated in the impending "Dark Ages" of human de-development of Civilization, and that a new and different kind of human being may emerge from the ashes of the old.

Overpopulation, over development, ecocide, and evolutionary selection, all will have unintended and unexpected consequences and side effects for the future development of both humankind and its system.

The blindness of our progressive pursuit of systemic development has always been a history of unintended consequence. But it is the consequences of the blindness and myopia of our systemic development that we will have to live with in the long run, whether this is a radioactive pollution with a fifty thousand year half life, no ozone layer, no natural primeval forests, no polar ice caps, no wildlife, no natural ecology, and no more mineral resources or fossil fuels.

The paradox of the alternative pursuit of human development is that from the structural standpoint of political economy, it is relatively inexpensive and easy to pursue.

It does not have the long-term dangers that are inherent in the eco-cidal side effects of systemic development, and it eventuates in the long-term improvements of human quality of life and greater relative equality. Its paradox is also that it leads to the development of vision, instead of blindness, and of understanding, rather than delusion.

We have a final choice to make in our determination of our own history on earth. We can continue to pursue systemic development at the cost of human de-development or instead choose the alternative course of switching to human development at the necessary price of systemic de-development. This is the lesson of our historical anthropology and anthropological history.

The Third Millennium (1999)

Essays on the Human Predicament

Hugh M. Lewis

Preface to the Third Millennium (2023)

Earthboundness and the Dilemma of the Global Commons

I wrote <u>The Third Millennium</u> about 23 years ago, in December of 1999 hurrying to finish the manuscript before the beginning of the new 3rd Millennium—a momentous event at least in my mind at the time.

There is little I would change in the text today, except perhaps to refine my thoughts somewhat regarding earthboundness and regarding theories of social authoritarianism.

We had just returned from China and in rereading the work now I am somewhat surprised that China then was not the main or explicit reference point to some of the text that it has since become. Of course, we were just beginning then our "reverse culture shock."

I had returned from China with a distinct and clear impression that there was probably little independent fact-checking on the Chinese population at 2000 A.D., and that the Chinese population was basically as small or large as the Chinese government wanted the rest of the world to believe. The presumption of trust in China is not something to be freely traded on a simple smile and handshake.

Thus my main conclusion was that the population was probably larger than most people believed. The One-Child Policy was not necessarily working everywhere the same way. Everywhere signs of this massive growing population showed itself—in urban migration to our local agricultural city that was driving almost a yearly doubling of that population as well as the size of our student body. But our agricultural city was directly upon a main railroad line to bigger and better places linking Central China mainly to the Chinese east coast.

Thus I had returned from China with a strong sense of urgency of exploring alternative perspectives linking to global circumscription.

In hindsight, almost now a quarter of a century later, if the Chinese government seems more aggressive territorially and on the prowl globally, then it is quite understandable from the population standpoint that the revolutionary tidal wave of rising expectations if not political equality, must keep pace with the developmental control capacities of the Chinese communist regime.

The Mainland Chinese government today is playing by a different set of rules than most of the rest of the world. In a world of peak finite resources, the Chinese follow the long-view traditional wisdom of taking care of their own first (and to hell with the rest.)

I would argue this perspective is intrinsic and inveterate to Chinese history and socio-cultural structure, both in the past and in the present, and most likely also into the near future.

For the Chinese, their huge population has always been their greatest and cheapest resource, and also their greatest potential liability.

In editing the work now for this publication of the work, I am also surprised somewhat that many of the ideas carried forward in an applicable way to unfolding realities in our contemporary world.

We just recently crested the estimate of 7.5 billion human souls on earth sometime around 2013-2015. Now in 2023, we have certainly surpassed the Club of Rome estimated "Limits to Growth" global carrying capacity set back in the early 1970s.

I never really trusted rough global population estimates based upon complex estimations derived from limited and uneven sampling.

We are looking by United Nations 2017 population update for the global human population to reach between 8.4 and 8.7 Billion by 2030, and between 9.4 and 10.2 billion by 2050 (the lower estimated trajectories being the best possible scenario.)

Carrying capacity of the earth, for richer or poorer, will have to be able to accommodate between 9.6 and 13.2 billion human beings on earth, after which population is expected to "slow down" in its growth and even off.

<u>Earthbound Perspectives</u>

Nevertheless now, whatever the actual size of current human population, which may be greater or less than we may realize through our formulas, we have no choice but to work with global populations beyond known carrying capacities of the natural earth, in the yearly confrontation with global dilemmas.

Furthermore, if we are to create a fairer and freer world for, any such global solution must include Mainland China and sub-continental India an intrinsic part of that solution.

Of course global carrying capacity is inversely proportional in super-complex ways to relative degree of global social-circumscription, and depends upon our cultural technological capacities and policies to effectively intervene and interfere with the natural world for the sake of human population growth.

A key set of factors governing these outcomes appears to be what might be referred to as human developmental momentum in certain socio-structural trajectories relating to urbanization, fertility, increasing quality and quantity of life, functional linkage between core and periphery (or urban and rural) contexts, and the capacity of urban core areas to effectively absorb population with employment opportunities for adults and educational, welfare and heath services for children.

This links to lowering infant mortality rates and lower fertility of young women overall, as well as with increasing average rates of longevity.

The larger trends are hopefully inspiring, at little, if not a too little too late—global population growth is beginning to taper off in most regions except for Africa. Urbanization of more than half the world's population has been reached within the past decade, and will continue to grow.

Female fertility rates will fall, and hopefully so will infant mortality rates, while average global human longevity should continue to slowly rise, barring global pandemics such as we first experienced with the global COVID 19 crises.

The rapid development of effective vaccines and its worldwide distribution was a clear and comforting confirmation of the power and efficacy of human cultural interventions, as long as we do not continue to take this for granted.

Introduction

It is quite natural in the year 1999 to look forward to the dawning of the Third Millennium, and its implications for humanity on earth—especially for people of the Judeo-Christian tradition because the concept of the millennium has long had vital connotations of the coming of a perfect age. Upon the edge of the 3rd Millennium, we can look both backward to where we have been, and forward to where we are now going to be.

It is quite legitimate to ask but quite impossible to answer whether or not humanity will even be here in another thousand years from now, and if so, then what kind of state and world will our distant descendants then occupy. If we assume that a generation of humankind recurs every 27 years, on average, then in a thousand years there will have been approximately 36-7 human generations upon the earth. We can look back to the condition of humankind at 1000 A.D. Europe was then just awakening from a dark shadow of a previous millennium of involuntary servitude and violence, of religious ignorance and feudal anarchy.

At the edge of the 3rd Millennium, we can see clearly several major difficulties looming upon our collective horizon. A great amount of ink has been spilled on these issues already. It is nearly enough now to list them in rank order of their importance: Global Population; Loss of Bio-Diversity and Mass Extinction; Militarism: Human Authoritarianism & Inequality: the Global Challenges of Human Development. This ordering is paradoxically in reverse of the predominate trends in spending and policies pursued by most governments and major organizations today.

A great deal of money and human energy is currently being invested in the pursuit of often short-sighted policies of economic development, and while other vast amounts of resources are consumed uselessly in vicious cycles of human corruption and in the maintenance of systems of structurally reinforced inequalities, and even more is wasted in building armies and destructive weapons. Proportionately very little effort or money is being spent upon solving more basic and in a sense more pressing issues of global pollution, loss of habitat and bio-diversity, and in concerted policies to control and alleviate the pressing problems of human overpopulation. These problems are all interrelated. They are the direct result of the rapid proliferation and success of the Human species on the earth, especially in the last few decades.

Upon the dawn of a new millennium we must ask ourselves honest questions as human beings about where we've come from, who we are and what we are doing in our world. We can make no more distinctions between black and white, Moslem and Christian, east and west. We can no longer afford the ethnocentrism and prejudice that had bound our ancestors to a long dark past of perennial violence and chronic suffering.

It is time as a single world of modern human beings that we formulate our new one thousand-year resolution, and these resolutions must be something we do not collectively forget before the following springtime. Our resolutions for the new century and the new millennium must now be built upon a deeper and more realistic understanding of what it means to be a contemporary human being on the modern earth.

As mass communications and the information revolution breaks down invisible barriers and bring us all potentially ever closer together, we cannot escape the daily evidence of our shared and common humanity. On television we see live satellite images of suffering and violence from the all corners of the world, and we know that it could just as well be happening next door.

Unlike our grandparents, we can no longer naively or with self-deception maintain the petty ethnocentrism, delusions of prejudice and hatred, and comfortable illusions of "our better world." It is our common and shared fate to become responsible members of the world community whether we wish to be or not. We have a collective identity and implicit responsibility to this global human community that we cannot freely shirk without a sense of having not done something right.

This responsibility is in the final analysis a democratic one--one that is based on equality and freedom of choice. It is our responsibility to exercise this freedom and to actively participate in the possibilities of this new found global democracy. The ground swell of global democracy, the natural outcome of the information revolution, is potentially a grass roots movement of major proportions. It is our new found responsibility to put aside our emphasis and attention to cultural differences and our preoccupation with separatist and divisive chauvinism, and to promote those qualities that are shared and common to all human beings—qualities of individual importance, of achievement and success, of family love, of courageous and heroic commitment to causes beyond our own selfish ends.

Like it or not, we are all connected together. Not only are we all connected to one another, but we are also all intimately connected, singly and in groups, and as a whole species, with our natural world and the larger physical universe. We cannot escape the fact and consequences of this sense of total, universal connection to our world.

We are greeted at the dawn of the Third Millennium with an immediate and pressing set of problems that we must resolve if we are to assure the future survival and well being of our progeny on earth. There is no single worst issue or separable set of little problems.

We are confronted immediately and dramatically by a single, large, complex problem that has an impending sense of urgency. Indeed, if we think about it, there is an overwhelming sense of immediacy that lurks in the background of all our lives. It is like a huge, black, ominous storm cloud that now overcasts the entire earth in a foreboding shadow.

It is the global imperative of the dawn of the Third Millennium that we must collectively face this common set of problems, or, by failing to do so, face the threat of disaster and eventual extinction. It is a complex synergy of many kinds of issues connected together that demand our attention and remedial action. Its complexity and chaos entail also that the solutions cannot be simple or straightforward to implement. But solutions are there, one way or the other.

At the dawn of the Third Millennium we are confronted with the imperative that we must change ourselves and our old ways of doing things that were oriented toward isolated selves in many isolated communities.

We cannot afford to simply continue in previous modes and maladaptive patterns of social behavior without in the long run dearly paying the piper and seeing our children led off into the mountain. We cannot afford to ignore these dilemmas and to delude ourselves that our actions do not have larger consequences in the world.

We really have no choice any more. To fail to change is to allow the world to run amok within the next century. We can believe that this will never happen; we can wish that it wouldn't; we can rationalize how and why it probably won't—but we must assume responsibility for the roles we can and may play in the future turning of events. And with the increasing interconnectedness of our world, there is also increasing opportunity for both constructive philanthropic acts as well as for mass destruction.

The dawn of the Third Millennium is a wake up call for all people to unite once and for all, to come together on common earth and deal together for a common future or to else suffer collectively a shared, tragic fate.

The argument is made in this book that the only reasonable solution to the common predicament of humankind is to unite together into a single world federation of nations. A genuine global government—a single world state that is powerful enough to enforce its rule of law over all individuals and single nation states.

It is true that the world is not quite ready to go this far, but it is imperative that this does happen sooner than later if humanity is to continue further without a great deal even greater of mass destruction and bloodshed than was witnessed in the previous century.

The danger of a single dominant world state is to risk the rise to power of a single tyrannical and totalitarian entity that controls all things. The only means of creating a world state that is relatively immune to this kind of possibility is to define it as a democratic institution in that the rule and routine of the law is placed above the control or influence of any human being, but is the common mandate of all human beings.

<u>Earthbound Perspectives</u>

Modern nation states themselves, especially those that are totalitarian and authoritarian in structure, cannot be entrusted to turn their weapons to plough shares. The effort at global unification must be at last a grass-roots ground swell—an effort, ultimately "of the people, for the people, and by the people."

It is the responsibility of all people, regardless of their nationality, religion, ethnic identity, to define a new kind of citizenship of the world—that transcends and comes before all other socio-political identities.

Legal citizenship to modern nation states that often demands absolute loyalty and coercive life-sacrifices of its constituency, must be made to yield its final coercive and violent authority before this larger and potentially more powerful sense of identity.

National citizenship must be subsumed and encapsulated as but one alternate identity within the global nation of humanity. The basis of this alternative identity is to be found in a common and shared sense of humanity.

This is both our destiny and our duty at the dawn of the Third Millennium.

Part I: Basic Problems and Prospects

In spite of all the advances of our sciences and technology, at the edge of the Third Millennium we are still almost as socially backward and undeveloped as we were at the beginning of the last century. Major political issues in the United States today are anti-abortion, prayer in school, creationism and possession of firearms.

China, containing one/fifth of the world's population, with misrepresented growth rates, remains still an essentially Orwellian world of big brother and newspeak—a totalitarian state controlled by only a very small percentage of the total.

All economies today remain based almost exclusively upon petrochemical and fossil fuel exploitation, even though this has been clearly demonstrated to be the major contributory factor to global warming.

Militarism, social authoritarianism and gross structural inequalities are not only prevalent in the world today, but in many respects are even more vicious and destructive in their consequences than they were one hundred years ago. Undoubtedly, the central problem that humanity faces in the 21st Century is the problem of humanity itself.

Chapter 1: Basic Dilemmas of the Global Imperative

There are a number of basic dilemmas now confronting humankind. Most of these problems are common knowledge, though the issue of their global interrelationship and complex negative feedback and synergism remains poorly understood.

These basic dilemmas include:

1. The problem of human over-population.

2. The problem of environmental circumscription.

3. The problem of militarism and authoritarianism.

4. The issue of ethnocultural differentiation & assimilation.

5. The problem of mass poverty.

And,

6. The problem of modern socio-economic development.

These problems concern basic structural issues that underlie the patterning of the relationship of humankind to the natural world. Structural relations are long-term patterns usually lurking in the background of the unfolding everyday landscape. In all their complexity they do not simply go away if ignored and they are fundamentally intractable to superficial and token band aid efforts at their resolution.

The problem of human population growth is obvious to everyone, but its basic importance has been lost to many people. The human population is doubling very quickly. In fact, no one knows exactly what the total population of the earth is now at the dawn of the 3rd Millennium, and probably we cannot really know. The United Nations had declared the 6 billionth baby born just before the new Millennium, but this number was largely symbolic and had most probably grossly underestimated both the actual rates of population growth and the total size of the human population on earth.

The hard evidence suggests that the published statistics are probably lower than the actual amount and that the rate of growth is greater than we estimate it to be. Human population is fundamental to the global issue because more than any single factor it drives the other problems as a basic, feedback mechanism.

By United Nations studies on human population growth, we cannot clearly measure global carrying capacity. By 2100 C.E. the human population on earth is projected at near or above twelve billion souls.

Whatever the actual numbers or the eventual long-term consequences of human population growth, it must be understood that this problem is a population time bomb ticking away in the background of all our lives. It has a delayed effect. We cannot know how long it will be before it goes off, but it can be seen in the structure of the long run that this is likely to happen sooner than later.

We are witnessing the beginning of the consequences of the real population explosion in our own time in subtle symptoms that are easily ignored. The increasing social pressure of population in core regions, the stress of social systems and the increasing pollution of local and regional environments, the loss of habitat and the retreat of wildlife from the oceans, fields and forests, all indicate a basic problem of global circumscription of the human population.

The population explosion is likely to really begin happening when the human population approaches or overpasses some hypothetical carrying capacity of the earth. Not enough arable land to feed the masses—too many people creating too much pollution.

Increasing but unknown levels of regional and global circumscription should place natural limits on the growth capacity of the human population. This would be reflected in increasing rates of starvation, malnutrition, disease and poverty, even if these are indirectly the result of human conflict and violence.

Just as we do not know the exact size of the human population, nor its real rate of growth during any one period, we also cannot really know what the finite limits of the earth's natural resources are, what its carrying capacity to support a huge human population really can be, nor when the limits of our own development and scientific technology may be eventually over stepped. These are basic but fundamentally unknown questions.

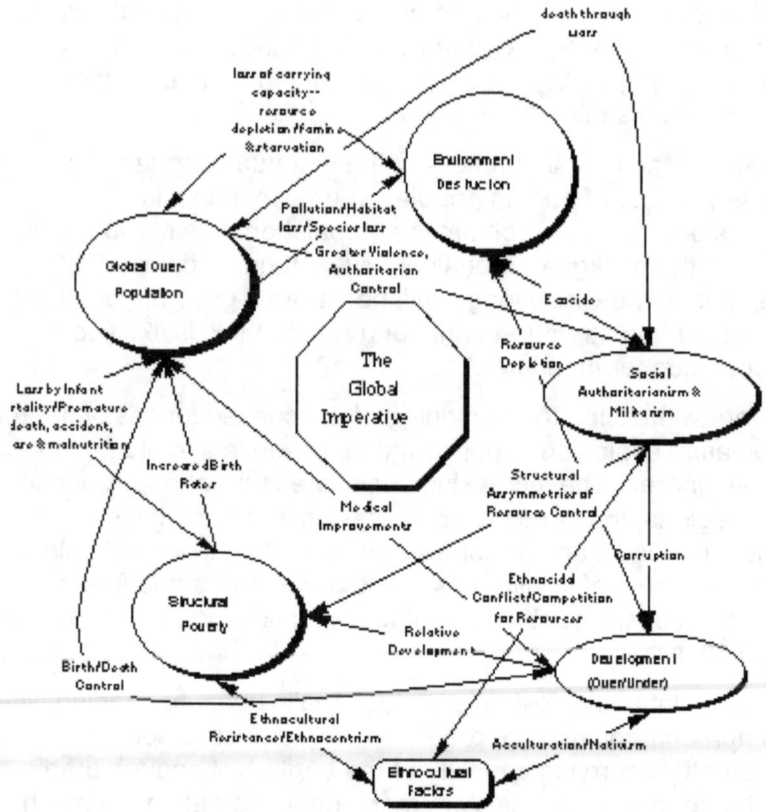

Hypothetical Interconnections of the Global System

But we do know that the human population is very large and growing larger by the day. We do know also that the global environment has been increasingly influenced and stressed by the presence and activities of so many humans. We also know that for whatever gains science may achieve on the frontiers of development, there are also many hidden costs that have not yet been measured.

To continue to deny these basic realities is to deny the truth and experience of our own everyday sensibilities. It is to put on our ideological blinders and commit our selves to narrow-minded and shortsighted political agendas that are doomed for extinction like anachronistic dinosaurs from a by-gone era.

To try to argue against these realities, and to preach attitudes and actions that are contradictory to their indications, is to push humanity and human civilization forward in a mad, headlong rush over the edge of the precipice of uncontrolled development during the first decades of the 21st Century.

We cannot rely any longer on any established governmental agencies in the world to communicate to us a truthful, fully honest and realistic vision of the world. In the long run, they undermine our sense of credibility in their reliability and validity as agencies and sources of sound and realistic information about the world.

But enough signals come through, even in extremely closed societies, to make it possible for any honest and sensible human to put the basic facts together in a logical way and to derive the kinds of conclusions that are in any reasonable analysis inescapable.

The population explosion will have a complicated delay effect and will be felt by increasing annual increments of stress upon our social systems worldwide.

As the average age of the human population grows younger with each passing year, and average life span increases for adults across the board, we must realize that the final count down has already begun.

As increasing numbers of youth reach adulthood, and reproductive age, their demands on the social systems around the world increase exponentially, changing in kind and focus, in volume and need, with each passing month of each succeeding year.

The problem of population itself is a complex issue and is not just a matter of birth rates and infant mortality rates. It is an issue that inevitably involves other kinds of problems. One of the most important points about human population is that, being a culturally organized species, all human beings have some kind of impact upon their habitat and lived environment, and human social systems in total have even greater cumulative impact on local and regional environments. This problem of the cultural impact of humankind on our environment brings to bear the second set of issues and that is the problem of environmental circumscription and ecological destruction of the earth's natural habitat.

We are all witness to these events that affect the background of our lives, and yet we continue in the same modes of behavior that originally cause and lead to these very results. We know it is wrong, but we cannot help it beyond token contributions to rather weak and flaccid, mostly symbolic, efforts to assuage our own sense of guilt.

And if we attempt to make a concerted effort, it is almost guaranteed that we will run headlong into the status quo of the established state powers that be and large private interests. We will realize just how powerful the petrochemical industry really is that fuels the global economy.

We can see how it controls government policy making, and conspires against people who induce changes that would be unprofitable for them. And this dilemma of structural inertia in the current system and of human social resistance to its change is central to understanding the solution to these dilemmas.

We can add to the list of the oil-suppliers and automobile manufacturers, the gun makers, the makers of tanks and armored weapons, and the producers of missiles and military aircraft. We can name companies, mostly based in the United States and Europe, which are some of the largest private companies in the world.

But behind this pattern of inertia and structural resistance to change, lies an even more perverse and pervasive pattern that I will call the pandemic of militaristic organization and mobilization and social authoritarian power structures that rely on the perpetration of military violence for the preservation of the hierarchical and asymmetrical order of nation states within the current world system.

Militarism is a very old story. Human beings frequently resort to organized forms of social violence to achieve their aims, protect their interests, and promote a stilted sense of communal solidarity and purpose.

It is not difficult to find numerous examples of such violence even in the most recent past or in the modern era. It is not unusual to find strong suggestion and evidence of inter-human violence in the fossil record. The history of human civilization is in fact mostly a bloody history of military conquest and destruction of one group of people by another.

Anywhere we go we can find corrupt governments backed by even more corrupt military people in control of entire nation states. Wars occur globally with a regular and expectable frequency.

It is necessary to understand that militarism is a kind of social pathology, a disease of the body politic that leads to a destructive orientation and eventual destruction. It must be understood also that, anthropologically speaking, authoritarianism is a panhuman pattern structurally characteristic of all developed social systems, and that it begets patterns of parasitic corruption and violence that result in obstructing positive social innovations.

Authoritarian power structures are all similarly characterized. They are anti-democratic and aggressive in establishing their own prerogatives at the expense of many others. More extreme forms shade off into dictatorship and oligarchic totalitarianism.

Poverty must be construed as a by-product and result of the dominance of authoritarian power structures in the world. If democracy begets economic growth and development, then it is clear that its opposite leads to stagnation and depression. Endemic poverty is the result of the chronic lack of access to basic resources, the lack of social productivity, and in the larger framework, the unequal distribution of productive resources and their by-products.

This uneven distribution is so pervasive and becoming so acute that in the underdeveloped countries, mostly those that belt the equator, there has emerged a permanent underclass of dispossessed people who increasingly dwell in absolute poverty.

<u>Earthbound Perspectives</u>

Poverty is also a vicious cycle and has its own internal mechanisms that aggravate patterns of endemic impoverishment. Endogenous ethnocultural patterns become established among the poor, in exogenously reinforced frameworks of structural inequality and exploitation, including a pattern of secondary gain, that leads to their perpetually reinforced dependency and structural inferiority within the confines of the larger systems. Poverty is a major problem because the poorest people in the world are also the largest source of population growth in the world.

The rich can blame the poor for the problems of the world, but along the way the rich must also acknowledge their strategic roles in the larger system and in the maintenance and administrative articulation and status quo of its structural inequities.

It is the structural imbalance and unevenness of the global system that is the primary exogenous factor producing poverty in the world today. Of course, poor people most often require authoritarian and military-style management, that asymmetrical requirements therefore justifies the pattern of authoritarianism and militarism in the world.

It is logical to conclude that development as we know it, is the final issue of consideration. It is held by many that only through development can we solve the problems of poverty and inequality in the world. But it has been recognized lately that development in the modern style that has most often disregarded the land and nature as an inherent natural resource base, has led to the systematic destruction of the environment.

At the same time, such development that disregards human development as little more than a productive resource to serve technology, also produces the basic structural asymmetries in knowledge, technologies and in the capacities for people to apply knowledge effectively to their adaptation in a changing global environment. This reinforces the asymmetry between the rich and poor, so that promotion of development is mostly a catch-22 benefiting a few at the expense of the many.

The global imperative is that the human system is now a complex one and is reaching levels of systemic super-criticality.

Comparatively minor and fundamentally unpredictable events can cause random underdetermined chain-reactions that spread and take their own course in destabilization of the larger system. The extent and consequence of these minor events affecting the profile of the overall system is unknowable, but they can be expected to occur with an increasing prevalence and frequency.

We cannot know how much the increasing super-criticality of the global system is being offset by factors of economic growth and integration and technological development that serve to stabilize the world system under its own mass, population momentum and complexity.

Whatever the actual case may be, it is inarguably clear that the entire set of problems of the global imperative describe a complex vicious cycle in that negative and counter-productive patterns reinforce violence and destruction, and positive actions tend to become precluded at birth. But the world changes in its own way. The same technologies that may enslave humankind to its own vicious system can also liberate us from ourselves.

The challenges are set down now clearly before us. The means to respond effectively has also been laid at our doorsteps but deserves and demands explication. Now it is time for us to think about these issues and then to act in a decisive manner.

Chapter 2: Cultural Selection and the Human Succession

To understand the history of the earth is to understand that it has witnessed a continuous succession of one natural regime of life after the other. Seas and oceans turn into swamps that become deciduous forests and then turn into deserts. Mountains gradually lift and slowly erode away and decay as continents imperceptibly shift and large land shelves sometimes shake.

Within each succession, there occurs a gradual biological pattern of extinction and speciation--new forms of life and selective regimes emerge in the new suite of changes and old forms of life based on previous adaptive patterns slowly give way and disappear.

The mountains, forests and farmlands that we know today were not the same ones of even a thousand years ago. Pine is replaced by spruce and cedar, spruce by willows, willows by slower growing hardwood trees.

Species of animal also constantly come and go on the global stage. We cannot know what the average life span of a species might be. Some say about four or five million years, but drawing a clear boundary around a species is difficult to do in space, much less through time.

The human species has emerged as the one dominant form of life on earth today. Second place must either go to rats, cockroaches, or some incurable virus, if that is even a life form.

We have attained our "God-given" place on the Great Chain of Being, but that is about all we really do know. The human species is not yet totally free of the vicissitudes of the laws of natural selection. Human extinction is perhaps an even greater possibility in the modern era than it had been at any time previously in its natural history.

The species of Homo sapiens is yet a biological being and cannot survive independently or separated completely and artificially from the nature that we have so sought to dominate and control. In our obsession and compulsion to exclude death from our own lives, we have so squashed nature into square holes that we have run the risk of cutting ourselves off completely from the natural foundation of our own being in the world and, hence, of our very survival in that world.

Like all masters, we are dependent and tied to the very thing that we attempt to dominate and control. We cannot do without nature without ourselves also perishing in the process. Therefore, if we destroy nature, we destroy ourselves, and it is this conclusion that makes of our late destructive efforts on earth a form of ultimate self-destruction.

The critical factor in understanding the natural history of the human species is our capacity for cultural adaptation to the natural environment. The original function of culture and its reason for emergence in the evolution of humankind was that it facilitated human survival, reproductive success and, eventually, our physical domination upon earth.

It is somewhat foolish of some "bio-cultural" anthropologists who seek biological foundations to our cultural patterning to ignore the vast prehistoric and historic evidence that points not to a pattern of biological determinism, that is what humankind left behind when our ancestors emerged from the cave, but to a pattern of non-hereditary cultural determinism.

Nature does not determine directly humankind or our social patterning. Humankind is increasingly determining nature and nature's biological patterning, even if often inadvertently and mostly in a myopic manner.

The term "world openness" has been applied to the human species as one of its key characteristics—behaviorally we have been freed from the fetters of nature, from its instinctual imperative, by the fact of our brains, our language and our cultural patterning. We have been permitted to reconstruct our environment to suit exclusively our own needs for survival.

It is this same pattern of cultural determinism that is at work today in driving modern human civilization and our predominance on earth as a single species.

So much has this happened that through our science we have gained control of evolution its self. We are now even manipulating the genetic codes of many species without regard to the long-term forces that produced these codes in the first place.

It is not to pass judgment on this process as good or bad. It is to state only that it is happening, and that it is an inevitable result of human nature to artificially manipulate and control their natural environments in ways that are fundamentally not the same as animal nature. We have gradually replaced natural selection with a process of cultural selection

Cultural selection can be found in the domestication of plants and animals. It was practiced even before this period with mammoth hunting and shellfish gathering that led to massive shell Middens, and mass kill sites of the largest game.

Cultural selection is an influence of human activity on the processes of natural selection on other species. It is also a process that has affected the evolution of the human species itself. We have turned the processes of cultural selection upon ourselves even more than we have practiced it upon other species. This has led to both our own destruction and our successful proliferation.

Cultural selection has been the single most important determinant that has led to the predominance of the human species upon earth, and the ultimate control the human race has on life itself. It has led to what can be called the era of hominid or global hominid succession.

This succession even has meant that whatever else nature has been doing, especially in the past millennium, it has had to yield increasingly to the encroachments and demands of a human-made world—an artificial world of concrete, asphalt streets, plastic factories, fences and pollution.

It is indeed absurd and hypocritical to continue to formulate policies and theories of genetic determinism and bio-cultural selection driving human social patterning while in daily life depending upon the very agencies and faculties of our own cultural construction and selection.

To argue this case is to simply and blindly ignore the realities of a human-made world. It is equivalent to the hypocrisy of preaching creationism in class, while using the products of science to teach anti-scientific doctrines, computers, projectors, and microphones that are part of the exact same science that gave us evolutionary theory.

The long-term survival of the human species will depend foremost upon our being able to find our selves an adaptive niche or plateau in the larger natural order of life. If we do not create for ourselves such a position in life's web, then we are setting ourselves up for both the destruction of the environment, and of ourselves, because we are ultimately tied to this environment for our own survival.

Hopefully, this adaptive plateau will be characterized by zero-population growth of the human species, and by obtaining natural limits of growth of our socio-economic development, a form of development alternative to the kind that we have so far advanced. Success at this stage of human development will not be measured in the degree to that we have overcome our natural environments, but by our ability for long-term survival within a natural world.

We can only wish for a return to nature. The fact of the matter is that it will not happen, at least not in the way that we know or understand it to happen today. It will probably happen in a different way perhaps.

If we humans should finally drop the bomb upon ourselves, or if some new strain of hemophagic virus should become virulent and epidemic, then we can look forward to the rapid end of the human succession and the gradual return of a new selective regime of nature.

We can only fantasize what this new suite of natural life would be like. I can imagine a 1950s science fiction movie with the irradiated rise of giant, human-sized insects and chitinous creatures with the strength of bulldozers and the intrinsic viciousness of sharks, mass producing at a phenomenal rate while feeding on the remains of an irradiated and mutated human population.

Chapter 3: A Brief Natural History of Humanity

An encapsulated natural history of humanity on earth is not an easy thing to write. It might be better entitled a history of inhumanity but it has not just been one of violence. History proper begins with the invention of writing, and really takes off with the printing press in the mid-15th century.

But to give a true consideration of humankind on earth we must push back the biological clocks at least 5 or 6 million years. Fossil evidence is gradually accumulating that point towards a divergence of a distinctly hominoid line at about this time. Interestingly, the first uniquely human trait to emerge at this time was the characteristic of bipedalism—that humans could walk, trot and run long distances on two feet, and did not need to use their knuckles or palms to help them keep balance.

This is an evolutionary feat. We can look to special brain structures in the medulla oblongata and the cerebellum that permitted this specialized activity to occur with an automatic sense of reflex and yet by virtue of our own voluntary power.

Quasi-tropic traits are those that exhibit a remarkable degree of plasticity and yet that affect to some extent the biological conditioning and subsequent evolution of the human species.

Coupled with bipedalism, there were three other sets of traits— freeing of the hands to perform other, more complex functions than trotting and climbing in trees; freeing the mouth to function in other ways than as an organ for eating and biting; and freeing of our eyes to scan and take in a wider horizon and broader field of view than is possible with our noses to the ground.

Though half facetious, this second set of traits is coupled with the emergence of other cerebral brain structures—special locations like Broca's area for speech and language apprehension, occipital regions for detailed visual pattern recognition, and the emergence of hand-eye coordination that permit wonderful feats of manual and pharyngeal dexterity.

It is clear that language was not a bio-cultural miracle—an all or nothing occurrence to have suddenly burst on the evolutionary scene with one mutated Eve. It probably emerged gradually as an increasingly sophisticated system of calls, names, and hand gestures.

Of course, perhaps Neanderthal and archaic Homo sapiens were more guttural than their modern descendants. Perhaps they didn't have the full vowel range or a complete set of consonants, but their language systems were otherwise no less deficient in basic communication needs than are our own today.

In time language was indispensable because it made survival easier and it therefore hung around a long time, promoting larger brains. Those who communicated best tended to be those who more readily apprehended the dangers of their world and responded more intelligently.

Selection favored the talkers. Another pattern that probably emerged 2-3 million years ago was one of gradually increasing infant dependency and slower development of human growth. This is another kind of those quasi-tropic traits that only interest anthropologists.

It is really a hen or egg kind of question. Longer periods of infant growth and dependency enabled longer, more complex learning that in time enabled bigger brains. Rapid selection for bigger brains was obviously the rage at this time, as there is a tremendous increase in cranial capacity from 4-500 cc. up to a phenomenal 1500-1600 cc. This increase appears to be steady and lineal, and points to the fact that something important was happening during the "stable" period of Homo erectus.

Related to this emergence was the wide adaptive radiation of hominid species. For the first time our precursors were to be found in large numbers out of the African continent, and in far-off places like Asia and the Pacific.

Also associated with this period is the distinctive use of flaked and chipped stone tools. The chopper chopping tool complex characteristic of the Chinese remains suggests that the adaptive radiation occurred at a fairly early period, and this tradition took its own course of development.

<u>Earthbound Perspectives</u>

Evidence has arisen that modern Homo sapiens began populating the earth about 80 to 50 thousand years before present, and relied heavily upon watercraft by which to do it.

Archaeologists tend to be rather conservative and data bound in their conjectural constructions of human prehistory. They tend to want to keep dates and achievements as proximal to the present as possible.

To grant the development of an extensive network based upon common adaptation to shared water-ways as a secondary mechanism driving early cultural development is something that Archaeologists in general are not prone to do.

To build a hypothetical reconstruction of such a waterways system when most of the evidence is washed away with the tides is anathema to building the past from the depths of the ground.

Nevertheless, archaeological evidence of the early peopling of the Southeast Asian Archipelago, the Australian continent and the New World, suggests that waterways had to be effectively breached in mass. It also suggests that long distance trading mechanisms had long been in place that may have indirectly integrated many regions of the globe.

The rise of pristine agricultural civilizations in the last 10 thousand years, and especially in the last five Millennium, were indirectly the by-products of an earlier and more extended period of waterway adaptation that circumnavigated the globe and that probably reached back a previous 30 thousand years in time, perhaps culminating sometime in the late Neolithic when sea-levels had reached their lowest levels.

The subsequent historical spread of technological civilization is common knowledge. It is enough to remark that by and large the conventional history of humanity has been a bloody military history of imperial conquest and colonial subjugation, and gradual emancipation of both the spirit, the minds and bodies of humanity from the social constraints and cultural bounds of its own making.

Perhaps we turn against nature with such fervor and zealous violence because we cannot really turn against our selves and our own cultural machinations. Nature and the fallacy of naturalization, a form of reification or misplaced concretization, is also a way of symbolically displacing and legitimating on a very basic level the fact that our cultural realities are of our own making.

Human cultural history has also been a long buried history of endless trial and enduring tribulation, of failure and folly, of ignorance and prejudice. We see only the few humanistic glories and scientific successes in the march of humankind like landmarks scattered along a distant road of broken backs and littered bodies and bones. This road has been built upon the back of nature.

It is necessary mainly to point out that the basic acculturative processes of civilization are trans-cultural, or acculturative, and trans-national in nature, and they are fundamentally irreversible in their largely unintended historical consequences except through total destruction. Once societies acquire a new invention or innovation that is beneficial, they will not willingly give it up.

The sweeping changes now being created by the advent of semi-conductor technology will penetrate and cause permanent changes in all of the furthest corners of the globe, and it will not all be monopolized by one computer software Mogul.

We cannot predict the exact consequences of this new technological transition. This information revolution has the effect of changing the developed parts of the world as much as they are altering the undeveloped. Its impact will be felt in almost every aspect of our daily and shared lives, and will reach symbolically deep into our conscious and unconscious life. But we can expect that the world will inevitably change for both better and worse.

Chapter 4: The Population Bomb and Global Circumscription

The main sign of the success of the human species is of course the size of its population. How big are we? The world has just recently celebrated the birth of baby 6 billion in Sarajevo, as officially announced by the United Nations, but there is something suspect and false about this business.

The statistics and methods are strangely secret--the lack of real evidence betrays a reality of false reporting. We honestly do not and cannot really know how many people there are, though we have been well over 6 billion and we, the human species, are probably in fact quickly approaching 7 billion.

We must understand the geometric aspects of this natural growth curve. At the time of the birth of the United States, in 1776, there was estimated to be about 2 billion people on earth. By the year 2012 we will be over passing the 7-8 billion mark. By 2050 C.E. global human population is expected to reach 9 billion.

Many claim now at the dawn of the 21st Century that there is no cause for concern. Many say now that the early 1970s "Limits to Growth" study with six billion as the human carrying capacity of the earth was in fact a very small number. Many put the old Malthusian theorists who make pronouncements of the population explosion as unrealistic dooms-day criers.

The total number of humans to have lived on earth is put at 70-80 billion, but we cannot really know this as well. We do not know how populated the prehistoric world was. Take the New World for example—population estimates for the pre-contact Americas vary from 2 to 20 million souls. We might apply this principle of variation to almost every region on earth in not so deep time..

The problem of population is that large numbers of people simply do not go away. Humans live for years, not just for months. Physiologically speaking, they all have about the same nutritional and medical requirements. If they do not eat enough protein or consume enough calories, they will suffer malnutrition. If they eat too much fat or carbohydrates, they will suffer over-nutrition.

The central problem of a large population is that of feeding itself, reproducing itself and surviving to a ripe old age. Invariably, populations will stress the environment in critical ways. Larger and larger populations must venture further and further a field to obtain the necessary resources to sustain the population and its growth rate.

In a global system, a huge population stresses the global environment, such that demands of large populations in one corner of the globe can have large effects on populations in other regions. Now the huge population of the Han Chinese, probably 1/5th of the world's total population, is also probably one of the least innocuous upon the world system—to a great extent its population is self-contained and self-subsistent.

It imports little rice and grain from other countries, unlike the United States whose much smaller population consumes a much greater proportion of the global natural resource base. But it is clear that no human population, in large enough size, can be inconsequential or entirely innocuous upon the earth's environment.

Relatively small populations—the 270 million in the United States and the 100 million or so in the commonwealth countries and in Japan (as of 2000 CE), are probably the world's greatest consumers, and thus their demands and needs can have far reaching global impacts greater even than those much younger and larger fast-growing populations of poorer nation-states and less developed regions of the world.

With development, we can talk about a concomitant need-inflation that is the result of increasing patterns of consumption and integration. Inflation of needs results from increased patterns of material and resource consumption and in turn leads back to increasing patterns of consumption. This pattern is fueled by increased development. It is a predictable pattern of global economic integration, and the human revolution of rising expectations.

This means that with increasing population in the world, coupled with increasing development, there will accompany the population explosion a resulting "revolution of rising expectations," especially when this is fostered and fueled by the mass communications media and by the global information revolution.

This revolution of rising expectations will also lead to greater revolutions of equality as more and more dispossessed poor people of adult-age begin demanding a greater place in the global system and a greater, more proportionate share of the earth's available resources.

It is doubtful that birth control in the form of voluntary and family planning programs are as effective as they ought to be. Religious resistance to such programs and basic ethno-cultural values of kinship that place a premium on childbirth help to demote such programs in some of the poorest and most populous regions of the earth.

Death control is an alternative strategy, but there is even greater moral resistance to its systematic implementation. As far as death control is concerned, medical developments in general are gradually but steadily prolonging the life expectancy of adults in most parts of the world, and rapidly lowering rates of infant mortality.

Death control may well take its own direction in a larger framework as new diseases born of human social patterns spread and cause their damage. The final or lasting effect that this form of natural death control takes cannot be known or estimated.

The plague in Europe and European-based diseases in the New World during the contact and post contact periods were significant factors in the massive reduction of these populations, far more than any wars, natural disasters or other forms of human violence.

Weapons of mass destruction make the prospect of death control by human violence increasingly expectable, especially when combined with the growing likelihood of political conflict and competition for resources indirectly resulting from both population growth and uncontrolled development.

Proliferation of weapons of mass destruction has been occurring on a large scale for the last half century, and this process is proceeding rapidly. It is in the long run an inevitable consequence. The paradox is that these weapons are now falling into the hands of leaders in some of the politically least stable regions of the earth.

It is hoped that increasing socio-economic development and integration will stabilize the world against this sort of violence. At the same time, there is an inherent deterrent value in the use of weapons of mass destruction because in general everyone is killed and there is no clear discrimination between allies and enemy.

On the other hand, there is an increasing potential for the use of such weapons in acts of terrorism that remain essentially beyond any political control. Terrorism is clearly waxing on the global horizon, as small, unstable and radical groups realize a greater potential to affect politics by random acts of violence.

A World War III that dwarfs the scale of destruction of all previous wars on earth cannot be predicted but this remains also a possible outcome of current patterns of military development.

The population explosion is not something that happens suddenly—not even in one night or even in one year. It will transpire gradually and perennially, over a period of two decades or so (2050). It will culminate in a climactic set of events that will most likely be violent and destructive. Thus it is an internal implosion event of the global system more than a literal explosion.

The real consequence of human over-population is that over-population is not just a local or even regional kind of event. It is a global phenomenon and is beginning to have real global consequences. As its result, we can refer to the phenomenon of increasing global circumscription—the human species over reaching its limits of growth everywhere and anywhere, and suffering the increasing restrictions, privations and consequences of this situation.

These limits will be felt increasingly in many different ways. We can look to an average decrease in the quality of life for most people—loss of opportunity, greater competition for even minor or trivial resources, etc.

At the same time, we can expect an even greater and growing disparity of class inequality between the richest and poorest people on earth. Not only will the number of poor people increase, but the wealth of the rich will also increase and become more concentrated in the hands of the few.

This is perhaps an inevitable process, as there exist no structural mechanism in place to prevent or compensate from its occurrence. The current capitalist world system is founded on basic structural inequalities of global resource distribution that were rooted to an earlier period of colonial imperialism. The post-colonial era has served the interests of the old masters economically. Only global scale warfare can alter the basic profile of these structural relationships.

At the same time, development efforts in the underdeveloped regions of the earth where the greatest and poorest concentrations of people are found, continue to run up against the perennial obstacles of corruption, cronyism, and nepotism that is the consequence of the control of authoritarian power structures.

The foreign policies of state of the developed nations do little to promote democracy in the third world. In fact, first world nations deliberately encourage the status quo of authoritarian regimes, as this tends to reinforce the larger status quo of the system with all its structural inequalities.

It leads to certain kinds of basic contradictions of the global system. The developed countries can enjoy the freedom of democracy because they are developed and wealthy enough to do so. The undeveloped countries must continue to suffer the tyranny of violence and authoritarian control because they are undeveloped. Certain powerful religious organizations are also implicated in this process.

Underlying this theory is the hypothesis that economics is a principle determinant of other structural and political patterns. Alter the profile and patterning of the distribution and utilization of basic resources, and you must concomitantly alter the political and social organization of the society in question.

The paradox is that before one can alter the basic profile of resource distribution on a global level, one must first change the pattern of resource-control that leads back to the question of global politics and social structuration.

Chapter 5: Global Environmental Circumscription

The second major dilemma faced by humankind at the dawn of the Third Millennium is the increasing amount of human impact on the natural environment of earth. Global circumscription of the natural environment is an increasingly apparent reality.

Many will argue that this impact is negligible and therefore relatively unimportant, just as they argue that human population is not really a major issue.

But global circumscription that is reducing our natural resource base very rapidly, and that is causing permanent loss of other environmental resources, as well as ecological disequilibrium, remains a persistent and increasing problem that cannot be honestly denied or forever avoided without dire consequences for all of humankind.

The critical issues of environmental destruction includes, in general:

> 1. The question of global warming, that seems to have been occurring at a steady rate at least since active monitoring began in the late 1950s.

> 2. The question of the bottleneck and loss of species diversity and the replacement of natural habitat for natural selection processes by human-made or artificial habitat.

> 3. The pollution, damage and permanent destruction of these natural habitats and the permanent loss of non-renewable resources available within these habitats. Desertification and soil loss are a part of this third dilemma, but we can also point to the eventual depletion of accessible petroleum and coal deposits, and the destruction of natural forests worldwide.

Global warming is not a certain trend. Long-term weather and climactic trends are difficult to determine. But the evidence of the melting glaciers and polar ice caps, rising sea levels and the increasing turbulence of the weather—unexpected draughts, unusual flooding, multiple hurricanes—all these patterns suggest that there has been a general shift in the global weather pattern towards gradual but steady increases in average annual temperature.

The case for global warming is mostly a case against the fossil-fuel industry, upon which the global economy runs. The burning and manufacturing of petrochemicals produces a number of gases that are toxic to nature, but it is not a clear case. Sea water levels are gradually rising each year.

On the other hand, nature may also have built-in mechanisms that serve to arrest or balance the patterns produced by humans, except that we perhaps may chronically debilitate these natural capacities by our development and deforestation.

The situation of global warming points directly to the dramatic effects of the human impact on nature, and that is the destruction of the natural ecosystems of the global environment.

We are now in a mass extinction event. We do not need to wait for another large meteorite to fall to the earth to wipe out the majority of mammals on earth. We are doing that ourselves. Of course the only species left to be wiped out by a natural global event would be the human species itself.

The destruction of the rain forests is the primary example of this damage assessment of human civilization, though it is not the only form that this destruction takes. The rain forest habitat is recognized as the richest and most diverse set of natural ecosystems on earth.

It is a concentration of life teeming with bio-diversity. The largest rainforest region is the Amazonian drainage system. This is followed by the rainforests of the island of Borneo and the numerous surrounding islands. These ecosystems have been ages in the making, but it has only been less than a century in its undoing.

The real loss this represents for science is the bottlenecking of the genetic totipotency of biological life on earth. As species pass into extinction with each passing year, natural habitat allowing for the speciation and production of new species is systematically removed to make room for pasturage, plantations and small farms, new roads, townships and hydroelectric projects, we lose irreplaceable biological information that is the product of billions of years of evolutionary history.

This loss of species diversity is critical, and can spell disaster for life as we know it, because it leads directly to the restriction of the ability of life in general to adapt evolutionarily and respond successfully in the long run to new changes and new environmental regimes. The factors that drive natural selection within a larger ecosystem are broken down. The ecological loss of this bio-diversity is a tragedy of the greatest proportions.

With the destruction of the natural environment and its rapid replacement with a humanly constructed one, the home for wild plants and animals is being destroyed.

Natural habitat loss is the single greatest contributor to the modern mass extinction of species on earth. Once disappeared, this natural habitat cannot simply or easily be repaired or replaced with an equally viable one.

Global circumscription is the unavoidable consequence of increasingly massive human population and the cultural impact on all natural environments. This impact occurs on many levels and is not completely understood. Indirectly it has been affecting even the remotest and least populous corners of the globe.

Circumscription is about the fragility and complexity of the relationship between the human species and its cultural adaptation and development and its natural contexts in the larger world.

It is about the ultimate finiteness and limitations of the natural earth and its resources, that limitations impose upper limits to both our cultural adaptation and our population growth.

The realization of those limits comes gradually but undeniably. As we strain these relationships we increase the risk of disturbing irreversibly not only the natural ecosystems upon which life on earth is made up, but also of destroying our own relationships and adaptability for survival in such systems.

Increasing global circumscription brings with it the realization of the natural limits of our human population growth and cultural development. We must learn to live within these limits and to abide by these limits if we are to continue in the world as both masters and stewards of all known life in the universe.

Chapter 6: Militarism

The history of warfare, and indeed most conventional history is de facto military history, is one of increasing scales of violence and involvement. All over the world, extensive evidence demonstrates unequivocally the basic social violence that human beings are prone to.

Almost all pristine civilizations were founded upon the rule of the sword over neighboring groups of people. Things have changed little, as science and technology has only made the killing more efficiently horrendous and impersonal.

Beyond seeing a military orientation, any military orientation, as a duty or an obligation, it is important to construe it as something else, as perhaps a necessary evil, but also as a kind of organized madness and culture of destructiveness that achieves no other purpose than death and destruction and that has no other function than promotion of the rule by violence.

In this matter, our armies are no better or worse than those of the enemy, as the end result remains the same. The necessity of war and of military styles of life entails a kind of tyranny of violence over people and over the natural world.

It must be acknowledged also that military organizations are for the most part unproductive and often even parasitical to the host society that supports it. Military organizations drain off expensive and precious resources, and tie these resources up as weapons and tools of violence and destruction--they produce nothing of lasting value.

This is maybe even truer in modern times than it was in early human history. The meaning of total warfare assumes larger and more grotesque and tyrannical dimensions with each succeeding generation.

This destruction extends beyond the bounds of human destruction to incorporate the massive destruction of the environment as well. Most governments, even the smallest and poorest ones, continue to spend the major portions of their national budgets on the purchase of new and expensive weaponry, resources that would be available and more wisely spent on more benevolent programs are drained away.

It is important to see militarism as a kind of social disease, a social pathology that affects groups of people with delusions and attitudes of in-group solidarity and out-group projection. Militarism is a product of human culture. It is a value system that is taught and learned and passed on from generation to generation.

That human beings have a proclivity towards violence, especially mass violence, is undeniable. This predisposition is well rooted in our deeper history, and suggests biological origins of the human species in contexts of competition and warfare.

The notion of militarism as a kind of social disease that has destructive consequences constitutes a kind of social theory about warfare and human violence. In this we must understand the patterns of socialization for aggression and enculturation of violence and tolerance of levels of violence.

Human aggression and violence are to be seen not so much as or only as innate instinctive drives. These basic drives have social direction, social definition, and cultural system, and are molded by cultural constraints, sanctions, rewards and incentives, that give it focus, meaning and tangibility in human behavior that it might not otherwise have.

How we show our aggression, and what we do with violence, and the tolerance and promotion for violence, is, in other words, culturally constructed and therefore also culturally malleable. It can be shaped in almost any direction that we wish to turn it to.

Organized and group violence as it is evinced in the modern form of warfare is different and separate from violent behavioral tendencies of individuals. The relationship between social patterns of violence and individual acts of violence is at best only indirectly and complexly related.

Militarism is a product of our social organization and social pressures to conformity. It is an institutionalized form of violence that, under special conditions, legitimates such violence on a massive scale. Underlying the military cult of violence is a kind of culturally embedded authoritarianism.

<u>Earthbound Perspectives</u>

It is a generalized worldview and belief system that power and force are intrinsically necessary and might makes right and that the world is indeed justly, inevitably ruled by the tyranny of force.

Militarism as a social disease is but one facet and symptom of a deeper sense of disorder that has long affected humanity. It comes through an emphasis on conformity to authority, especially forceful and potentially violent and punitive authority.

It also entails the de-emphasis and devaluation of the role and development of the individual in the world, especially as a naturally creative and independent being in the world.

In this sense, violence is a form of frustrated creativity that is innate to the human psyche—one that results in a compulsion toward destructive violence and a pathological preoccupation with control, death and the symbolic forms and results that violence takes.

In other words, human beings are so violent and destructive, not so much because they were born that way, but because they learned how to be this way as the result of their socialization, enculturation and integration into violent and warlike societies.

Human beings have an innate aggressiveness that is related to their sexual and creative drive. This aggressiveness can be sublimated to a great deal of productive and creative energy, but also it can otherwise be frustrated and rendered into something perverse and violent.

Military social organization and the mobilization for social aggression on whatever level or scale, entails the maintenance of certain ideological symbolic structures, of ethnocentrism, and of internal authoritarian power structures that are based on asymmetrical structural hierarchies.

It entails fostering and maintaining socially and subjectively on an impersonal level certain closed rigid and dogmatic mind-sets, values and worldviews that preclude alternate orientations or the possibility of adaptation or adoption of a greater variety of understanding.

It entails a kind of behavioral conditioning on lower order patterning of defensive mechanisms and response that preclude the possibility of more sophisticated and differentiated forms of response.

Humankind pays a heavy price for its social organization for violence in many ways. Not only do military organizations parasitically consume basic resources and expend energy and technology for fundamentally destructive and counterproductive purposes, but it also limits, constrains and distorts human development and the human resource base that is available to a society.

The paradox and dilemma of our orientation for social violence is that we require military style organization to effectively defend ourselves from other people and societies who adopt an aggressive, military way of life.

Pacifist appeals to a common humanity frequently do not work with madmen and totalitarian dictators as necrophiliacs who thrive on death and destruction. In a world where violence is always a very real and sharp-edged possibility, violence always begets more violence, and only the foolish and innocent fall victims to the conqueror's sword. Emancipation often entails taking up the sword to break the chains of bondage.

The real challenge therefore is how to effectively constrain military violence in the world and maintain sufficient but minimal defensive military organization in the world, without becoming the victims or servants of our own military predisposition or of others.

Furthermore, this must be accomplished on a global or trans-national level, and in a genuinely democratic way. This has not yet been accomplished except through rather imperialistic means of one nation or the other achieving hegemonic military control over the world.

Just as civilization has grown and advanced, so too has militarism, as a kind of social affliction of state civilization, also developed and evolved into a form much greater and in many respects more terrible than it has ever been before.

We do not anymore need to imagine the horrors of nuclear holocaust to see and feel the real power and terrorism of militarism. We can find it now even in conventional warfare that can be waged with pinpoint accuracy and extreme lethality from a safe, push-button distance.

Rarely any more do people need to engage in hand-to-hand combat and bloodletting to realize the consequences of warfare. Rarely now is combat confined only to a small group of professional soldiers. Usually modern warfare involves as its victims innocent children, average citizens and just about any body else who happens in harm's way. The weapons that have become more accurate, precise, long-range, and lethal in one way, have also resulted from and in their uses in a far less discriminating pattern of mass destruction involving "collateral damage."

Chapter 7: Authoritarianism

Authoritarianism is the psychosocial disposition of people to adopt a strong, anti-democratic and hierarchical disposition in relation to other people.

Authoritarianism is a fact of human nature and human culture. We are all potentially authoritarian and every society has aspects of authoritarian control in the world. In face, authoritarianism on some level is necessary if we are to live in an ordered and fair society, relatively secure and stable.

The human capacity for authoritarianism is derivative of the human capacity for aggression and for its compulsive repression, control and sublimation into other aspects.

Socially, it is the human capacity to control and manipulate others unfairly—a projection of our own compulsive repression, and a derivative function of structural asymmetry in society. It is a very deep-seated and fundamental aspect of human nature.

Authoritarianism has several aspects. Authoritarian people value conformity over individuality. They value strict punishment. They value shows of strength and brutal solidarity. Authoritarian personality tends to be dogmatic, closed minded and prejudiced towards out-groups.

Symbolically, they show strong attachment to and dependency upon external symbolism, especially in the concrete and literal sense. They show little capacity for abstraction, lateral thinking, or a tolerant attitude towards human differences.

Psychological authoritarianism refers to those personality characteristics that lean towards bigotry, prejudice, and hatred of out-groups, especially as measured upon the classic F-Scale inventories. Different varieties of authoritarian attitudes have been recognized based on response patterns to different kinds of attitudinal inventories.

Authoritarian character tends to be more compulsive than usual, and more egocentric. Also, they tend to be under-achievers in normal social life that means that they also tend to be afflicted with low self-esteem and a poor sense of social status and ego-identity, feelings that they frequently over-compensate for in seeking dominant positions in hierarchical structures of society.

Social authoritarianism refers to several recognizable types of government, most commonly found among undeveloped nations, in that rule is by a small autocratic oligarchy or even a single dictator, who is in control or is controlled by the military.

Authoritarian power structures refer to the pattern of authoritarian behavior accreting into administrative positions of power and prestige in governments tends toward monocratic rather than poly-cratic power structures.

Anthropological Authoritarianism must be understood as the cross-cultural and comparative aspects of alternative forms of authoritarianism in the world, and an elucidation of what can be considered the panhuman capacity and predisposition for authoritarianism, as well as the structural aspects of authoritarian social organization and socialization for authoritarianism that are shared by all societies on some basic level.

Authoritarianism as an inherent facet and distinctive patterning of humanity has not been studied as such by anthropologists, though many anthropologists have remarked upon and noted its occurrence and pattern in the larger world.

Authoritarianism can be said to be characteristic in one form or fashion of all societies on earth, although its expression and elaboration varies considerably between different cultures.

Some groups enhance and elaborate violence, social asymmetry and authoritarian tendencies, while others tend to play it down and suppress its expression culturally. There are many variable factors that influence its expression and historical development in society, and this creates a complex explanation for its occurrence.

Needless to say, studies of enculturation indicate that authoritarian patterns of socialization are deeply rooted to a particular cultural orientation, but vary systematically with other related factors in fairly expectable ways. Thus anthropological authoritarianism does have a more general paradigm of understanding, at least on a hypothetical and theoretical level.

Authoritarianism is not uncommon. In fact evidence suggests that in many circumstances it is the rule and not the exception, lending credence to the notion of Homo hierarchicus. People psychologically and socially tend towards the abuse of their power over other people when in positions of minor superiority or control. This is often unconscious, or at least unconsciously compulsive or motivated.

Authoritarian people tend to adopt certain ideological belief structures that symbolically reinforce and legitimate their attitudes and actions--these belief structures are characterized as closed-minded and narrow in focus, rationalizing and self-serving in expression, auto-compensatory and self-fulfilling in pattern.

Authoritarianism is a social patterning that is mostly the product of primary and secondary socialization, particularly, I believe, socialization for aggression. The predisposition to resort to violent aggression as a means of resolving conflicting issues is a suggestion of the lack of development of more sophisticated ego-control mechanisms that would otherwise effectively channel innate aggression and socially induced frustration in more constructive directions.

Authoritarianism is also culturally reinforced. Success based upon authoritarian characteristics is frequently rewarded in most state societies, even in contexts that are ostensibly open and democratic in orientation. People value symbolically the appearance of strength and dominance, even more than the cunning of intelligence and the wisdom of good temper.

Symbolic forms reiterated and frequently portrayed in the mass media appeal to a lowest common denominator that reflects this basic authoritarian orientation. Cultivation of non-authoritarian value orientations is marginalized and construed as a form of weakness and vulnerability. Thus it connotes, among other things, a predisposition to failure.

But the cultural reinforcement of authoritarian orientations is more basic and insidious than this. People do not need to be muscle-bulging weight lifters to be capable of blind and violent conformity to the narrow norms of a society. Violence and tolerance for violence is acquired and valued, often surreptitiously, within a society. It is a social psychological phenomenon of mass appeal that bypasses intellectual reason and appeals to the gut-level of instinctive aggression.

We can all secretly be supermen no matter how weak and plain we may really be, or no matter how perverted the expression of our secret desires may become. Thus we have cases of successful figures of society, obsessive-compulsive to the extreme, beating their wives, abusing their children, and committing violent atrocities to strangers.

The holocaust in Germany is only one example of many in the modern era when a supposedly rational and well-ordered society can run amok with authoritarian actions. It is perhaps the clearest modern example of how blind obedience to conformity can be fostered among children, women and otherwise good-hearted adults, and how, in the name of duty, this can be subverted to systematic evil. But this can happen to any society—no modern society is fundamentally immune to its possibility.

It is a paradox that the striving for competitive achievement that is an earmark of developed societies, tends at the same time to foster a kind of compartmentalized competitive authoritarianism that, in its extreme form, leads to an undercutting of achievement by the strength of compulsive repression that may especially hinder the higher-level development of cognitive-behavioral faculties.

Achievement must therefore be understood as a culturally defined, culturally sanctioned value. Being relative to its cultural construction, achievement is usually a social value on that one's ego-identity and status-identity in a society is based and rewarded through resource acquisition and opportunity.

The emphasis on achievement that is constrained in specific social settings and contexts, may preclude the development of other achievement orientations in alternative ways, and can result in the long run in a form of distorted or exaggerated achievement orientation that is driven by the fear of failure more than the desire for success.

Chapter 8: Socio-Structural Inequalities

Inequality is a fact of life. Many inequalities are rooted in nature and physical differences cannot be undone. To be born physically or mentally handicapped is a fact of life that cannot be simply reversed. Cultural practices and social institutions exist to either exacerbate the basic inequalities of life, or to attempt to reverse some of these basic differences between people to create a context for the realization of greater equality.

The concept of equality is, like that of human rights and human freedom, an ideal that exists as a possibility in the best of all possible worlds. It is like a perfect triangle—though rarely seen in nature, we cannot deny its mathematical and a priori truth. The source of this sense of equality, and its demand on earth, comes from the same source as does the understanding of human rights and freedoms.

It springs from the subjective experience of human suffering and from the sympathy we extend unselfishly to others. This inter-subjective capacity of human beings to share the experiences and feelings of others in the world is what separates us off as something more than mere animals. At the same time, because it is not necessarily innate or fixed by nature within us, it creates also the possibility of its denial and failure.

Equality is an ideology that is touted by almost all nations, but is realized in fact by very few. Absolute equality is an unrealizable ideal. The emancipation that human beings have struggled for through history and sometimes won was a greater degree of relative equality.

The realization of greater rights, freedoms and opportunities are for people who are in a structurally inferior position in a society and who perceive and believe these differences in their identity. The demand for equality often leads to the overturning or toppling of an entire state system, as happened in the French Revolution or later the Russian Revolution.

Social inequality is inevitable in a stratified state system, because state organization requires the concentration of administrative authority and the separation of classes along occupational and marriage lines.

It is inevitable in a stratified global system as well. To expect it can ever be otherwise is unrealistic. It is not a question of creating a completely fair system of total equality.

Such an attempt leads to dysfunctional and counterproductive communal experiments that fail in the long run either because they turn into totalitarian entities to "get the job done" or else nothing gets done because no one has the authority to enforce state decisions.

The central issue is a question though of creating relative conditions of greater or lesser equality in any one area, of constraining authority and the effects of authoritarian power and control in ever narrower margins, and of inducing the kinds of freedoms and cultivating the kinds of responsibilities in more parts of more people's daily lives, such that inequality eventually may become not so disparagingly blatant as it is today increasingly becoming.

The realization of the notion of equality is a relative one. We can speak of averages and relative degrees of equality achieved in any one situation or place, compared to other similar cases. But as relative deprivation, it underlies one worldview of social reference and relative idealism.

In order for equality to be realized more broadly on earth, it is necessary that we redefine our human identity of our selves and others in the world, to see past all the myriad differences of people, and to enlarge the symbolic scope of our sense of community to encompass all people on earth.

This entails relinquishing or at least playing down nationalistic and ethnocentric prejudices that place our own kind before others' interests and separate our selves and our communities from other people of other communities. This redefinition must be done on a broad global scale. It can only come from the realization of the basic humanity all people share.

Enlarging the circle of our shared identity in the world also entails that we expand our sense of self-identity as individuals in the world. We are not just exclusive members of any particular grouping of humankind, but on a basic and shared level we become implicit members of all groups.

We must become capable of seeing ourselves in many different kinds of people and of learning to walk in the moccasins of many roles and types. This entails that we must relinquish some of our basic compulsions and inhibitions that serve to restrict us and channel us along narrow self-serving pathways in life.

The realization of human equality in the larger world entails a realization that all people have both good and bad, that all people are equally capable of doing good and bad things in the world. We are none of us so innocent that we are free of guilt and responsibility to try better, and few of us are so guilty that we absolutely forfeit completely our rights to our humanity completely.

The notion of equality is an ideologically normative one, yet it is an unavoidable argument in human development. It is an ideal that we either regard as valuable or not. Even the writer of the Declaration of Independence and many of the framers of the US Constitution, some of the most important statements ever made about equality, kept slaves.

This was the basis of an unresolved issue over equality that led a hundred years later to a bloody civil war. The problem of inequality and equality is indeed a statement of the history of human civilization. Human civilization was to a great extent founded upon the blood and sweat of slaves and the inequities of involuntary servitude.

Slavery still exists, and involuntary servitude takes other uglier forms. Coercive structures that impel people to live and do things they would not otherwise do have changed with the rise of the world system. But coercion and exploitation of human labor and reinforcement of structural and social inequalities remains a fact of life in the beginning of the 21st Century.

It is important to separate the issues of social and structural inequality. Social inequalities are what one notices in everyday life in the class based distinctions and pretensions that so many people adopt in relation to one another.

Structural inequalities are more pervasive, more perverse and usually occur unnoticed in the backgrounds of our lives. They are the inequalities of opportunities, the impersonal and systematic discrimination based on category or quota, the inequalities of advantage, education, and information.

Altering the structural system that reinforces and creates basic inequalities in the world cannot constructively be accomplished overnight. Any major revolutionary change in this regard can only have consequences that are more destructive than constructive, and that may end in a system more tyrannically coercive and violence-based than even the current world order.

Reform of the structural system is had in small bits and pieces and is a cumulative process that begins in everyday life and in common places, extending itself gradually to a grand scale and momentum.

Different forms of equality are recognized. We can talk about political equality, social equality, economic equality, and ideological equality. Many regimes pay much lip service to ideological equality, but in fact promote programs of great actual inequality and violence.

A large proportion of humanity today lives in conditions of blanket ideological equality guaranteed by their state, when in fact the degree of totalitarian state influence and control is extreme.

Ideological equality in itself does little without the actual instantiation of equality on earth, but it does create the symbolic justification and presumptive preconception that is prerequisite to the greater realization of equality in the world.

The grant of one form of equality does not necessarily entail all forms. What we strive for is finding greater relative equality, while working for the realization of greater potential equality.

Authoritarian control can never be completely eliminated in state organized societies. It must be narrowly delimited and restricted in its scope and degree of control it may assert in our daily lives.

Without a doubt, greater equality cannot be achieved in the system until the tyranny and disease of violence and authoritarian power control is lessened in the world.

Greater human equality in the world cannot be realized until a world state is created that will provide the structural framework protecting and promoting such equality. As long as people remain divided into ethno-national groupings, there will be wars, totalitarianism and human inequality.

We can argue what form such a single world state should take, but without a doubt it must be democratically organized, for only in a genuinely democratic state where the average citizen is given political freedom to vote and decide independently, and powers of individuals are regulated and restricted by the fair and just rule of public law, can the setting exist that will allow the realization and expression of genuine human equality.

Chapter 9: Ethno-cultures
Acculturation, Differentiation, Stratification, Assimilation & Integration

Ethnoculture is the distinctive cultural identity situated in place and in period of time that defines itself at least in part in relation to other, alternative groupings.

It may in fact be a distinctive sub-grouping of a larger cultural identity—as per se a national culture or an ethno-national cultural orientation.

Ethnoculture tends to be local in orientation and distinguished by detailed traits commonly shared and acknowledged by the members of the grouping.

We all share some sense of ethnocultural identity and heritage that is in part what we inherit from our parents and grandparents, and also what is the consequence of our own histories and the impinging of the larger context on our everyday lives.

Ethnocultural identity often embodies some model of kinship and a familial framework that is core to its constitution and symbolic articulation in the world.

It is this relational network that makes ethnocultural identity such a basic part of our experience—so much so that we tend to accept it as natural or "God-given."

In fact, we are bound within our ethnocultural identity on very basic levels in our preferences, speech patterns, appetites, and aversions, and we cannot easily escape or forego these patterns even if we try to.

Ethnoculture is a concept of human identity that situates the individual as a social animal in the nexus of a web of interpersonal relations and a culturally defined context from the time of birth until final death.

Ethnocultural identity tends to be distinctive and unique for individuals and for different groups of people who share a suite of basic traits. It is inherently differentiating through time and across space, and leads to greater division and discrimination between people based on relatively minor and superficial qualities or characteristics.

Through our ethnocultural experience, our attitudes, views of the world and response patterns to our experience of the world are shaped and constrained in fundamental ways, and this mostly in an invisible way, and mysterious force in our lives largely pre-structures and determines the kinds of relationship we will maintain with the world throughout our lives. It situates us definitely in everyday life in both time and place. It locates us in certain, undeniable provenience of the stream of human life.

Why not culture and why ethnoculture. The name "ethnoculture" is not intended as a politically correct term or to highlight the notion of "multiculturalism." Ethnocultural studies are systematic and distinct—the subject and objects of their research are clear, and the methodologies that demarcate its sub-disciplinary boundaries are unique to it self.

Ethnoculture is to Cultural Anthropology as Ethno-history is to History writ large. Ethno-culture attempts an ethnographic description and ethnological explanation of a distinctive grouping of people primarily in endogenous terms the people's own terms, and particularly in relation of the prototypical individual to a larger context of relations with other groupings and in the identity of the group in literature.

At the same time, it seeks to locate the individual subjective experience in the framework of the larger historical and cultural realities impinging upon the group, as well as the range of both individual and group variation found within a particular ethnocultural orientation, both over time as well as across space.

Ethnocultural studies tend to be analytically detailed, systematic, engaged explicitly in minutia, as well as comprehensive and nonexclusive in scope, and integrative or systematic in framing the small in relation to the large. Its excoriation of meaning and information in the patterning of people's lives borrows much from the older paradigms of culture history and philology.

Ethnocultural differentiation is a natural process of groups to splinter and split apart and to define an essentially separate identity as against the host or parent body.

<u>Earthbound Perspectives</u>

Like the related processes of linguistic differentiation, ethnocultural differentiation is a natural process of cultural development. Because it is essentially an historical or what Boas would have called a cosmographic process, it is one that is complex and un-predetermined.

Ethnocultural differentiation is contrastive to the larger historical processes of acculturative fusion and assimilation that occurs especially when more powerful or cosmopolitan societies come into contact and relation with more closed and localized groupings.

Transculturation processes of human civilization also tend to run against the grain of more normal and "natural" processes of ethnocultural differentiation. The uni-dimensional culture of modernization is an example of how very different groups of people will converge on certain specific traits because of their common sharing within a larger global exchange system.

At some level, people are still prone to go to fight with one another over minor symbolic or cultural differences, because competition and group identity dictates conflicting relations between groups, even if in fact they share common language, clothing, cars, etc.

That the concept of ethnoculture may be important to understanding our Global Imperative has escaped the critical notice of most people, though wars of increasing violence based mostly upon ethnic difference and differences of ethnocultural values such as religious belief, are still occurring and are quite persistent.

Ethnocultural differentiation and stratification are in fact occurring at a greater rate than ever before, and we are having to bear more and more directly the consequences of this increasing human pluralism in the world.

Most of this differentiation is politically organized from above by a few elite who seek dominance and exclusive control over a narrow resource base, and are contrived by vested interests who attempt to mobilize groups based on their sense of ethnic identity and solidarity.

Differences between people become highlighted and marked as boundary maintenance mechanisms. Groups work together to provide mutual advantage, often at the expense of well-defined out-groups. Thus, ethnic stratification has become a new kind of political-social-economic game of manipulating peoples worldviews, attitudes and actions for some kind of gain in the larger world.

At the same time, the possibility and potentiality for increasing integration within the global system also presents itself in world society. The possibility for overcoming prejudices and discrimination based on the ethno-schismogenesis and exaggeration of in-group/out-group boundaries is much greater as people can more freely share their own subjectivity to a broader range of people via the Internet.

People hold dearly, often violently, to their parental cultures, especially when they feel these are threatened by rapid change or by the presence of alternative out-groups they little understand. These feelings of intense attachment and identity are very fundamental in our self-awareness, and these often lead to great violence in the world.

Ethnocultural stratification can be referred to as the long-term structural relations that are established between different ethnocultural groupings of people, especially when these relations tend to be asymmetrical in structure and non-reciprocal in a political or economic standpoint. Ethnocultural stratification tends to be diagonal and it occurs as much within ethnocultural groupings as between different or distinct ethno-cultures.

Ethno-classes are sub-groupings within a society that distinguish themselves by the interconnections between class and ethnocultural identity—members of the same general ethnoculture may be separated nonetheless by occupying different class categories or profiles.

Ethnocultural assimilation refers to the process of the absorption of one ethnocultural grouping or its traits by another, often dominant grouping, and by the loss of identity of the original ethnocultural orientation and the adoption of the ethnocultural patterns of the dominant group.

Ethnocultural acculturation refers to the process of exogenous borrowing and change that is the result of contact between different ethnocultural groupings in time.

Ethnocultural shock is the result of sudden loss of original or support ethnocultural contexts, as with immigration, refugees, or destruction in the face of natural disaster or human aggression.

Ethnocultural integration is the process of creolization between different ethnic groups, often entail intermarriage, or amalgamation, or the mutual symbiotic coexistence in a common setting of two or more ethnocultural groupings, often exchanging or sharing affinities with one another.

Ethnocultural aggression & conflict is frequent and often very bloody. It is rooted in hate and intolerance that defines prejudice and ignorance about others. It is rooted in stereotypes that dehumanize the other as something less than human. It is rooted in structural competition for resource that can appear to threaten the survival of a grouping. It is rooted in a demand for group solidarity and conformity that excludes all possibility of alternation and that seeks to reinforce its boundaries by targeting out-groups as a rallying point.

It is true that ethnocultural violence is not waning in the modern world, but is actually on the increase as more and more people come into collision and competition in the global market place.

Chapter 10: World Systems—Open and Closed

It is commonly understood and acknowledged that we live within what has been defined as a capitalist world system, dominated by the core countries of the United States, Britain, Japan, and France. We can consider it on a grand level as a kind of economic imperialism in that foreign policy and economic trade relations are reinforced through trade sanctions, embargoes, etc., and sometimes even through the use of military intervention.

The actual extent of development of the World System remains somewhat questionable. Only several communist countries remain effectively outside of this system, and there are a few "rogue" or pariah states as well that do not function fully within the framework of the system.

The global system itself is largely an undetermined one, as much as the major players like the United States, Japan and Great Britain, would like it to be otherwise. This means that ultimate control over its development is largely absent, and no single entity has achieved a complete monopoly of control in the international arena. In fact, from a political and an economic standpoint, it is very much a chaotic system that frequently runs out of control.

What drives this global system? First, a huge and powerful military with state of the art weapons technology, and a near monopoly by the core nations on nuclear power and nuclear weapons technology. Secondly, there is a heavy, almost exclusive dependence on fossil-fuel technology that drives development and powers the heavy industry of the system.

Third, the First world countries effectively maintain academic and government-sponsored leadership in science and technology, in particular, now the vanguard of the information revolution and the biological revolution.

Fourth, a well established banking and credit system that has been focused within the industrialized nations and has served to concentrate a vast amount of wealth and control of resources in certain core places.

The world system is in fact not a new thing. Previous world systems have been around a long time ago. These systems are often construed as imperial civilizations, and indeed they have frequently been so.

The traditional Colonial European Kingdoms—first Portugal, Spain, England, France and the Netherlands, vied for power and control on the high seas, in the frontiers of the New World and in the spice markets of the Old World.

Later, with industrialization, this developed into another kind of system in that raw materials came from the colonial entities to be transformed into commodities in the home markets.

The modern World System is the by-product of two world wars, a long Cold War that is not quite finished, and a shifting arrangement of socio-political and economic allegiances and treaties between the many nations of the world.

In the modern system, Japan and Germany, albeit transformed through reconstruction as democratic entities, compete successfully with the old established ex-colonial superpowers. New up and coming nations enter into the competition for global markets and resources, albeit in lower-class positions.

The current world system is characterized by economic structural integration in the face of ethno-national stratification and increased differentiation between groupings of people. This lower level ethno-cultural differentiation can be understood to be related to class closure at the upper strata of this system, through economic opportunities and marriage patterns.

This partial closure of the global system entails, among other things, that social mobility from the lower to the upper levels are extremely controlled and circumvented by a variety bureaucratic and authoritarian mechanisms, and that symbolic identification within the system must be in other forms than that of achievement in terms of competition.

Ethno-national identities are competing common interest groups that utilize their internal networks as leverage for achieving mobility within the system. Symbolic identification and constraints at the group level preclude individual participation of the members in a larger framework of resource competition.

Principal competitors are construed as alternative ethno-national groupings, and not as the overarching controlling interests, that are, for the most part, effectively invisible in most contexts of everyday life except in very marked circumstances.

At the same time, structural integration is marked by a kind of economic acculturative assimilation of modern values that are defined and dictated by the global market economy. Like ethnic stratification at the bottom, economic assimilation into the system encourages and enforces ties of dependency upon the normal structural relations of the system.

Unequal and non-reciprocal ties that tend on average to systematically disadvantage the poor in relation to the wealthy. The poor are taught daily through the commercial hype of the mass communication media that they must emulate the life-styles of the rich to achieve status, success and happiness. Indeed, even the core values of what it is to be beautiful, rich, and successful, are manipulated by this same system.

Though the world system is a powerful one, it is by no means an infallible or absolute system. It remains basically open-ended and unfinished though it is also highly uneven and structurally unbalanced in favor of the elite. However powerful or asymmetrical in its structure, the World System is in fact a self-organizing one and is, in the structure of the long run, a basically unstable one.

It is composed of no single nation or entity that has enough strength to enforce a confederation of nations. It is an increasingly complex system and economic integration entails crosscutting interdependencies between different nations that can both enhance stability and at the same time lead to super-criticality. In such an environment relatively minor events can create chain-reactions spanning the globe that can result in major systemic reactions.

The basic structural openness of the world system can be both a boon and a bust for its continuation in the long-term. Destabilization and break down can occur relatively rapidly, but the economic costs would be tremendous and inhibiting.

On the other hand, its openness permits a degree of flexibility that allows new nations and new organizations to come into the center of the stage for control and competition. This can be both stabilizing and destabilizing, but it does entail that the so-called "world system" might adapt itself to new arrangements in the long run.

World systems are nothing new. What is new is the extent and actual global qualities characteristic of the new world system.

Most of the globe is being effectively integrated at some level and in some way into the global system, and this system is a modernizing one that entails a foundation of sharing of basic technological amenities and worldviews whatever else the differences of culture, language and worldview. Only a few regions on earth today are beyond the reach or purview of this system.

Structural integration of the world into a single system is inevitable and will continue to happen. The possibility for its break down and for World War is also always present in the background and complex chaos of the system.

It is up to ourselves in the final analysis to determine that kind of system we wish to establish for ourselves on earth, and how much control and power we are willing to grant it over our lives.

If we do not act soon to decide these issues, the likelihood of the long run is that somebody else will decide for us, and then the results will probably be less than satisfactory for most people on earth.

The potential benefits of structural integration of the world far surpass the advantages of maintaining competitive and conflicting national differences and promoting ethno-schismogenesis in the world.

The costs of ignoring the imperative of global integration are simply too great. Indeed it is also a part of our global imperative, that we must in the long run pay the price of greater human inequality and suffering in the world.

236

Part II—Basic Principles and Progress

A better world in the 21st Century begins within our selves, and extends systematically out through our families, our communities and our homelands to encompass the entire globe. New technologies offer us new opportunities to realize greater freedoms and greater human potential in the world today. The realization of greater freedom and human productivity is directly related to enhanced global development and to democratization of human society.

At the same time, the potential for greater realization of human potential also entails a concomitant realization of greater individual and social responsibilities to act in an appropriate and adaptable manner, both in relation to one another and in relation to the earth itself. Our imperative is to change or to perish. The destruction of the earth's habitat is the destruction of humankind on earth. The earth is our home, and we have become its stewards.

Chapter 11: Alternative Development

The future of the world is open-ended and underdetermined by the current powers that be. It can turn in any one of many possible directions. It can lead humanity to disaster, that is the greater likelihood if we continue in our current modes of adaptation unaltered, or it can lead us the realization of greater good in the world, if we make a collective effort now to change our worse habits and adopt newer, saner ways of doing things.

It is clear that the predominant system that is controlled by vested interests have a commitment to the status quo that will stand in the way and create resistance to any significant attempts at fostering alternative development.

These powerful interests have the resources to effectively prevent any kinds of changes in the world that they perceive as being contrary to their own private interests. But this is a temporary situation in the world, and the common interests of humanity are in the final analysis their own best interests as way.

Alternative development must be accommodative of these orientations and interests groups, and not contradictory to them-- but at the same time efforts at alternative development must not yield to these interests or to allow our primary objectives to become compromised and rendered ineffective because of such top-down and inside-out our outside-in resistance.

Modern development and modernization as we have known these to be are not so much inevitable as they are politically and economically promoted and therefore permitted to continue in the way that they have. Many vested interests have huge stakes in the game of development.

But conventional development in the way that it has been unfolding is without a doubt not necessarily the best possible hypothetical future to behold. It is not without its own intrinsic contradictions that make our whole-hearted and unquestioning acceptance of its mandate more than a little uncomfortable and in the long run futile.

The future can unfold in any possible number of directions, and it is worthwhile in the brief period remaining before it does do so, to seriously consider some of the other options that may be available for humankind other than those that have been placed before us by the powers that be.

There is a great deal of media-hype and information control that is dedicated to creating the illusion that the predominant world is the only possible way, and that any other way is not efficacious or unworkable. Many of the basic technologies upon which alternative development could be founded have been around for a long time now—at least as long as the fossil-fuel industry.

The ignorance and prejudices, rooted in common sense that would resist such alternative development are in fact the by-product of this tremendous effort to hard sell the contemporary system as inevitable, desirable, and even natural.

It is paramount therefore that the promotion of alternative development attempts to counter and reverse some of this public attitude away from the consonance of the system and social inertia to basic change.

Success of the human species in the Third Millennium will in the long run depend on how much it can promote alternative forms of development during the first half of the 21st Century.

These alternative forms involve alternative power technologies primarily derived from solar energy, and upon the widespread adoption of basic democratic social innovations that lead to greater equality in the world.

Alternative development is therefore a critical issue affecting the destiny and future course of human history. Alternative development includes as well a clearer notion of Human development.

The issues of promoting Human development are inextricably tied to the promotion of alternative development such that one will not be successfully achieved without the other.

The object of alternative development is to provide an alternative direction for world development and global integration other than what has been the predominant mode of the modern era in the 20th Century.

<u>Earthbound Perspectives</u>

Alternative development does not aim to replace or displace the current patterns of development that are mostly based on the petrochemical and military industries, so much as to complement these with a greater range of viable and profitable alternatives that are less violent and destructive of our world.

Part of the function of alternative development is therefore in a sense mediation between the host world system and the natural and human world in global, regional and local senses.

It makes continued fossil-fuel development possible and tolerable, indeed sustainable, by placing brakes and constraints upon this development, and by reinforcing the current energy system with a safer and more sustainable substitute.

Alternative development consists of a number of factors working together. Development of eco technologies and eco-cultural orientations that depend upon these technologies is an important step in this direction. The success of these technologies and cultural orientations depends on the scale of their adoption in the world, and therefore upon their active promotion among different peoples of the world

Alternative development in part also involves alternative human development, and a redirection of the meaning of human development in the world. Human development has mostly meant "human resources" in the production systems of the past. It has rarely been construed as a kind of right, as something that is its own goal and objective in the overall <u>qualitative</u> improvement of the human condition.

As a side note, an extension of human development entails the promotion and eventual adoption of more democratic institutions in the world, and a concomitant withering of authoritarian power structures. Economic well-being and vigor depends on open and free market systems and upon the incorporation of greater numbers of people into the decision-making process.

Promotion of alternative development requires redirection and cultivation on a mass level of alternative human values and views of the world. Human valuation is seen as an essential ingredient of the world system, underlying economic value and structural patterning on earth.

240

It entails, among other things:

      1. The promotion of Pacifism

      2. The collective realization of Earthboundness

      3. The development of Techno-ecology and Eco-technology

      4. The cultivation of Eco-culture

      5. The realization of the Information Revolution

      6. Promotion of alternative Human development

An alternative vision of the future sees a return to reliance on solar energy sources and spin-off technologies of these alternative energies to drive our system, and less reliance on the fossil fuel based technologies that have predominated, especially in the 20th Century.

To some extent, it sees a return to steam-power, but not driven by the burning of dirty bituminous brown coal. Upon this alternative energy base we can see the gradual rise of new kinds of buildings, streets, and cities that are made of alternative materials other than timber and concrete.

We can envision air-craft that fly into outer space beyond the grip of the earth's gravity, and cars that reach speeds in excess of 300 miles an hour--effectively turning a trip across the continental United States into a single day's drive.

These are not fantasy visions of a science fiction writer. They are in fact the possible and better technologies that are available to us today. It also sees powerful personal computers and software that are cheap enough and available enough to be distributed more evenly and more equally in the world.

The lack of initial profitability construed in the development of these technologies must be understood against the background of the increasing incentives and desirability of these technologies, and in fact, in the lowered cost of such technologies once they reach the optimal level of mass production and global distribution.

This lack of profitability and high cost thresholds to initiating alternative development are more apparent than real, and are biased by the predominant capitalist point of view that sees profits as primarily short-term gains.

Such technologies in fact tend to be lower net cost in operation and to involve longer lifecycles of its components. The gain of such an alternative system is cumulative and gradual, but its development, once it takes root, will grow exponentially and in the long-term, quite rapidly.

Chapter 12: Non-Violence & Pacifist Revolution

What are the values of pacifist philosophy? The concept of nonviolence entails a non-destructive approach to life. How shall we measure our destructiveness? By our capacity to do harm, and control the patterns of the world arbitrarily—to bring to an end to life.

We can say that in a basic sense the world system that we currently live within is fundamentally a violent and destructive one. Many of its processes eventuate or cause the destruction of a great deal of life on earth. It has been happening at such a rapid rate and to such a great extent in the world that we can no longer blithely chose to ignore it or the consequences.

Promotion of the values of pacifism is a difficult thing to do in a world full of aggression and violence. The principles of passive resistance require a kind of courage and self-sacrifice that is uncommon to the average human being.

Few exemplars have existed to lead the way in this regard. And there have always been too many Hitler-types who would easily kill off every Gandhi in line without a twinge of remorse or second thought. On one hand the world must be protected from the innate aggression of madmen like Hitler—thus the doctrine of pacifism must embrace a policy of active, strategic defense.

Likewise, we cannot carry the concept of ahimsa, or non-violence, to the absolute extent that we refuse to deal effectively with a swarm of locusts eating our crops or with a strain of virus killing our children. We swat a fly in the house when it annoys us, and we smash a mosquito engorged with our baby's blood, but this does not make us violent in the world.

Violence that we seek to undo is the structural and social patterning that results in violation of humanity's basic rights and in general and deliberate destruction of and erosive effect on the environment on a massive scale.

On the other hand, the use of violence in any form or fashion, even if restricted to defense, entails the risk of its misuse as well and thus a vicious cycle of violence begetting more violence. It is true and perhaps unavoidable that by adopting methods of violence to counter and defend ourselves from violence, we are rendering ourselves our own worst enemy.

The sad conclusion about the reality of widespread violence in our world is that it forces us to become violent to defend ourselves--removing from us our responsibility and freedom of non-violence.

Pacifist revolution is not defined only by the value strategy of passive resistance, but also by the concerted strategy of resistant activism—it entails a kind of aggressiveness and defensiveness that is essentially non-militant.

The best military strategy is an indirect approach that decisively or cumulatively wins war with the least amount of destruction and bloodshed. In the long run, everyone loses in the violence of war—therefore diplomacy that successfully accomplishes the sort of goals is preferable to going to battle.

Pacifism is a valuable, indeed, a precious doctrine. It must be practiced as much as it is preached, and tempered by the sober realization that humankind will probably never be entirely free of violence. It is a cultural orientation, an alternate orientation other than the predominant modes of national chauvinism that are promoted in the name of patriotism and loyalty under a single flag.

As a cultural pattern, it is something to be learned and taught. Parents must learn to put into practice its basic principles, and then to try to teach these principles through example, modeling, emulation and valuation, to their children. Teachers have the same task to teach their students. Likewise, leaders must instruct their people.

Concomitant to the principle of non-violence entails we must also cultivate an attitude of openness and tolerance to human differences and cultural variations in the world, as we are increasingly confronted with such differences and their consequences in our lives.

Openness and tolerance must be construed not just in a passive way of live and let live, but in an active form of curious enjoyment and appreciation and positive evaluation of human differences in the world. One of the great religious doctrines of the world, the concept of universal love, must be applied in our daily lives and extended to every person.

The principle of nonviolence and the promotion of active pacifism in the world thus entail another set of values that we must embrace in the world, and this is the value of self-sacrifice, charity and generosity in the world.

The concept of greed, hedonistic pleasure and unbound profit incentive that underlies so much of the capitalist system must be construed in a basic and fundamental sense to be contrary to the principles of pacifism and eventually leading to destructive consequences that are entailed in the exploitation and theft of other people's property or energy.

Just as pacifism does not necessarily preclude the intolerance of Hitler, it also does not necessarily preclude the dynamic and beneficial aspects of an open capitalist market system. As it is not a contradiction to defend human rights against the violence of a Hitler, it is also not contradictory to promote profitable orientations through the organization of labor and capital in the world system.

But this must be accomplished without corruption, exploitation-- achieved through honest hard and intelligent work. Gaining of value for all is the ultimate purpose of human development— value gained within the system should not be exclusively or primarily at the expense of others.

What does a pacifist revolution of the 21st Century look like? It is an ad-hoc, grass-roots organization of common people as equals, regardless of their station or class in life, regardless of their language or national affiliation, working together for a common cause—the cause of world-peace and world justice. Working with the knowledge that without justice there can be no lasting peace, and without peace, there can be no true justice.

At the same time, we must all be brought to the final realization of giving up our immature and somewhat childish preoccupation with the tools and weapons of violence—that violence is something easy to accomplish but impossible to ever undo.

We must reach inside of ourselves to unlock the deep-seated compulsions that tether us to our violent toys and obsessions, and to release more creative forces in our daily lives. Thus a pacifist orientation entails a relinquishing of the symbolism and means of violence in our everyday life, and a deliberate, conscientious exploration of our own creativity and hidden potential in everyday life.

The alternative system must promote this effectively in the world, providing leadership and an organizational framework and alternative cultural context that will allow people to securely and safely adopt alternative value orientations without fear, without discrimination or violence.

This has always been a tall order, a well-neigh impossible requirement. But in the modern world at the dawn of the 21st Century, it is now not only a realistic and realizable possibility; it is becoming a necessary imperative.

Much of what must be resisted emanates from what can be called human nature. It is so basic and so embedded in our world and our identity, that we even feel threatened by the suggestion that it may be wrong or lost. The refusal to bear arms under circumstances of national fervor over war will be construed not only as an act of cowardice or desertion of duty, but it will be treated as a crime against the state.

At this level, the state is exercising its ultimate coercive authority over its constituency. It is the power to arbitrate the life and death of its people. It is at this level perhaps that this form of coercive authority, what is the privilege and power of nation states in the modern world and that leads to so much violence in the world, must be primarily challenged. This coercive authority of the state stems from the rights of states to make war to defend their independence and territorial integrity that stems from the independent sovereignty of states.

But if the rights of states are ultimately even if indirectly derived from the rights of individuals within the states, and if individuals either tacitly or actively yield their rights to the state for the sake of the protection and promotion this citizenship provides for them, then it follows that actions by the state that deprive its citizens of their basic rights and freedoms are unjustifiable and lead to the potential forfeiture and delimitation of state authority.

This is a difficult question. It is clear that Hitler's aggression that ended in World War II was an illegal abuse and transgression of legitimate authority by the German State. To a great extent the German people were either induced by blind collective delusion or by fear to conform to his dictates and the systems coercion, or else to suffer a cruel death.

On the other hand, American involvement in Vietnam is less clearly an act of overt aggression, though its continuance and escalation lead to a great deal of unnecessary destruction and violence.

But it falls upon the shoulder of the people themselves to decide and determine the limits of legitimate authority of its states, or any states. The problem is that once instituted, states in fact yield a great deal of control and power over its constituency, and most often, individuals are in a very weak and disadvantageous position to enforce their ultimate prerogatives over the state.

This is why in totalitarian states, as in modern communist China, the right to congregate in large numbers outside of state sanctioned activities is generally denied its people.

Total warfare that is characteristic of modern warfare, that involves the mobilization of entire nation states and all their industrialized resources, is a consequence of the potential totalitarianism of the modern state.

Again, Hitler's Germany is a clear example of this. But even very democratic and otherwise usually non-aggressive nations like the United States can at times adopt fairly totalitarian orientations in the world that result in total warfare. The world witnessed this in Vietnam.

At the dawning of the age that, with the horizontal proliferation of weapons of mass destruction, and with the kinds of technological refinements of modern warfare, we cannot and do not have to afford to continue with mobilization and means for making total warfare. The eventual outcome of such warfare is unthinkable for every rational human being.

<u>Earthbound Perspectives</u>

It is possible though to return the problem of defensive warfare to the business of highly trained and well-equipped professional elite, much as we rely on well-trained policemen and detectives to protect us and guard our rights and freedoms in the world.

The means for organizing relatively small military organizations that can effectively enforce world peace without committing the world's resources to total acts of ultimate self-destruction have been at hand for several decades now.

What is missing is the willingness on the part of nation-states to do so, because of the yielding of their own power and independent authority in the world this would ultimately entail. The peacekeeping forces mounted by United Nations efforts are usually a joke, ineffective even in preventing small arms violence by ill-equipped militia forces.

Such development would require a joint commitment by the world's major powers to supplying the technology and expertise required for such a global police force. It would also entail a genuine commitment to a global democracy and to a strong paradigm of states rights that do not preclude the realization of individual human rights.

In a world composed of powerful private interests and many petty authoritarian dictators, this is perhaps asking too much.

Chapter 13: Human Rights and States' Rights

Human rights are always a silent, chronic background issue in our lives.

We struggle every day without a clear sense of what they are or what they entail morally in our world. And yet they are extremely important because they structure our relations with others in the world.

They set limits to what we can and cannot do with others, and what others can and cannot do with our selves. We mostly only know them when we really lose them or when others violate our sense of our rights.

It is obvious that totalitarian governments in the world must by definition be anti-democratic and thus must actively demote and devalue the role of human rights in the world, and want to convince their subjects that human rights are either a threat to the state or a conditional privilege arbitrarily granted (or taken away) by the state.

The issue of states rights deriving ultimately from the sanctioning and mandate of the people, the collective will of the people, so to speak, and being ultimately constrained by and legitimated by basic natural, human rights, remains an important normative and philosophical point to develop, because a lot of real things in the world hinges on its justification.

The power of independent nation states is derived from and granted, however implicitly, by its people. It is limited by its responsibility to protect and uphold the rights and interests of its people.

The nation state is usually construed as a corporate entity whose organizational life and imperative is greater than the needs or rights of any individual within it, or even greater than the sum total of the rights of the individuals who compose it. It is governed by a regime supposedly legitimate and representative of the will of the majority of people.

<u>Earthbound Perspectives</u>

At this point of its development, a state changes from being "of the people, for the people and by the people" in a direct and active sense, to becoming "over the people, above and beyond the people."

This mandate of state authority is usually derived on the grounds of protecting or promoting the national cultural heritage of the people that is held to be greater than the biographical lives of the people who compose this heritage.

Much of this is ideological rhetoric and symbolic construct that has no necessary a priori justification—it is collective illusion fostered by the state as a means of secondary legitimization of its institutions and policies.

It is at this level of "no-man's land" as with the gray regions of secondary and derivative human rights that the possibility for prevarication and manipulation of rights and powers mostly occur and for which few clear solutions actually exist. It is this gray area of derivative rights and privileges that lead us to extended courtroom battles.

It is unfortunate in history that all too frequently vested and corrupt political interests have an undue amount of power and influence, and deliberately and underhandedly exploit and exaggerate issues of ethnic identity and solidarity and out-group threat and scape goats, for their own empowerment and aggrandizement in the world.

Most people appear too often to be susceptible and easily persuaded and led in this way, and leaders not only realize this mass weakness, but presume upon it in many of their policies and platforms.

Human rights is the only valid universal meta-ethical doctrine that exists for humankind, not because there is some natural imperative or mandate that makes it so, but because we in our history have collectively agreed to make it so.

We know human rights mostly by their violation. We know it by our long history of slavery and the violence of aggression and totalitarianism the leads to the human loss and violation of rights on a grand scale.

Human rights are a semi-explicit doctrine ultimately about the fundamental value and worth of the human being, as both an individual and as a member of a larger society, in the world. It states that this value and worth is in some sense absolute and inviolable. We cannot justly put arbitrary limits or impose cultural constraints over it or its implementation in society.

The concept of human rights has gradually expanded over the decades, especially in relation to modern development, to embrace a broader range of issues and basic areas of life. These include in a general sense the rights to life, liberty, property and the pursuit of happiness.

More specifically we recognize the rights to freedom of speech, assembly, religion, defense, etc. Among the basic rights as laid down in the American Bill of Rights, we can include several others that have subsequently risen to the fore as vital social issues.

These include the rights to a home, to a job, to equal opportunity, to vote, the freedom of expression, freedom of privacy, freedom of information, the right to alternative life-styles, the right to health, education and basic welfare of our families.

State's Rights, the sovereignty, territorial integrity and independence of ethno-national groupings, are the symbolic and de facto extension of human rights, applied to the rights of groups to form for themselves and freely operate as separate and independent communities presumably upon native and natural territorial claims.

Because the paradigm of states rights ultimately derives from the doctrine of individual human rights, the domestic analogy of individual rights becomes a viable and appropriate model for understanding the interactions and normal relations between states.

Because states' rights are derived from basic human rights, the power and moral, meta-ethical legitimacy of a nation to assert its prerogatives is fundamentally constrained by these same basic individual human rights.

Nations cannot justly forfeit or alienate basic human rights, though they frequently do so. At the same time, no nation has the privilege to consider itself above or beyond the purview of the basic paradigm of human rights.

The Nuremberg Trials and many war crimes trials subsequently have demonstrated the value and intrinsic importance attached to the doctrine of basic human rights by the international community. The case of cultural relativity cannot be justly made against the assertion of human rights either, especially if we mounted medical normative arguments of human health and well-being.

Cultural variability in the interpretation of constraints, rights and responsibilities varies widely between different groups of people, but upon a meta-ethical level the actions of all states, either domestically or internationally, is fundamentally constrained, and judged in history by the doctrine of inalienable basic human rights.

In the international arena, there is a place for an institution like the United Nations to enforce the doctrine of human rights and to keep peace among nations. The United Nations has grown in its effectiveness over the last decade, but it remains still limited and fundamentally weak to enforce its mandate even among relatively weak nations, unless it is backed up by the military might of its more powerful sponsors.

The mandate of the United Nations will be made stronger and more effective when it is able to enforce its rule with a heavy hand among a genuine federation of nation-states that cannot legally act outside of this union.

Chapter 14: Human Rights and Anthropological Relativity

As anthropologists, we have a moral obligation to search for some sense of realistic resolution to the dilemmas posed by ethical and cultural relativity for the doctrine of human rights.

We cannot as professionals simply pose this problem and challenge the world to find a solution to it and then simply walk away from it claiming our professional ethics and disinterest of objective inquiry.

Anthropological relativity of value and worldview is a realistic fact of human life—Roman slaves were little better than cattle, and people regular put to death in the Coliseum was a normal and popular, if somewhat brutal and bloodthirsty, form of entertainment.

Even in the modern era it is not difficult to cast about and find similar examples of cultural practices that test our sensitivities and sensibilities and understanding about what basic rights and violence are.

International and national practices in human trafficking and black markets and smuggling come to immediate mind. I would include in this the controversial issues in contemporary American society over gun control--when youth walk onto a campus carrying automatic weapons designed only to kill people.

Communist China today claims cultural relativity of its long and ancient history--modern communists appropriating for their own purposes and empowerment and long heritage of traditional Chinese civilization, as it justifies totalitarian policies that lead to massive human rights violations and to wide scale corruption. It even goes too far as to define human rights as capitalist promotion of democracy and as a threat to the normal social order of the Chinese people.

To deny the relativity of values on some level, even if just for the sake of philosophical argument and conjecture, is to side-step the centrally critical issues of real importance, that are the relative status of human rights in the real world, and the limits of variation or of tolerance of states and leaders that the world community and humanity seeks to define in relation to human rights.

There is a great deal of room for interpretation and misinterpretation of what are basic and derivative rights and freedoms, responsibilities and the limits of authoritarian domination.

But if we honor and respect alternative cultural traditions that may place different valuations on people and their freedoms, at the same time, we also all implicitly recognize and on some level acknowledge the basic limits to authority and coercion in any society, beyond that there is only intolerable violation and cruelty.

From the standpoint of a meta-ethical doctrine of universal human rights, we all of us, as equal members of humanity, have a moral obligation to respect and uphold some notion and practice of this doctrine, that ultimately transcends and places limits on the relativity and variations of the pattern of culture.

To claim cultural identity and relativity, in other words, does not exonerate us from the moral constraints of the doctrine of human rights, and places basic conditions and limitations on the amount of cultural variation that we can ethically tolerate.

Though headhunting and ritually prescribed cannibalism was a common cultural trait in Oceania, incorporation of these tribal societies into a larger world system of relations entailed that this pattern be arrested and prohibited. Slavery and human sacrifice in Africa is another endemic cultural institution that, from a human rights standpoint, was construed as intolerable and was eventually eradicated.

Chapter 15: Earthboundness

Earthboundness can be described as a subjective and collective state of mind. It is the realization on some level of our being of our inherent limitations on earth, and of our vital relationship and dependency to earth, hence it is a growing understanding and a new sense of responsibility to caring for and managing the earth in a manner that is good both for it and for ourselves.

The earth is our home, like it or not. We can make it a mess—we can destroy it, or we can clean it up and set it back in order.

It is a common realization similar to the one that people of Columbus's age perhaps had when the earth was demonstrated to be round and interconnected east and west. Earthboundness can be a sense of the isolation of the planet earth in a vast and almost boundless universe. It can also be a sense of our common place in the greater natural scheme of things.

Astronomers and astrophysicists search the edges of the universe for the big bang, but philosophers must still ask the question of what lies beyond all of this.

And yet we are temporarily, for all intents and purposes, still tethered with our feet on solid little earth. This shared realization of our finiteness and the finiteness of life on earth, of the earth's resources and of our own longevity and tenuousness on earth, impinges upon the things that we do and how we view the world in many ways.

Earthboundness is a steadily increasing realization of our responsibility, individually and socially, to the earth, to its stewardship as caretakers. This sense of responsibility is something that we cannot simply escape or ignore even if we choose to. It is always in the background of our lives like a gigantic question mark looming over the horizon.

We must also realize that what we are in charge of taking care of is not simply our own to do with as we please. This has been our common problem for many centuries so far.

Our sense of responsibility is as renters. Mother nature is our landlady. We are realizing increasingly, especially as we enter into and take control of the world of the gene, that we cannot simply manipulate nature in anyway we see fit.

Earthboundness is a very basic alternation of our collective world-view that is tied to the growing realization of the finiteness of the world and of the constraints of the human condition in the world. It is in a sense a preconception—a collective pre-understanding. It comes before and basic challenges our rational faculties for understanding and relating to the world.

Perhaps, for many reasons, we are in fact "seeing" the world differently from the way our ancestors and distant cousins saw the world. This fact of altered perception of our world entails that we must reformulate our symbolic and ideological structures that were rooted to an earlier sense of vision and wisdom and relation about the world.

I call this new point of view "earthboundness" because I believe that the dawning shared realization of the limits and boundaries imposed by our basic relationship to the earth and our ultimate dependency to the earth, is at the core of this altered conception of reality.

We are increasingly feeling and learning about these limits and boundaries in ways that our forefathers never could have known. With this new point of view, comes a growing awareness of new responsibilities and also of new kinds of freedom that is the by-product of our technological civilization.

Earthboundness as a worldview is probably the first collective understanding that is genuinely or potentially pan human—one that is shared by all people together. It transcends all previous religious philosophies and ideologies. It is because part of the earthbound perspective is the common realization that we are all in the same big boat together drifting through the vast empty seas of space.

Worldview is important because it orients us every morning, and allows us to sleep well every night. It helps to render coherent and orderly the multitude of experiences and perceptions. It provides us a common set of attitudes and symbolic framework by which we can communicate, explore new experiences, and test out our subjective feelings, opinions, and sense of reality against those of others. Without a coherent worldview, at least implicitly, our sense of reality would be quite disordered and even destructive.

So far, the earthbound perspective exists but only in the background of our lives. We all know it is there--the same sense of the earth's problems and our relationship to the earth is taught in China as it is in the United States. And yet, as a coherent, clear view of the world, and of our place within it, it has not yet been in itself rendered explicit enough.

Earthboundness is also a state of mind, but more than a world-view, it is a state of being in the world. It is not a transient state of being—it is a habitual, regular and everyday way of living. We know that gravity is a subtle but extremely powerful force of nature that keeps us mostly right side up.

There is no more direct evidence of our earthbound condition than when we clumsily drop something from our hands or trip and fall to the ground. It reminds us, among other things, of our humility before the forces of nature. We thus kowtow before nature without our willing to or not. We are embarrassed, but we need not really be.

Because we are in some small measure rational beings, what we think and believe is important to our lives. It gives us a sense of order and direction, and sometimes even, we act upon this sense of order in ways constructive or otherwise.

Earthboundness has several components. Earthmindedness, that in its explicit form allows us to think, feel and hopefully talk about our relationship to the earth in a variety of ways, and Earthbeing, that is a hopefully conscious way of living when we come to accept in our everyday lives our sense of earthbound being.

It is like the second thought we have when we go to toss out a piece of rubbish paper.

We make sure it goes to the proper place rather than anywhere-- we do this even if at first it requires a little extra attention and energy on our parts, until it becomes a matter of routine or habit.

Earthbeing has a deeper sense of meaning. It can be construed as a state of being in the world that is not vicarious, but immediately apprehended in the apperceptive recognition of our own position and place in the world—of our own sense of being in the here and now. It entails a giving up of the illusions of ego-attachment, of fetishes, of impulses that are dangerous or harmful. It entails the cultivation of a spirit of being in a natural state, with our selves, with one another, and with the larger world.

Earth-being therefore has wider implications for our socially constructed world--for our cities, our skyscrapers, our freeways, our suburban sprawls, our slums and ghettos. We must ask ourselves the honest question of what these are in our lives.

Of course, a great deal of money is invested in advertising over the television to get people to accept and desire things that perhaps are not completely consonant with an earthbound way of living. We are told that bigger, faster and newer trucks are better than smaller, older and slower ones.

It becomes a question of our status-identity in the world. If we own the fetishes of capitalism, then we are, at least for the moment, somebody important. It is difficult to resist the social pressures to affluence and to conformity. There appears little counter-voice or basis for alternation of value that enables us to independently feel comfortable and unthreatened about our selves and our own ego-identity in the world.

This pressure occurs on a symbolic level in our everyday lives. It affects how we see and feel about our selves and our worldview. It is inescapable if we are to participate successfully and normally even in a minimal way with everyday society, especially in the most developed regions of the world. It is constant and unyielding, like the fast lane of a busy freeway.

Earthboundness therefore at some level will entail a reassessment, reevaluation and perhaps a revitalization of our symbolic structures in a way that yields a view and orientation to the world that is more consonant with being in the world, that is less vicarious, less attached to material fetishes and the corrupt sense of power and good this brings with it.

It may entail a new found simplicity, a conscientious return to a simpler way of living that is less cluttered with the compulsions that drive us such long distances to acquire greater wealth and the status symbols that money buys. It will therefore entail a new sense of humility, and a disdain of the ephemeral vanities that the modern world is made up of.

If this sounds like good Christian eschatology, it can also just as well be basic Buddhist or Hindu values as well. In fact, earthboundness knows no clear religious boundaries. It transcends all previously known religious doctrines, and, in the process, incorporates many of the basic values.

Chapter 16: Global Eco-culture

Eco-culture is a new form of general, pan-human cultural orientation based on the possibilities of social integration represented by free information exchange of the Internet, and by the eventual promotion of alternative primary institutions of production as well as consonant alternate secondary social institutions of symbolic legitimization and social organization.

Institutions of primary production include solar-based energy sources and extended electrical technologies derived from solar power, alternative intelligent and automated technologies of production, and secondary institutions of social organization and legitimization.

It also entails on a subjective, phenomenological level, the promotion of orientations in everyday life, by our habits, the choices we make, our conversations and interactions, that are conducive to a non-violent and symbiotic relationship with the natural world.

Lip service has been paid to the emergence of a modern global culture constituted mostly in the capitalist market place, that is increasingly erasing ethnocultural and national boundaries of identity.

This modernization is apparently having an assimilative effect of bring all styles of art, architecture, fashion, and products of manufacture, into a common form or mold—streamlined and similar no matter where they are produced or designed. Very little of this new material culture of world civilization is in fact conducive to or a part of a genuine global eco-cultural orientation.

Eco-culture in fact does not exist on a very wide or widely shared basis, but a general need and platform for its emergence does exist today. Much of what passes in the name of environmentalism is in fact a form of market-oriented appropriation of popular themes and consciousness.

But eco-culture is not about environmentalism or environmental activism per se. It is a new form of environmental conservation effort upon all levels together: local, regional and global.

It is not only about camping out in trees or protesting nuclear tests. It is about the cultivation of alternative life-styles that lead to a grass-roots movement—a ground-swell, that predetermines basic consumer attitudes and habits in the global marketplace, that redefine basic market values and reorients economic development toward new avenues that are considered more healthier than what is currently promoted.

To unhook the average consumer from the status hype of new large cars, new clothes, sporting apparel, etc., and to symbolically refocus cultural attention toward alternative status and more mature life-styles would be to liberate a great deal of humanity from the chains of economic coercion and constraint that fetters them to the modern system.

To provide the average consumer with a viable set of reference points and a context and identity that allows them to better redefine their basic values and attitudes in relation to the system, more independently and more fulfilling of their lives in a meaningful way, is essentially to undermine the authoritarian power structures and the status quo of the current system that demands and expects absolute conformity on very basic levels.

Eco-culture must be more than a mere ideology, or a vague philosophy of empty words—it must be defined by our collective actions and shared involvement in the real, material world, by its transmission to our children and by its institutionalization in our global social order.

In this regard, promotion of eco-culture is an activist program, and to some extent attempts to encourage a revolution, albeit a pacifist, or non-violent, global social revolution in all that we do.

Eco-culture is by definition global in perspective. We cannot see it as regionally isolated or preferential to a particular place or period of time. It exists for every human being equally.

The present world system as it exists, divided politically into over 200 independent societies of competing nation states, must not only allow eco-culture to develop, but eventually help to promote its development in the world.

Without a doubt, active promotion of eco-culture on earth will encounter much resistance, some of that may be violent. Change in conservative and asymmetrical social systems is always met with forceful resistance, especially when the new changes threaten the status quo of the power-relations that already exist within such systems.

Eco-culture is therefore a global culture, but it is alternative to the predominant mode of global culture as it exists today as the product of the capitalist development of world civilization.

Eco-culture therefore is antithetical to many of the manifest and promoted values of modernism that exist in the world today-- values that are largely defined by class and status acquisition of material fetishes and fads.

Eco-cultural development is not anti-modernism or counter-cultural. It is simply alternative, different from the main stream of this development. It is in some ways complementary to this mode, and in other ways antithetical to it.

It must be understood that eco-culture and its promotion is not reactionary or antithetical to the established order of relations. It effort is to provide to the world an alternative way of development on all levels of social and cultural integration that is designed to complement and reinforce the established order, while at the same time minimizing the most adverse effects of this order.

Eco-culture can be described as a new way of living, a new world-view, a shared set of primary and secondary institutions and symbolic systems of conceptualization that is more consonant with our sense of earthboundness and more symbiotic to a steady-state of natural evolution on earth.

Development will continue on earth—but the driving force behind this development and its main strategic direction in the aggrandizement of the power of a few, must change, and the ultimate foundation of this development must also as a consequence be changed.

The compulsions to power, to status, to acquisition of material wealth and resources that has long driven capitalist development, the mass appeal to common human vanities, to vicarious enjoyment, to thrill seeking, must give way to a more sober and more sophisticated behavioral dynamo of human social motivation and evaluation.

Many of the values of eco-culture have already been defined in the context of this work--pacifism and non-violence, universal tolerance, creativity and openness, charity, generosity, honesty, thrift and productivity. Other values must also be seen in relation to this orientation--frugality, the golden mean, and the old-time capitalist values of hard work, punctuality and industry.

The development of eco-culture on earth will entail therefore a kind of peaceful revolution, a casting-off of the chains that tie us to the big world system, and a conscientious declaration of independence. This revolution will be slow in coming, but inexorable in its consequences.

Part of the dilemma of its realization is that most of the poorest and dispossessed people on earth only want to become wealthy and rich, and would not give up this dream for values that remind them too much of the humility of their own disadvantaged backgrounds in life. The real resistance to the promotion of this kind of alternative orientation will not come from the wealthy, but from the poorest, people.

Eco-culture must be about global equality in a maximum sense. It must be about freedom in a way that has not yet been realized. It must also be one that permits people greater latitude for achievement and acquisition than they would otherwise enjoy, even within the normally developed system.

Eco-culture will be something that we teach to our children-- something we value enough to teach to our children. Our children will have to grow up into it as if it were natural. But how to teach something that is alien even to ourselves, that we poorly understand?

Cultivating eco-cultural values and a consonant way of life must on some level entail reconciliation of a host of discrepant realities between the world as it is,   and the world as it could and should be. We must battle with this issue everyday in many basic ways.

Chapter 17: Human Development

Human development is a critical concern of the 21st Century. There are billions of people on earth, but the promotion of human development lags far behind the promotion of economic and technological development.

Most often, human development issues take second-place, or are in fact demoted in favor of frequently shortsighted strategies that aim at quick economic development. Governments, institutions and most people themselves cannot be trusted to be unselfish enough to want to promote human development beyond token symbolic efforts.

The need for human development is increasingly acute in the world, and the consequences of its promotion or continued demotion in the world may prove fatal or critical to the successful long-term adaptation of the human species on earth in the 21st Century.

With so many new people on earth, the demand on resources and the requirements for development that strives to improve the average quality of life for all human beings is growing greater and greater by the minute, while the predominant system remains for the most part negligent and disconcerted in its efforts in this way.

Basic and derivative human needs, upon that human rights are based, are increasing in direct proportion to the increasing size and environmental impact of the global human population.

Humans are seen, in light of the capitalist world system, as simply "resources" that can be developed primarily in terms of their efficiencies and productive capacities within the machinery of the global manufacturing and market system.

Their social qualities are directly tied to their relative position in the global ladder of socio-political-economic success. They are profiles and broad sets of needs to be met. They range with profiles on a natural medical continuum of human variation.

Human beings are not simply resources. They are the ultimate ends of all development, and human development is not merely a form of economic development, but is a goal in itself. We strive to promote human development in the world or else fail to do so, primarily because it is fundamental to the definition of what it means to be human on earth.

Human beings, collectively, are the primary determinants and sources of all value on that the modern world system is built. Even economic values, in the final analysis, are derivative of basic human value.

Human development is in fact a human right that is owed to each and every person. The promotion of human development in its more genuine aspects does not debilitate or take away from economic development.

Rather, its greatest consequence is that promotion of human development in societies creates the preconditions to the greater economic growth and development of that society, especially when that development is based on institutions that create greater equality between stratified classes of people in a society. This holds true whatever the traditional cultural pattern or historical heritage of a particular society.

Much that has gone on in the developing countries in the name of economic development has in fact resulted in increasing stagnation, corruption and greater violence. Programs currently aimed at human development are often compromised in their structural organization and function.

By their relative positioning within the global system, such programs are such that they are rendered corrupt and false in their representations to the world, and even frequently tend to the demotion and interference of genuine human development rather than the other way around.

Promotion of genuine human development liberates people from the constraining forces of the system they live within and allows them to accomplish their life goals. It provides new opportunities for people to realize a better life and to pursue their dreams as fulfilled human beings.

The challenge before us is how to promote genuine human development in the world. Human development is more about the realization of innate human potential on an individual level, and about the average social improvement on a social group level, than it is about the alleviation of social "problems" that are themselves the result of structural asymmetries in a larger system and of embedded ethnocultural patterns on an interpersonal level.

It begins on the proposition that beneath the skin, on a deeper level, all people are basically the same, and in general, expect and want and value the same basic kinds of things in life.

The cultural form or the symbolic expression of these needs and expectations may vary widely, as does group identity and patterns of group solidarity and goals.

But these kinds of differences on deeper analysis tend to be relatively superficial and comparatively superfluous in comparison to the pan-human cognitive and normative framework that is derivable from the typical existential predicament that most people find themselves within, especially now within the modern world system.

Human development derives from the fact that human nature is in fact inherently creative in orientation, and that it is not normatively healthy unless it is allowed to develop its fullest creative potential. We cannot, beyond the meeting of basic needs, dictate to all people or even any people what is best for them in terms of their own development.

All people must be permitted and allowed the opportunity to realize this for themselves without social interference. The focus on the individual is a radical hypothesis in a world where most traditional civilizations and culture demote the position of the individual to group identity.

This is the basis for the justification of the human value strategy of promoting human development in the world. It is rooted in a social philosophy that is basically philanthropic.

Human beings are born good and innocent, and are taught, directly or indirectly, to be bad. Not only are humans basically, by definition, fundamentally good but they have on average much greater potential than most of them realize in their life-times, for a complex variety of biographical and social reasons.

<u>Earthbound Perspectives</u>

Human development is therefore a grand value strategy that is contrary to reliance on militaristic strategies of the threat of force. Indirectly but in a very real sense it affects economic production, because, by raising human value, expectations and quality, this value translates into greater productivity and the realization of greater differentiated economic value, which in the final analysis is the social realization of human value in the first place.

Promotion of human development in the large world entails therefore the wide scale adoption of what Denis Gabor referred to as social innovations on the secondary level of socio-cultural institutionalization.

These social institutions are primarily educational, and human service related organizations. Fostering new institutional arrangements in the world is no simple or straightforward task.

The most difficult aspect of this is inducing people otherwise set in their ways to accept new ways of doing things.

 Conservatism of traditional cultures worldwide, and all the attendant ethnocentrism found within these different orientations, have the inertial effect of resisting adoption of innovations on a scale that these would be effective in the world.

The question of how to do this is a top priority in the development anthropology game. Fortunately, no single private interest has made a monopoly on this topic, for if they did we can be sure that there would only be more of the same old modernization!

The realization of human development in the first place depends upon the freedom of humankind from the tyranny of violence and from the constraints of the threat of violence in everyday life.

Furthermore, it entails the realization of individual independence and the protection of individual human rights in most social contexts. These are fundamental prerequisites to building a foundation for human development in the world.

As far as the promotion of human development in the world, it is true that we are our own worst enemies. Human development begins at home and in our selves. We must work on ourselves first, and not worry too much about what others are or are not doing.

Indeed, our cultural conformity and socialization frequently entails the embedding of unconscious repression and compulsions that foster our authoritarian relation with the world in very basic ways, and that limit our own development as human beings.

Creating the preconditions that encourage and provide direction for this kind of alternative and individual human development is a requirement of society in general, but it comes to full force in the familial context of the home environment.

Human development entails leadership training, alternation to more acceptable modes and values of living, rehabilitation and remediation; it entails achievement reorientation, motivational training, retraining and acquisition of basic and advanced skills in a variety of directions.

Human development entails enhancing both the average quantity and quality of life for all people. The level of human development is measured and determined by this panhuman standard.

We cannot assess the level of attainment in human development by comparing average Americans with average Chinese or Malaysians--such comparisons only show us, more than any thing else, how far we have still to go.

Quantity of life in terms of access to wealth and resources and quality of life in terms of basic indicators like relative health, well-being, education, etc., are indeed interdependent sets of factors. We cannot ultimately improve the quality of life without somehow first increasing the average quantity of life. At the same time, we cannot simply enhance the quality of life by merely augmenting material possession or acquisition.

Chapter 18: Techno-Ecology and Eco-Technology

Modern industries were quick to jump on the new biological revolution that enabled genetic manipulation of corn crops. They did so myopically and without regard to the possible long-term or possible indirect consequences of human interference in the genetic transmission of biological information—the encoding of life itself.

They did so only in the selfish desire of capitalizing on a new form of technology. Genetic manipulation is a clear and stark example of the effect that modern scientific technology is having upon the natural ecology of the earth—at many levels and in many different ways.

The history of capitalist development reveals that most of it has been by definition short-sighted because it was always based simply and only on terms of rapid and immediate profit-maximization—or rather a strategy of the nearest possible short-term gain—seemingly very much a part of human nature. This basic ethos runs headlong against the problem of the global commons.

Modern technologies indeed create and foster their own kinds of ecology on the earth, as many otherwise feral species of life are forced to adapt to the new human-made conditions imposed on their natural habitats or else pass rapidly to extinction by habitat loss and extreme resource competition.

These new human-made ecologies prove usually to not be very adaptive in the long-term. They tend to have destructive and imbalanced consequences for natural ecologies in the larger framework and the suites of species that normally make their homes within these regional contexts.

Eco-Technology can be defined as the alternative technologies, such as the primary institutions of production of food and fuel, that promote more sustainable large-scale adaptations of the human species on earth, or at the very least are less destructive of an eco-cultural orientation than are the currently predominantly fossil-fuel based technologies.

These primary alternative institutions are basically solar-powered, either directly or indirectly, along with a host of spin-off technologies that are derivable and exclusively dependent upon these alternative energy resources.

The information revolution has made this new kind of technology not only more possible, but potentially even more efficacious and even more profitable than traditional-styled technologies!

As Buckminster Fuller was fond of remarking, information is anti-entropic, and if we are to understand the synergism of an alternative system of basic and advanced technology, then it must be understood from the standpoint of its structural-functional integration derived from information technologies and the possibilities that this new kind of cybernetic integration creates.

Eco-technologies have a primary derivative source—solar energy—either directly or indirectly utilized by a variety of means. Upon this general source of energy, technologies that are efficient and ecologically efficacious are elaborated as viable alternatives to the common forms available today.

The wide-scale adoption and development of these alternative primary institutions set up a new foundation for alternative development outside of the present system and yet that remains complementary to that system.

The challenge is the development of an alternative eco-technological infrastructure that is complementary to the existing fossil-fuel economy. Many of these alternative technologies have been around for a long time, but the justification for their lack of implementation has been the availability of less expensive alternatives and the high cost of their initial infrastructural development.

This is only partly true, and disguises the real issue that has been involved in the promotion of alternative eco-technologies. The large oil companies and derivative companies of automobile and truck, heavy and industrial equipment manufactures, would not want forms of competition to enter their lucrative market place that might in the long run undermine their own profits and profitability.

In fact, in the long run, if properly designed, eco-technologies would actually be far more efficient and less expensive than the current petrochemical based industries.

The promotion of these alternative technologies does require some rethinking and rewiring of the system—old money will die and new money will be born. Even more, it requires a general receptiveness and willingness of current socio-political systems to adopt these kinds of programs.

If the new alternative technologies can be cultivated and allowed to rise to the fore, then the old Industries of oil and coal combustion would become eventually relatively limited and specialized industries.

The promise of these programs promoting alternative development is that, relatively speaking, they are non-destructive of the natural environment, and produce far fewer harmful side affects that the current state of technology.

They would be designed for the long run, to operate on a regular or continuous basis without the need for constant inputs of huge amounts of coal or oil. Because on average they would tend to be long lasting, steady and relatively reliable, many of the issues that are contemporary to the petrol-chemical industry, such as the rising cost of gas at the pump, or the need to exert military presences in hostile foreign countries, for example, would eventually simply become irrelevant.

The focal foundation of techno-ecology is the elaboration of solar and gravity powered technologies, and the advanced application of these technologies to the viable and economical solution of practical problems in the world.

Spin-off technologies would also be forth coming from promotion of this development. Furthermore, new development based on these technologies can be directly applied to accomplishing scientific objectives that have not otherwise been obtained.

Alternative development will succeed in rendering global social organization more complex and occupationally differentiated. The structural dynamics of panhuman social order would take on new dimensions and new orders of magnitude as greater amounts of power become available to more people at less cost and greater net efficiency.

It may also remove some of the foundation stones that currently influence militarism and current asymmetries in the world order—competition for access and control over mineral deposits and basic energy resources or food production zones, for example.

The real challenges faced by alternative techno-ecological development is not its cost-effectiveness, but rather the organized resistance it will receive from many super-powerful lobbies and private interests that mandate government policies and manipulate public awareness and opinion.

But these challenges can be effectively met, and in time, their resistance will wither away in the face of a growing global receptivity and demand for cheaper sources of power and their by-products and technological spin-offs of these sources.

The sooner the human race gets unhooked on fossil-fuel consumption as their primary source of power, and becomes hooked on alternative solar-hydrogen sources, then the sooner the foundations for world peace and for pan-human development can be better secured in the world.

In a Buckminster Fullerian design revolution of "more for less" rather than entropy producing "less for more." In the meantime, we must concern ourselves with dealing with a world of our own making, but not completely of our own choosing.

For such alternative technology and development to occur, it is clear that governments on all levels must become more cooperative and willing as participants in this effort. Promotion of such development will entail the joint extension and integration of regions world-wide that have little to do with political boundaries, much as the information revolution based upon the Internet has had little to do with national boundaries of culture, language or communications.

At the same time, governments alone cannot be relied upon to assume the initiative for beginning new programs of alternative development. The people themselves, as global consumers and producers, must assume the initiative and put the real power in their own hands.

Chapter 19: The Information Revolution and the Dawn of the Information Age

The advent of the movable type printing press in 14th Century Europe spelled the beginning of a major cultural revolution and the dawning of the Renaissance. The availability of books to read led to fresh perspectives and a new accounting of worldview that was the birth of science, capitalism, modern art and architecture and the exploration of the world.

With the advent of the PC and global Internet services, we have been in the midst of a new kind of revolution, that of the electronic information age. Conventional textual storage and printing operations have been rendered fairly obsolete as the primary means of information transmission and storage.

We do not now know the full implications or possibilities of this new age, but it is happening upon the dawn of the Third Millennium. Many spin-off technologies have yet to be discovered or invented from the possibilities presented to us by this breakthrough in digital information storage and processing.

One of the yet untapped possibilities of this information revolution is that control and manipulation of mass information, upon that modern nation states have used as a means for mobilizing and controlling their constituency, is being rapidly and effectively undermined by the free, immediate access to information via the web.

Censorship and propaganda upon which modern totalitarian states have depended for the manipulation and control of the masses is being rendered obsolete—an anachronism of a frequently brutal 20th Century.

At the same time, individual people, given instant access to the entire globe, have the potential for making their own voices heard. The social consequences of this new information revolution may prove to be greater than the technological inventions that will be forthcoming from it as well.

The information revolution promises new foundations for social exchange and integration and moderation of worldview on a level heretofore impossible. For the first time means are directly placed in the hands of people who can act privately, as individuals, in a potential forum and network that is worldwide in scope.

People have the means now for voting directly on issues and for making their own voices heard around the world. Under such conditions, totalitarian and repressive governments, even secret agencies in otherwise democratic nations, are finding manipulation and control of the truth to be more difficult than ever. There are huge stakes involved in this game of mass communications and information manipulation.

Information organized and transmitted electronically and digitally has a different form, function and topographical organization than did the previous form of printed information. Its presentation, its processing and its impact is also changing in basic ways.

We can talk about the continuous reshaping of our worldview—a reorganization of how our attitudes and values about the world and of our own identities and the identities of others within it. Old boundaries of our prejudice and ignorance must yield and wash away under the flood of new information available through the Internet.

Electronic Information storage entails that a new form of electronic literacy will take precedence over the previous form of textual literacy. This transformation of consciousness is an unavoidable consequence. Practically any kind of information of any level or quality will become available to anyone who has access to the Internet.

The means of organization and presentation of this information will change in fundamental ways. The old outline form will yield increasingly to a new "electronic stream of consciousness" that will beget a style of learning and thinking that is based upon its interconnectivity with the virtual world.

This new worldview is a global worldview. It is a global collective consciousness that we plug into each in our own way and on our own time schedule. The structure of our social system is becoming increasingly intelligent, and synergistic in a super-organic sense.

As this informational capacity increases, communications become instantaneous around the globe and more direct than ever before. At the same time, people and organizations grow in their sensitivities and sensibilities about the world.

As our worldviews and collective attitudes and values are being reshaped, so too will our actions and what we do also become redefined thereby. This is an inevitable process. Thus the information revolution will have teleological and behavioral consequences that will penetrate and influence almost every aspect of our shared and private lives.

These changes are inevitable. They will come regardless of government actions to prevent it. As more people connect up to the global system and share in its values, as the virtual system itself becomes more intelligent and responsive to the queries and needs of people, the system and its culture will begin to define itself more clearly and in a more differentiated sense. We cannot stop this process from now occurring.

 We can only perhaps shape the direction in that it goes, and the overall consequences it may have in our personal and public lives.

But the current electronic information revolution will have many more consequences than we can now imagine. They will eventuate in a degree of applied automated intelligent systems that will have the consequence, as did early industrial revolutions, of freeing many more people from the drudgery of hands-on work. Increasingly, people, liberated from the repetitive, mindless drudgery of the assembly line, will be given the opportunity to "make work" on-line.

Within a capitalist framework, this can result in the problem of the commons and in the displacement and mass unemployment of people by new, more intelligent machines.

This entails that political and economic reforms must keep pace with the rise and growth of electronic literacy and connectivity in the world, or else the potential for spreading the gap between haves and have-nots, or those in the know and those who remain outside of the information loop, and for fostering greater asymmetries and inequalities within the system, will be realized in a way never before imaginable.

<u>Earthbound Perspectives</u>

It is for this reason that the information revolution must have greater entailments for change than just technological invention and development.

We must apply the same lessons we are learning in the information technologies toward inducing social innovations and new patterns of human development that effectively compensate, indeed are better than, the losses experienced in the transition from an old fossil-fuel service economy to a newer automated digital information economy.

At the basis of the information revolution is Buckminster Fuller's anti-entropy formula—information through knowledge and communication creates synergistic patterns that defy the thermodynamic law of chaos. New information technologies create new values and new sources of value—these are invariably human in essence or meaning.

The Internet will be a form of symbolic integration of noetic human reality. We can effectively make something from nothing in the virtual world. It creates the possibility for new levels of integration and differentiation within the system that both empower the individual and realize greater resource potential for all individuals.

By means of the Internet, human beings have the capacity as never before to define their own sense of value in the world, to realize their own individuality and creativity, and to influence and participate in the important affairs of the world as equals.

Political organization takes on new meaning and scope over the Internet, when many people can meet in a collective virtual forum to deal with issues of mutual concern. We no longer need to depend upon periodic elections to choose representatives to do our bidding for us.

Obsolete are the dictators and military tyrants of the 20th Century who ruled by the threat of violence and destruction. They have no place, no room, on the Internet except by futile attempts to control its access and by lame efforts to propagandize their own violence.

The Internet provides means for directly accessing the will and conscience of the people far more cheaply and effectively even than the penny-presses of the late 19th Century.

It presents people, all people the world over, with the infrastructure and structure, as well as the opportunity and the possibility for achieving a new level of structural integration in the world, one that transcends all previous styles and methods of doing so. It remains up to the people themselves to try to achieve this new form of organization.

This global reorganization of human social relations entails that people must assume a collective orientation in a system that is largely self-organizing. Old forms of political organization cannot be trusted to dis-enfranchise themselves in the prospects of realizing a more stable global unity.

In the final analysis, the information revolution becomes the revolution of the people, for the people and by the people. It becomes the freedom and responsibility that people must realize for them selves by means of the Internet.

Chapter 20: Global Culture, Global Society & Global Civilization

We must look to the beginning of the Third Millennium as the rise of a new human orientation that transcends previous national horizons and ethnic chauvinism. It presents us the possibility of a new age human, the age of a global-human.

To be viable, global culture cannot be the unidimensional form of culture represented by modernity and modernization that is the exclusive product of capitalist development and participation in the world capitalist system.

It must become an alternative culture that permits a wider range of variation and tolerance for basic ethnocultural differences. Structurally, it must provide all people with greater latitude and freedom of choice in defining their relationship to the overall system. It must help to empower people at all levels.

The possibilities of the Internet and the information revolution are the foundation of a new cultural patterning that is by definition global in worldview, and individual and local in its manifestation and consequences, and that transcend all previous cultural boundaries and orientations that were fixed to locally specific or regionally exclusive orientations.

The possibility for the rise of a new global culture is at hand that now transcends national cultural boundaries. It is not just any particular national cultures, but, at least by definition, any and all national cultures.

Many of the institutions upon that previous national cultures have been based will be rendered simply inconvenient and obsolete by the realization of new possibilities through the information exchange of the web.

The rise of global culture entails a merging together of the differences and the adoption of a common pattern of living that is transcending many of the basic boundaries that have separated people time immemorial.

We can no longer afford the petty ethnocentrism and chauvinism of a bygone era. These attitudes and prejudices will seem increasingly discrepant as more and more people hook onto the Internet and as the Internet explores is greater levels of information & knowledge integration.

We regularly use products that have been made by hands on the other side of the globe—often composites of sub-component manufactured and assembled in many corners of the world. And many of the products that we use are pretty much the same whether they were bought and used in the United States or in Russia or Uganda or Chile. Wars and the constraints of the present system remind us continually that the global system is not quite there yet, but it is well on its way.

We can make out the outlines of global society already. It is without doubt a stratified society. Global stratification is increasingly cutting across ethnic and national lines to separate the few winners from the many losers. As much as it is an increasingly stratified society, it will also become increasingly differentiated. It will enable a kind of modular articulation that reaches to the level of the individual and the small group.

As much as the new information and communication technologies allow for global integration across previous boundaries, they also entail an inevitable process of increasing differentiation of the global system in ever-finer units of production and control.

The hyper-specialization that was the earmark of the 20th Century will yield to a new kind of generalization that is focused upon the increasing realization of greater capacities of the individual who is no longer restricted to a single monotypic regime of work.

Global civilization is a shared, trans-cultural process that incorporates increasingly more people on the earth. As more groups become, one way or another, members of the global society, we are forced to ask ourselves the central questions of what kind of system we want it to become. To fail to actively participate and opt collectively for an open and democratically organized system means that by default it will become an increasingly closed and autocratic system.

<u>Earthbound Perspectives</u>

The currently emerging global culture is a stratified one. It is defined as a modernized culture that is materialistic and technological in orientation. It is also really accessible only to the few privileged elite of each society that enters the ranks of the world system.

Most of humanity still remains locked in local parameters of structuration. Modern culture is primarily also Western ethno-national culture, as it derives from European styles and capitalist based economics. Promotion of modern culture as a global commodity to be bought and sold is the source of a great deal of acculturative stress and storm for many relatively undeveloped societies in the world.

Acculturative pressures that stem from the metropolitan cores of the developed world have mixed results. It is rarely politically coercive, or directly assimilationist, but it is often indirectly so through the manipulation and control of resources to the national governments.

It has substituted the direct forms of political coercion common in the colonial era to the indirect but far more effective means of socio-economic coercion available by mass communications and economic policies affecting trade relations and international markets.

Acculturation in the post-colonial era does not aim at direct assimilation, but at indirect accommodation into the global system of diverse ethnocultural groupings in a manner that preserves the original status quo and asymmetrical hierarchy of the original order.

It must be understood that the trans-cultural processes of civilization have always been "globalizing" even in the early proto-historical periods of humanity. Civilization catches on and takes hold and does not regress.

Of course, there are dark ages where knowledge is forgotten, but in those interim periods of the loss of one civilization, the seeds are sewn invariably among the far-off tribes of the world for the eventual rise of an even grander order of civilization.

Once the secrets of silk production leave the isolated realm of China, silk becomes not just a Chinese monopoly, but a common possession of all humanity. So be it with Pentium processors and micro-software.

The knowledge, technology and communications that drive this global culture is having an effect of imposing a process of modernization upon all people regardless of the differences and isolation. This process of modernization has a homogenizing influence. It makes cars, clothes, and modern values very similar in almost any airport in the world.

It is also creating greater disparities between those in the main stream and the many fragments of humanity that remain disconnected on some level.

Part of the wonderful thing about the emergence of the global culture is that increasingly the individual has potential to have a greater influence on the overall patterning.

With globalization, there is implicitly a globalization of our responsibility. We can no longer act completely separately or with an exclusive sense that the consequences of our actions will not be felt around the world in one way or another.

We cannot behave in ways believing that our behavior will escape notice and attention around the world. At the same time, it is creating new opportunities and possibilities for acting and for the realization of our actions.

It thus puts upon us, individually and collectively, the new challenge of measuring up to the possibilities in a productive and philanthropic way. We live now in an interesting time.

Individual actions can help to define new patterns in the world. The complexity and chaos of the emerging global system permits a kind of human butterfly effect. People must recognize this potentiality and try to organize their actions in a way that can have positive consequences for humanity.

Chapter 21: Beyond the 21st Century

All indicators point to the fact that the fate of humanity rests in the balance of the early 21st Century. Totalitarian governments even now are in secret collusion in sales with one another of both conventional, modern weapons and with weapons of mass destruction.

These governments, controlled by very few of their national populations, maintain strict ideological and behavioral conformity of their constituencies through symbolic manipulation and censorship control of the mass communication media and educational institutions, and rely structural on the rapid mobilization of their people especially against targeted out-groups in order to maintain their own stability.

These governments for the most part remain outside the normal league of the Nations that are participating as full members of the modern global system. To the extent that they are systematically marginalized and excluded from full participation within this system, they can be seen as unstable elements in the structural self-organization of this system.

The consequence of this is that historical happenstance can twist quickly the fate of the world, by the election of a mad military dictator, by the radical actions of a terrorist group, by a violent coup d'état, or a reactionary movement of an extremist political party or mass movement. This type of scenario can rapidly ignite a World War III and bring to an end the current structural stability of the global system.

As we approach quickly the edge of our collective world history, basic unchanged conditions of overpopulation, environmental circumscription, poverty, authoritarianism and unrestrained militarism, create the supercritical conditions that would be ripe for such scenarios to occur in. They set the world stage for such catastrophic chain reactions to occur.

It is vitally important that we learn to look beyond the next decade, even beyond century, beyond the bounds of the lives of our grandchildren, to what kind of an earth we wish to leave to our posterity. We must begin betting on the very long run of humanity, and put aside our own shortsighted preoccupations with profit-maximization and seizing the market moment.

The question of our long-term, collective fate, is an important question, and will not eventually go away by our continuing to ignore it. We have an increasingly earthbound sense of responsibility to try to answer this question, and this sense of responsibility is gradually dawning on our collective horizon.

We have a choice, we can work together towards or better world, or we can, by default of our own passivity, allow the world to continue to go in the direction it has been taking. If it does so, all significant indicators point to the fact that it will not take very long to realize a worse fate for humankind.

Our responsibility is not only to try to see beyond the current predicament of humankind, that is in the final analysis mostly arbitrary, constructed, and politically constrained, and to try to understand this predicament in all its detail and complexity, but we must also try to take action, both individually, and collectively, to attempt to rectify the global situation before it is finally too late.

We must work together in this effort. The means for us to do so have presented themselves in the final hour. We have the information and increasingly the technology for using that information. Now we must put it into practice in ways never hitherto realized or realizable.

We do it not for ourselves, for our own aggrandizement and wealth. We do it for our children and for our posterity. When we say "our" we do not know any limits or boundaries of our collective identity—we mean all people, regardless of the color of their skin, their heritage, their history, or their choices and actions in life.

We do it for our greater sense of humanity and for the long-term good of all humankind. We do it because we are human and we share in this basic identity a collective relation to all other people on earth.

This book has been written in the perspective of the long-term view of the world. It seeks to see beyond the next century, not so much in detail as in general scope. To deny the large storm clouds gathering on the common horizon of our world at the dawn of the 21st Century is to do a disservice to humanity and to our posterity. To know that something foreboding is looming large on our horizon and to fail to act is to commit a kind of crime, a crime of neglect.

We make choices everyday that can affect, both individually and cumulatively, the final outcome of our collective destinies. We live in a world and in an age where the potential for our actions to have a global impact is much greater than ever before.

As this book demonstrates, there are clear answers to these questions. We do have alternatives, and they are not simply windmills on the horizon. These choices and the solutions they represent are not simple ones. They are immensely complex, but they are in the end analysis finite puzzles that are capable of definite solution and resolution.

It is fitting that this work should end with a proverbial clarion call—a call to arms—not of weapons, but of interlocked hands bearing help to the disadvantaged of the world, and barring the violence of the corrupt upon the innocent victims of their evil designs. This call to peaceful revolution is not a call to greater violence, but a call to seeking alternative life-styles that share some basic features in common.

These include a common commitment to the improvement of the human race, to preservation and promotion of the earth's natural environments, to the realization of alternative technologies that do not erode and wear away the foundation for our own survival on earth, and to more responsible involvement in the decision making that is necessary to secure a better world.

Afterward (2023)

We are entering the second quarter of the 21st Century and the effects of global-social (or "glocal") circumscription seem only gradually beginning to be felt in human historical time that has accelerated to the speed of light. Indirectly, the evidence linking to global warming is basically and scientifically irrefutable, even if its denial is commonplace and promulgated consistently and replete through the popular media.

The United States, world leader in global change, seems to have socially tried to step back to yesteryear and never-land, resurrecting lost causes in race-based ethnocultural identities, adopting quasi-neo-fascist political orientations, seeking abortion bans, seeking reintegration of church and state and thus subverting systematically vaunted public institutional frameworks, fighting for the right not to wear face masks to protect others from transmission of a deadly global pandemic virus, and still in mass denial over the facts of global warming, domestic mass killings and extreme vertical economic stratification.

This has all been happening in the background context of developing urban areas world round and exponentially increasing global human population. The international world community is perhaps closer to nuclear war than it has probably been since the early 1960s.

China's rising star was somewhat stained by the COVID 19 pandemic, and yet China is adamantly unapologetic about its part in the pandemic. In a sense, China must be and remain stubbornly Chinese, else as a nation it would be a huge loss of collective face and historical civilization possibly requiring internal recomposition of the state powers that be.

Appendix A: Universal Natural Rights & Human Responsibilities

Human rights are the responsibility of all people as both individuals and members of all other groups, as well as of individual nation states to uphold and protect. There are few if any overarching human agencies in the world to reinforce such a doctrine or to protect people from its abuse.

There is substantial variability in the interpretation of these rights, and this has been put forth as a claim upon the cultural relativity of value systems underlying a rejection of a call for universal human rights as a legitimate meta-ethical system for the organization of human normative behavior.

China is a perfect example of such a case. Students in China are typically taught, as a matter of state policy and cultural sanction, to believe that human rights is to be equated with irresponsible freedom and license that leads to the undermining of the moral and legal order of a society. Therefore human rights are rejected officially and categorically as a cultural prerogative as an anarchist doctrine interfering with the state.

Similarly, China has an official anti-democracy doctrine that outlaws non-state sanctioned religious beliefs and practices and that banishes any non-communist political parties. Democracy is taught as being a kind of conspiracy of Western capitalism and Imperialism.

Most students of China, even well educated ones, firmly believe official anti-rights doctrine to be the truth of the matter, and are largely misinformed as to the basic doctrine of human rights, though they often fell in their personal and family lives the contradictions and constraints of living in a society that does not value human rights.

Of course, this serves the interest of a very corrupt and anti-democratic elite, bolstered by the largest land army in the world, and who has one of the worst human rights records in modern history.

Only in cases today involving usually international migration and international labor, are questions of human rights extended beyond the purview of one nation's states own citizenry to embrace an expanded model for its application across international boundaries.

The only other instances are in those cases of usually humanitarian intervention when nation states grossly violate the rights of many people, or, in the case of international aggression, when one nation violates the territorial sovereignty and independence of another nation without provocation.

The world has changed rapidly since the earlier doctrines of human rights were promulgated: it has changed even more since the post-war era that was overshadowed by cold-war tensions and inherent competition between superpowers.

Today, whether we acknowledge or accept as this paradigm legitimate or not, we live within an expanded paradigm of basic human rights. Many legal precedents in International and domestic cases have served to outline and solidify the foundation for a doctrine of universal human rights. First, we cannot clearly or completely enunciate a doctrine of basic human rights without first appending a complementary doctrine that states basic human responsibilities.

In most cases, questions of human rights are not black and white. There is a tremendous gray area in the legal definition of human rights in which many lawyers make a good living in the manipulation of basic rights, and often in their hedging and dodging between the letters of the law. Legal codes in many cases do not adequately address issues of human rights in either a fundamental or a derivative sense, and many may actually exist in violation of basic rights.

I would include on my list the following items:

- The right to health
- The right to housing
- The right to work
- The right to social security & welfare
- The right to education
- The right to property

- The freedom of expression
- The freedom of thought
- The freedom of livelihood and pursuit of happiness
- The freedom of choice and sexual prerogative
- The right not to be abused, either physically or psychologically
- The right not to be misinformed
- The right not to be conscripted for involuntary service or servitude.

It is important in the world for most nation-state systems and non-state entities to adopt a meta-ethical paradigm based upon the acknowledgement of the universal efficacy of natural rights.

Natural rights extend from doctrine of human rights and responsibilities, and encompasses all relationships of humankind with nature, including especially other people.

This paradigm is expostulated because it is necessary to define and set clear precedents and limits by which human development and social action in the world can be judged, sanctioned and, hopefully, self-constrained.

It is difficult to define a paradigm of rights without also making explicit a set of basic human responsibilities. We are responsible ultimately for our own actions, no matter the context or the social motivations for such action.

The Nuremberg Trials of the Nazi War Criminals demonstrated in International Law the principle that knowledge creates responsibility. Further, we have a fundamental responsibility to seek to know, and to know honestly.

We understand our ethical situation and dilemmas in life because, as human beings, we are creatures of knowledge, and we have human civilization that is founded upon our capacity to know.

Ultimately, we seek a global human identity in the world that defines all of humankind as equal. The realization of a global social worldview and sense of global collective responsibility and identity is the beginning of a transcendent world civilization founded upon the principles of peace and universal equality.

Universal Human Rights & Responsibilities

15 Universal Human Rights & Responsibilities

15 Universal Human Rights

1. Right to Life

2. Right to Liberty & the Pursuit of Individual Happiness

3. Right to Due Process of Law

4. Right to Political Equality

5. Right to Ethnocultural Equality

6. Right to Habitation & Territorial Sovereignty

7. Right to Health and to be treated for disease by others without obligation.

8. Right to Work and to receive a fair wage for one's Work.

9. Right to Education

10. Right to Religious & Ideological Freedom

11. Right to Material Possession & Well-Being

12. Right to Individual Dignity and Self-Worth

13. Right to a Speedy and Fair Trial & not to be incarcerated without such a Trial

14. Right to Democratic Self-Government & Political Self-Determination

15. Right to Open & Free Knowledge & Information

15 Universal Human Responsibilities

1. Responsibility to exercise one's own rights

2. Responsibility to heal sickness & suffering

3. Responsibility to nurture the young

4. Responsibility to non-violent action

5. Responsibility to education and to be reasonably informed and open minded

6. Responsibility to serve and uphold the laws of one's community (i.e.)

    a. one's family

    b. one's nation

    c. the human race

7. Responsibility to intervene in violence and protect the innocent

8. Responsibility to seek social justice

9. Responsibility to work in a constructive manner to human development

10. Responsibility to healthy living

12. Responsibility to respect & protect all life

13. Responsibility to Democratic

participation in self-government

14. Responsibility to promote
open, unbiased learning and
knowledge

15. Responsibility to uphold and
respect the rights of all human
beings.

All government programs and policies of all nation-states and sub-national corporate entities need to be constrained and sanctioned in accordance and respect to this basic doctrine of human rights and responsibilities within the following meta-ethical paradigm:

1. Basic Human Rights and Responsibilities are interpreted in dynamic balance with one another, and there are many derivative rights and responsibilities that are forthcoming from their interpretation that applies in limited contexts and cases.

2. Human violence is defined as the unnecessary use or threat of destructive force, social constraint or coercion/persuasion in the violation of basic human rights and responsibilities.

3. The central agenda of this doctrine is the realization of greater human potential and possibility through universal tolerance of human difference and the active promotion of human development, both individually and upon collective levels of human social organization.

4. For every rule stated, there are an unknown number of possible exceptions, conditions, extenuating circumstances, and resulting interpretations and applications that nevertheless do not violate the spirit of the implicit principles involved.

5. There is therefore mandated by the doctrine of human rights and responsibilities a general attitude and behavioral predisposition of generosity, openness, respect, tolerance and forgiveness.

292

It should go without saying that one's own rights generally leave off where another's responsibilities begin, but this is a central point in the balancing of rights and responsibilities that many people and governments seem to have forgotten.

It is true for instance that in some "rights-based" societies like the US, criminals with high-priced lawyers often gain greater attention to their rights and interests than their victims, because there has not been a balanced definition or emphasis upon human responsibilities.

On the other side of the coin, in some traditionally "responsibility-based" societies like China and India, individual human rights are frequently sacrificed and violated, and even go unrecognized or tabooed, for the sake of the preservation of a strong sense of social responsibility, which by the way becomes chronically violated anyway by the abuse of privilege and power and the maintenance of double-standards and hypocrisy of office.

It also remains quite true that these rights and responsibilities may be variously interpreted by different people with different backgrounds, agendas, viewpoints and orientations.

It becomes therefore the case that the gray areas of the interpretation of these basic sets of rights and responsibilities serves as both a ground of contention, possible conflict, compromise, exploitation, violation and even misappropriation, misrepresentation and the dysphemization of the actual exercise of human rights and responsibilities in applied settings. =

The "Right to Life" is a wonderful example of an inherently ambiguous basic statement that can be used by ideologically vested and closed interests to promote their own agendas in the world.

The interpretation of these rights and responsibilities therefore becomes more critical to their realization and the promotion of human development than their legal codification and formal definition.

The answer to this kind of dilemma is the realization that the basic doctrine of human rights and responsibilities serves not only as a basic anthropological charter for humankind, but as a general ethical code of conduct in which rights and responsibilities, variously interpreted, variably expressed under conflicting and existentially uncertain circumstances, constitutes a kind of meta-ethical system for individual and community behavior.

It therefore provides a template for human social action, organization, relation and definition of well being, and at least implicitly sets the standards for defining and measuring relative human well being, conduct and its consequences in the world.

For instance, promotion of human development, both individually and collectively defined, emerges in this framework as a certain high priority that cannot be responsibly ignored in the world.

Different rights and responsibilities of self and others operate and condition one another in a complex way in variable settings and under different sets of conditions. The system in part or as a whole always remains open to interpretation, discussion, revision conflict-resolution, adjudication, legislation and compromise.

The doctrine of universal natural rights represents a meta-ethical and logical extension of the doctrine of universal human rights. As with everything else, things can be argued both ways and nothing is incontrovertibly set in stone. There are of course gray areas in the articulation of development that will be manipulated by interests capitalizing on development

Universal Natural Rights & Responsibilities

Ten Universal Natural Rights	Ten Universal Natural Responsibilities
1, The Universal Right of Life	1. Universal Non-Violence
2. Right to Non-Interference	2. Responsible Intervention
3. Right to Natural Selection	3. Responsible cultural selection
4. Right to resource conservation and protection	4. Responsible environmental design and natural resource conservation
5. The right to explore and research in natural systems	5. Responsibility to stewardship: to controlled experimental intervention

<u>in natural systems</u>

<u>6. Right to protection and conservation</u>

<u>6. Responsibility to protect and promote living systems of all kinds</u>

<u>7. Right to medical intervention and rehabilitation</u>

<u>7. Responsibility to medically intervene</u>

<u>8. Right to natural ecosystem and ecological diversity & health</u>

<u>8. Responsibility to protect, promote and conserve biodiversity within healthy ecosystem frameworks</u>

<u>9. Right to area and territorial freedom and safe passage between natural territories</u>

<u>9. Responsibility to provision adequate space, territory and natural territorial integrity, as well as provisioning of passageways between designated territories free of human traffic.</u>

<u>10. Responsibility to monitor and promote natural biospheric systems and maintain adaptive equilibrium of these systems upon multiple subsystem levels</u>

Appendix B: Statement on Techno-Ecology and Eco-Technology

Modern industries were quick to jump on the new biological revolution that enabled genetic manipulation of corn crops.

They did so shortsightedly and without regard to the possible long term or possible indirect consequences of human interference in the genetic transmission of biological information—the coding of life itself.

They did so only in the selfish desire of capitalizing on a new form of technology.

Genetic manipulation is a clear and stark example of the effect that modern scientific technology is having upon the natural ecology of the earth—at many levels and in many different ways.

The history of capitalist development reveals that most of it has been by definition short-sighted because it was always based simply and only on terms of rapid and immediate profit-maximization--or rather a strategy of the nearest possible, short-term gains.

Modern technologies indeed create and foster their own kinds of ecology on the earth, as many otherwise feral species of life are forced to adapt to the new human-made conditions imposed on their natural habitats or else pass rapidly to extinction by habitat loss and extreme resource competition.

These new human-made ecologies prove usually to be not very adaptive in the long term—they tend to have destructive and imbalanced consequences for natural ecologies in the larger framework and the suites of species that normally make their homes within these regional contexts.

Eco-Technology can be defined as the alternative technologies, such as the primary institutions of production that promote more sustainable large-scale adaptations of the human species on earth, or at the very least, are less destructive of an eco-cultural orientation than are the currently predominant fossil-fuel based technologies.

These primary alternative institutions are basically solar-powered, either directly or indirectly, along with a host of spin-off technologies that are derivable and exclusively dependent upon these alternative energy resources.

The information revolution has made this new kind of technology not only more possible, but potentially even more efficacious and even more profitable than traditional-styled technologies!

As Buckminster Fuller was fond of remarking—information is anti-entropic, and if we are to understand the synergism of an alternative system of basic and advanced technology, then it must be understood from the standpoint of its structural-functional integration derived from information technologies and the possibilities that this new kind of cybernetic integration creates.

Eco-technologies have a primary derivative source—solar energy—either directly or indirectly utilized by a variety of means. Upon this general source of energy, technologies that are efficient and ecologically efficacious are elaborated as viable alternatives to the common forms available today.

The wide-scale adoption and development of these alternative primary institutions sets up a new foundation for alternative development that is outside of the present system and yet remains complementary to that system.

The challenge is the development of an alternative eco-technological infrastructure that is complementary to the existing fossil-fuel economy. Many of these alternative technologies have been around for a long time, but the justification for their lack of development has been the availability of less expensive alternatives and the high cost of their development.

This is only partly true, and disguises the real issue that has been involved in the promotion of alternative eco-technologies. The large oil companies and derivative companies of automobile and truck manufactures would not want forms of competition to enter their lucrative market place that might in the long run undermine their own profits and profitability. In fact, in the long run, if properly designed, eco-technologies may actually be more efficient and less expensive than the current petro-chemical based industries.

The promotion of these alternative technologies does require some rethinking and rewiring of the system—old money will die and new money will be born. Even more, it requires a general receptiveness and willingness of current socio-political systems to adopt these kinds of programs.

If the new alternative technologies can be cultivated and allowed to rise to the fore, then the old Industries of oil and coal combustion would become eventually relatively limited and specialized industries—a few functions accomplished more efficiently by gas or other forms of petro-chemical combustion than otherwise, hence being irreplaceable by alternatives.

The promise of these programs promoting alternative development is that, relatively speaking, they are non-destructive of the natural environment, and produce far fewer harmful side affects that the current state of technology.

They would be designed for the long run, to run on a regular or continuous basis without the need for constant inputs of huge amounts of coal or oil.

Because on average they would tend to be long lasting, steady and relatively reliable, many of the issues that are contemporary to the petrol-chemical--cost of gas at the pump, for example—industry would eventually simply become irrelevant.

The focal foundation of techno-ecology is the elaboration of solar and gravity powered technologies, and the advanced application of these technologies to the viable and economical solution of practical problems in the world.

Spinoff technologies would also be forth coming from promotion of this development. Furthermore, new development based on these technologies can be directly applied to accomplishing scientific objectives that have not otherwise been obtained.

Alternative development will succeed in rendering global social organization more complex and occupationally differentiated—the structural dynamics of pan-human social order would take on new dimensions and new orders of magnitude as greater amounts of power become available to more people at less cost and greater net efficiency.

It may also remove some of the foundation stones that currently influence militarism and current asymmetries in the world order—competition for access and control over basic energy resources, for example.

The real challenges faced by alternative techno-ecological development is not its cost-effectiveness, but rather the organized resistance it will receive from many super-powerful lobbies and private interests that mandate government policies and manipulate public awareness and opinion.

But these challenges can be effectively met, and in time, their resistance will wither away in the face of a growing global receptivity and demand for cheaper sources of power and the by-products and technological spin-offs of these sources.

The sooner the human race gets unhooked on fossil-fuel consumption as their primary source of power, and becomes hooked on alternative solar sources, then the sooner the foundations for world peace and for pan-human development can be better secured in the world. In the meantime, we must concern ourselves with dealing with a world of our own making, but not completely of our own choosing.

For such alternative technology and development to occur, it is clear that governments on all levels must become more cooperative and willing as participants in this effort—promotion of such development will entail the extension and integration of regions world-wide that have little to do with political boundaries, much as the information revolution based upon the Internet has had little to do with national boundaries of culture, language or communications.

At the same time, governments alone cannot be relied upon to assume the initiate for beginning new programs of alternative development--the people themselves, as global consumers and producers, must assume the initiative and put the real power in their own hands.

Appendix C: A Preliminary Definition of the Global Commons

The global commons has emerged as a critically vital concept of the global system and the global systems framework. Yet it is historically a relatively new concept.

What is sought in an explicit sense is a concise and well-formulated definition of what are the global commons and what is the central concept the global commons in relation to other forms human systems or natural systems.

For a large part, the global commons seems to include the broader concept of "public domain." The concepts of global and human heritage may also be important to the designation of artifacts, archaeological or historical sites, that belong rightfully to the greater global commons.

1. Humankind is a single species on earth.

    a. Human cultures, including ethno-national cultures

    b. Individual people and civic groups or groupings of people as a class or categorization.

    c. Global culture

    d. Human language including writing systems

    e. Human knowledge

    f. Science and Technology

    g. The Global Internet

    h. Human heritage, including historical, biographical and genealogical knowledge.

    i. Artificial Intelligence and robotic applications

2. Living systems are earthbound systems.

    a. Biological systems: including species specific populations, ecologies and biomes

    b. Conservation and sustainable stewardship of living systems as both a food source within eco-trophic frameworks, and as a source of genetic variation and evolutionary wealth.

    c. Establishment of protection and conservation zones for natural biological systems, undistributed by human activities, with substantial travel corridors interconnecting such regions providing the capacity for multiple species to traverse globally to new areas and zones and to continue speciation.

3. Global territorial spaces include:

    a. The high seas, "inner space" and the lands beneath them, including the shallow reefs and reef systems, and including the North Pole

    b. The fishery and living resources within the High Seas, including coastal estuaries and major lacustrian, fresh water systems of lakes, deltas, major Rivers, tributary systems and watersheds.

    c. The Antarctic.

    d. The upper Atmosphere.

    e. The earth's interior.

    f. Outer Space, to include the Moon and the outer special regions between and around the Earth and the Moon

It seems that resources can and perhaps should be listed and inventoried as belonging to the Global Commons, even if such resources in a specific sense are also otherwise designated as belonging to other frameworks or entities in the world.

Not all resources can be thus listed—certain wild flora and faunal resources, especially culture evasive species, can be listed but not itemized except perhaps through population estimates and census surveys or sampling.

Earthbound Perspectives

A subspecies of tiger or lion, pushed to the edge of extinction, might be listed as a resource of the global commons under a critical category that would warrant special protection measures.

Vital to the success and survival say of endangered large predatory felines would be the design and provisioning of ample conservation areas incorporating ranges of such large predators, and providing means of travel between protected area and away from danger zones.

While this multiple listing and claims would be a source of contention and potential conflict, such inventories of systems would yet be important to the establishment of a global judiciary framework for the adjudication and conflict resolution of these discrepancies.

In short, a framework of systematic listing of Global Commons Resources would provide the precedence and context for the development of effective global laws and order in the prohibition of some forms of "crimes against nature," "crimes against humankind," "crimes against life."

But creating and maintaining a listing is not quite the analytic-synthetic, prescriptive-descriptive definition of the global commons. I offer a quick take:

> The global commons are entirety of all those resources and resource frameworks of natural systems as they are found on earth and beyond, however much they may also be designated by cross-secting claims, by which the development of human systems in a sustainable manner requires de facto careful consideration and long-term caution for the sake of permanent preservation.

Intrinsic and central to the notion of global commons seems to be the idea of relative global health of sustainable systems. One measure of this has been devised in the form of the "global footprint" as a rough diagnostic of the total yearly impact a nation-state is currently having upon the global environment.

In order to avert any future global crisis as a result of human competition and aggression, a new set of rules and laws would have to be formulated and agreed upon by at least of the majority of the world's people as relating to the global commons, both directly and indirectly. I can imagine a legitimate requirement for a form of global law and thus also an efficacious global judiciary to interpret and enforce global law.

Appendix D: Notes and Queries on a Minimalist Framework

Steps toward a more rational life-style

Some one recently asked me, what is a "minimalist" framework. Being a job interview, I was not prepared for this kind of question, but it did cause me some reflection afterward, and for me to ask myself what I meant by this. Perhaps he thought less of me for this, or for lacking a clear answer, as he never called me back for the job, one way or another.

What is a "Minimalist" Framework?

I would define a minimalist framework as one that is independent of the huge leviathanesque Capitalist World System, in which one's habits, life-choices, life-style, perception of needs, and sense of status and well being in the world, is not dependent upon false advertising, commercialism, hype, double or multiple standards, or the exploitation of oneself, others, or the environment.

I would identify a minimalist framework as essentially a non-violent lifestyle. It is one in which we seek to cultivate good habits that do not bring harm to one's self, one's community or one's environment. We can be a pacifist and essentially non-violent in the world, even if we step once in a while upon a bug (by accident) or we sometimes deliberately swat an annoying fly who does not belong inside.

We must gain a living, we must live, but we do not have to have our values, our standards of living, or very sense of happiness and well being, be manipulated by others who have only profit and exploitation in mind.

Tips for Cultivating a More Minimalist Lifestyle

I would say a minimalist framework is the cultivation of a life-style that is not only non-material (hence, hopefully, a bit more genuinely spiritual) but also I would say vastly simpler and uncomplicated. Fetishism and the compulsion to have and mindlessly consume, to always seek immediate gratification, is essentially as unhealthy as it is a road to unhappiness and discontentment—one can never be finally satisfied if one's "needs" are always met upon demand.

Here are some Hugh-tips for cultivating a minimalist way of living, especially for the class-conscious consumer (I would put them in some kind of order, but I think maybe they don't need "ordering"):

- Cut up extra credit cards—keep only one or at most two for holidays and emergencies.
- Plant trees whenever and wherever possible.
- Cultivate a green thumb lifestyle.
- Become a suburban gardener.
- If one wants something, put it off at least a month or two, and see if one still needs it so bad.
- Give extra trees to neighbors to plant.
- Mulch one's garden clippings.
- Earthworm one's vegetable garbage.
- Drive a smaller car.
- Eat slow food slowly.
- Eat more chicken, less cow.
- Eat fish, fruit and nuts, and fewer candy-bars and TV dinners.
- Xeriscape one's yard.
- Put in drip irrigation systems.

- Read a book rather than watch television.
- Turn off extra lights.
- Open the windows more.
- Acclimate oneself to the transient temperatures of the day and the night.
- Dress appropriately for the weather.
- Dress to un-impress.
- Collect used books.
- Spend more QT with one's family.
- Turn off the computers.
- Slow Down—put off until tomorrow what you need to do today.
- When in doubt, don't.
- Learn to more easily recognize what is doubtful.
- Eat simple and basic things.
- Drink more water, fewer beverages.
- Save one's pennies, nickels and dimes in a piggy bank: "From the Pocket to the Piggy."
- Life's usually a big joke, so laugh it all off.
- People are normally stupid, and are not meant to be taken too seriously.
- Build a bird feeder and hang it up in your newly planted backyard tree.
- Use a nice hand can opener.
- Use a nice hand coffee grinder.
- Be a skeptic and an "unbeliever."
- Question everything and anyone.

Affluenza and the Addiction of "Maximization"

If we are to better understand what is a minimalist lifestyle, we might benefit from contrasting it to the things it is not, and the things it is intended to counter-act in the world. I would call affluenza the obsessive-compulsive neurosis of modern living, made possible in world in which over-consumption is not only easy to do, but often hard not to do.

Of course, affluenza is more than just about over-consumption of fast-food and big automobiles. A consumer based society that tries to maximize production and consumption, mandates and constrains patterns of habitual over-consumption regardless of indirect or long-term consequences.

We are beset by commercialism as well as by the reciprocal expectations of others as to how to achieve status in our world-- by the kind of car we drive, how we dress, who we associate with, what we can or cannot conspicuously consume, etc. It is about the never-ending quest for status acquisition, the competition for success in the eye's and mind's eye of others, and the attempt to feel good about oneself and one's world through a form of vicarious fetishism.

Affluenza also translates into a kind of never-ending status quest, a kind of no-holds-barred socio-political competition for position and status, often at almost anyone's or everyone's net expense, and it is about working hard at not working too hard. The appearance is greater than the substance, and appearing to be busy and hardworking outweighs actually being busy and hardworking in a non-distracted and non-dilatory sense.

The dividends of successfully managing a case of affluenza can be large—a large home, a large life-style, a large ego, and a large pocketbook. But affluenza can also be terminal and easily run amok.

FINI

Earthbound Primers

1.   Earth Spirits, Earth Songs
(1992-1995)

2.   Earthbound Essays
1992

3.   Earthbound Perspectives
(1991-2000)

Lewis Micropublishing Series
& Poor Hugh's E-Press

1. General System Notebooks

2. Indie Anthropology

3. Robidoux Stories

4. Hugh's Versography

5. Earthbound Primers

6. West Indie Tales

7. Mil-Anth Studies

8. Global Edge Studies

9. Poor Hugh's E-Press

10. Lewis Micropublishing Miscellanea